SPINOZA
JEWISH

MW00324443

Over the last two decades there has been an increasing interest in the influence of medieval Jewish thought upon Spinoza's philosophy. The essays in this volume, by Spinoza specialists and leading scholars in the field of medieval Jewish philosophy, consider the various dimensions of the rich, important, but vastly under-studied relationship between Spinoza and earlier Jewish thinkers. It is the first such collection in any language, and together the essays provide a detailed and extensive analysis of how different elements in Spinoza's metaphysics, epistemology, moral philosophy, and political and religious thought relate to the views of his Jewish philosophical forebears, such as Maimonides, Gersonides, Ibn Ezra, Crescas, and others. The topics addressed include the immortality of the soul, the nature of God, the intellectual love of God, moral luck, the nature of happiness, determinism and free will, the interpretation of Scripture, and the politics of religion.

STEVEN NADLER is the William H. Hay II Professor of Philosophy at the University of Wisconsin-Madison, where he is also a faculty member of the Mosse/Weinstein Center for Jewish Studies. His previous publications include *Spinoza: A Life* (Cambridge, 2001), *Rembrandt's Jews* (2003), *Spinoza's 'Ethics': An Introduction* (Cambridge, 2006), Volume 1 of *The Cambridge History of Jewish Philosophy* (co-edited with T. M. Rudavsky, Cambridge, 2009), and *A Book Forged in Hell: Spinoza's Scandalous Treatise and the Birth of the Secular Age* (2011).

SPINOZA AND MEDIEVAL JEWISH PHILOSOPHY

EDITED BY

STEVEN NADLER

CAMBRIDGE
UNIVERSITY PRESS

CAMBRIDGE
UNIVERSITY PRESS

University Printing House, Cambridge CB2 8BS, United Kingdom

One Liberty Plaza, 20th Floor, New York, NY 10006, USA

477 Williamstown Road, Port Melbourne, VIC 3207, Australia

314-321, 3rd Floor, Plot 3, Splendor Forum, Jasola District Centre, New Delhi-110025, India

79 Anson Road, #06-04/06, Singapore 079906

Cambridge University Press is part of the University of Cambridge.

It furthers the University's mission by disseminating knowledge in the pursuit of education, learning and research at the highest international levels of excellence.

www.cambridge.org
Information on this title: www.cambridge.org/9781108455282

© Cambridge University Press 2014

First published 2014
First paperback edition 2018

A catalogue record for this publication is available from the British Library

Library of Congress Cataloging in Publication data
Spinoza and medieval Jewish philosophy / edited by Steven Nadler.
pages   cm
ISBN 978-1-107-03786-1 (hardback)
1. Spinoza, Benedictus de, 1632–1677 – Influence.   2. Spinoza, Benedictus de, 1632–1677.   3. Jewish philosophy – History – To 1500.   I. Nadler, Steven, 1958– editor.
B3998.S72127   2014
199′.492–dc23
2014024242

ISBN 978-1-107-03786-1 Hardback
ISBN 978-1-108-45528-2 Paperback

Contents

Contributors

JACOB ADLER is Associate Professor of Philosophy at the University of Arkansas.

STEVEN FRANKEL is Professor of Philosophy at Xavier University in Cincinnati.

WARREN ZEV HARVEY is Professor Emeritus in the Department of Jewish Thought at Hebrew University of Jerusalem.

JULIE R. KLEIN is Associate Professor of Philosophy at Villanova University.

CHARLES MANEKIN is Professor of Philosophy and Director of the Joseph and Rebecca Meyerhoff Center for Jewish Studies at the University of Maryland, College Park.

YITZHAK Y. MELAMED is Professor of Philosophy at Johns Hopkins University.

STEVEN NADLER is the William H. Hay II Professor of Philosophy and Evjue-Bascom Professor in Humanities at the University of Wisconsin-Madison.

HEIDI RAVVEN is Professor of Religious Studies at Hamilton College.

T. M. RUDAVSKY is Professor of Philosophy at The Ohio State University.

KENNETH SEESKIN is Philip M. and Ethel Klutznick Professor of Jewish Civilization at Northwestern University.

Abbreviations for works by Spinoza

CHG   *Compendium grammatices linguae hebraeae* (*Compendium of Hebrew Grammar*)

Ep   *Epistolae* (Correspondence)

Ethics   *Ethica* (App = Appendix; ax = axiom; c = corollary; def = definition; dem = demonstration; p = proposition; s = scholium; roman numeral = part)

KV   *Korte Verhandling van God, de mensch, en deszelvs welstand* (*Short Treatise on God, Man, and His Well-Being*)

NS   *Nagelate Schriften* (1677 Dutch translation of OP)

OP   *Opera Posthuma* (1677 posthumous edition of Spinoza's unpublished writings)

PPC   *Principia Philosophiae Cartesii* (*Descartes's Principles of Philosophy*)

TIE   *Tractatus de intellectus emendatione* (*Treatise on the Emendation of the Intellect*)

TP   *Tractatus Politicus* (*Political Treatise*)

TTP   *Tractatus Theologico-Politicus* (*Theological-Political Treatise*)

Introduction

Steven Nadler

Once upon a time, Bento (in Hebrew, Baruch; and in Latin, Benedictus) Spinoza was regularly seen as a thinker in a Jewish philosophical tradition.[1] In the century after Spinoza's death in 1677, the "Jewishness" of his philosophy was virtually taken for granted. It was considered, however, primarily a matter of Spinoza's relationship to ancient and medieval Jewish mysticism. At the end of the seventeenth century, for example, it was not uncommon to regard Spinoza's philosophy – especially the *Ethics* – as deeply imbued with kabbalistic and occult themes.[2] In the eighteenth century, Jacques Basnage, in his grand *Histoire des Juifs, depuis Jesus Christ jusqu'à présent* (1705), included Spinoza in his discussion of kabbalah, which he sees as the source of his "obscure and mystical" ideas.[3] Later that century, Solomon Maimon asserted that "kabbalah is nothing but extended Spinozism,"[4] an opinion that the great twentieth-century scholar of Jewish mysticism Gershom Scholem would second.[5]

---

[1] I speak of *a* Jewish philosophical tradition rather than *the* Jewish philosophical tradition mainly because I am not so sure there is such a thing as the latter, given the diversity (and possible incompatibility) of philosophical traditions within Judaism.

[2] See, for example, the two books by J. G. Wachter, *Der Spinozismus im Juedenthumb, oder die von dem heutigen Juedenthumb und dessen Geheimen Kabbala Vergoetterte Welt* (Amsterdam, 1699), and *Elucidarius Cabalisticus sive reconditae Hebraeorum philosophiae recensio* (Rome, 1706). According to Wachter, the kabbalah is "Spinozism before Spinoza."

[3] Basnage 1716, Book IV, Chapter 7. Popkin (1992, 387–409) provides a possible explanation as to why other early modern figures believed Spinoza's philosophy to be kabbalistic.

[4] See his autobiography, *Solomon Maimon's Lebensgeschichte von ihm selbst beschrieben*, Part I, Chapter 14 (Maimon 1793, 162).

[5] See Scholem (1941, 258). This tendency has continued, to some degree, in recent scholarship. Thus, Levy (1989), despite his recognition of the importance of Maimonides to Spinoza's philosophical development, and apparently without intending to assert that Spinoza was an unqualified mystic or a kabbalist, nonetheless believes that Spinoza's "pantheism" comes from earlier, mystical trends in Judaism. "The pivotal concept of Spinoza's metaphysics – the intellectual love of God," he insists, "derives its origin . . . from mysticism" (28). To be fair to Levy, he does insist that "the comparisons between Spinoza's thought and the kabbalah must, however, be treated very carefully and *cum grano salis*" (30). See also Brann 1977 and Hubbeling 1977.

I

Seasoned Spinoza scholars now view this as a seriously distorted picture of Spinoza's philosophy. While there certainly are elements of his metaphysics, epistemology, and moral philosophy that may strike *us* as "mysticist" – in part because they are rather opaque to interpretation, as well as often couched in a mystic-like vocabulary (witness Spinoza's use of the term 'intuition' for the highest kind of knowledge, and his extolling the "intellectual love of God" as the path to happiness and salvation) – any careful reader of his writings will be struck by the arch-rationalism that deeply informs his thought.

Of course, it is easy to see in Spinoza precisely what one wants to see – in this sense, he functions as a kind of intellectual Rorschach test. Spinoza has been a hero or a heretic to a remarkable variety of causes. There seem to be as many Spinozas as there are audiences seeking to appropriate him for their philosophical, political, or religious ends. There is the "God intoxicated" Spinoza of the German Romantics, a pantheist who saw the divine throughout nature; and Spinoza the immoral atheist, a man vilified by his contemporaries as the author of what one overwrought critic (referring to the *Theological-Political Treatise* called "a book forged in hell with the help of the Devil." There is Spinoza the Jewish reformer and Spinoza the anti-Semite. In philosophy, Spinoza is said to be a Cartesian, a Hobbesian, a Platonist, an Aristotelian, a Stoic, and a Machiavellian, among other persuasions. He is also a socialist, a Zionist, an anarchist, a Jeffersonian republican, the source of the Radical Enlightenment, and so on.

Missing from all of these portraits, however, is something that captures not so much what Spinoza represents to others, but an essential feature of what he authentically is: a metaphysical, moral, religious, and political thinker who belongs to the history of Jewish philosophy, a true secular modern who simultaneously assimilates, transforms, and subverts an ancient and religious project.

Despite attempts to "marranize" Spinoza's personal experience,[6] his upbringing and education took place within an open, well-established, albeit (because of its historical *converso* roots) not always perfectly orthodox Jewish community. It is true that his parents had been through the *converso* experience, in Portugal and, in the case of his father, France. But Spinoza himself grew up under the watchful eyes of the rabbis of Amsterdam's Portuguese *kehilla*: he attended the elementary school of

---

[6] Yovel 1989. For a critique of Yovel's reading, see Van Bunge 2001.

the united Talmud Torah congregation, paid his dues as an upstanding member of the community, and (after taking over his father's mercantile business) most likely continued his adult studies in the Keter Torah yeshiva run by the congregation's chief rabbi, the Ashkenazic import Saul Levi Mortera.

In July 1656, however, Spinoza was expelled from the Amsterdam Portuguese community with the harshest writ of *ḥerem* (ostracism) ever issued by its leaders. The only extant documentation of this event, the *ḥerem* text itself, refers to his "abominable heresies" and "monstrous deeds," but it still remains something of a mystery why exactly Spinoza was punished with such extreme prejudice. It has been suggested that the cause of his expulsion lay in certain financial irregularities – in particular, because he went outside the jurisdiction of the Portuguese community to the Dutch authorities in order to relieve himself of debts he inherited from his father, in direct violation of the community's regulations.[7] However, in light of the vitriolic language of the *ḥerem*, its extraordinary harshness when compared with other expulsions from the period, as well as the reference to "abominable heresies," it is hard to believe that it all amounted to merely a legal matter. More likely, it was a question of ideas – in particular, just the kind of bold philosophical, theological, and religious views that Spinoza would begin expressing in his written works within a couple of years.

Be that as it may, the expulsion order was never rescinded, and Spinoza lived the rest of his life outside any Jewish context. In fact, he seems not to have had any residual sense of Jewish identity. In his writings, he goes out of his way to distance himself from Judaism, and always refers to the Jews in the third person – as "them." Nor does he exhibit any fundamental sympathy with Jewish history or culture; indeed, he seems to harbor a degree of hostility to the Jewish people, about whom he has some very unkind things to say.

And yet it can hardly be said that Spinoza's break with Judaism was perfectly clean and complete. Things are rarely so black and white in the history of ideas, least of all with as deep and complex a philosopher as Spinoza. While he may no longer have thought of himself as a Jew, and while he even had great contempt for Judaism and other organized sectarian religions, it cannot be denied that Jewish texts, history, and thought continued to play an important role in Spinoza's thinking – so much so that Spinoza can rightfully be considered a Jewish philosopher, both because his

[7] See Vlessing 1996.

ideas exhibit a strong engagement with earlier Jewish philosophy and because in his major works he philosophized about Judaism.[8]

For a long time, however, a reader of the literature on Spinoza would have had little reason for thinking this. Scholarship on Spinoza in the late nineteenth century and much of the twentieth century, especially in the Anglo-American tradition but also to some degree in France, the Netherlands, Italy, and Germany – when scholars even took account of context – was focused almost exclusively on the seventeenth-century philosophical background: primarily Descartes and Cartesianism, but also Hobbes, Leibniz, and others, including fellow Dutch thinkers of the republican political persuasion. To be sure, this is an extremely important framework for understanding Spinoza's thought, and the result of this scholarship, in books and articles, was great and influential insights into his philosophy.[9]

Moreover, it would not be fair to say that the Jewish context was completely ignored in this extended period. It is nearly impossible to write about the TTP without discussing Maimonides, primarily because Spinoza explicitly takes the author of the *Guide of the Perplexed* to task for his account of the interpretation of Scripture. Thus, works of European scholarship such as (Rabbi) Manuel Joël's *Spinoza's Theologisch-politischer Traktat auf seine Quellen geprüft* (Breslau, 1870) and Leo Strauss's *Die Religionskritik Spinozas als Grundlage seiner Bibelwissenschaft* (Berlin, 1930) include comparative analyses of Maimonides and Spinoza on Biblical hermeneutic, the relationship between reason and revelation, and other issues.[10] Meanwhile, Leon Roth's short but valuable book *Spinoza, Descartes, and Maimonides* (Oxford, 1924) recognizes Maimonides' influence upon Spinoza in matters beyond just the theologico-political; indeed, at one point Roth suggests that on certain topics "Maimonides and Spinoza speak . . . with one voice" (143–144).[11]

Above all, there is the magisterial work of Harry Austryn Wolfson. In his two-volume *The Philosophy of Spinoza* (Harvard, 1934), Wolfson insisted on intimate connections between the ideas in Spinoza's *Ethics* and the doctrines of medieval Jewish rationalists such as Maimonides and Gersonides,

[8] Thus it seems perfectly right that Spinoza should appear in most recent histories of and "companions" to Jewish philosophy, either as the culmination of the medieval tradition or the beginning of the modern. See, for example, Frank and Leaman 2003.
[9] Bennett 1984 and Curley 1969, as well as Alquié 1981 and Gueroult 1968.
[10] See also Pines 1968. More recent studies of the TTP that take due note of Maimonides include Chalier 2006, Levene 2004, Preus 2001, and Verbeek 2003.
[11] Likewise, Pines (Maimonides 1963, xcviii) has claimed that Maimonides' God is "perilously close to Spinoza's attribute of thought (or to his Intellect of God)."

as well as other figures. It was never any secret that Spinoza had closely studied the *Guide of the Perplexed*. But to claim that the highly opaque, extraordinarily difficult *Ethics*, which (unlike the TTP) does not once mention any other thinker by name, was also influenced by what Spinoza read in Maimonides – as well as in Gersonides' *Wars of the Lord*, and in the works of Judah Halevi, Abraham ibn Ezra, and Solomon ibn Gabirol – was a bold and original thesis. One need not accept all of Wolfson's conclusions, particularly when he suggests that most of Spinoza's philosophy is nothing but a kind of pastiche of earlier Jewish, Arabic, and Latin-Scholastic thought or when he claims that Spinoza was concerned to defend what Wolfson regards as certain traditional rabbinic doctrines (such as the immortality of the soul). But it can be said that Wolfson's study opened the door to seeing Spinoza as a thinker deeply engaged with Jewish philosophy, and not just because of some perceived echoes of kabbalah or because Spinoza engaged Maimonides head on in the TTP.

Throughout the twentieth century, then, it was certainly not unheard of to look at Spinoza's ideas in a Jewish philosophical context, and perhaps even to think of him, in some sense, as a "Jewish thinker." There were a few exceptional examples of learned scholarship that took account of the Judaic intellectual milieux and textual traditions to which Spinoza, alone among major early modern philosophers, had access. Moreover, virtually every "History," "Encyclopedia," or "Companion" to Jewish philosophy published in the last hundred years has seen fit to include some discussion of Spinoza.

Still, something seemed to be missing. Only a small number of scholars took up Wolfson's challenge in a serious way in the decades after the appearance of his book. Analytically oriented philosophers, more concerned with dissecting and evaluating Spinoza's theses and arguments (to be sure, often with great results), were only rarely interested in the historico-philosophical context, and not at all in the Jewish philosophical angle. The shortcomings of this approach were particularly evident when scholars expressed frustration over their inability to make sense of one or another important but apparently mystifying features of Spinoza's metaphysics, epistemology, and moral philosophy – for example, Spinoza's doctrine of the eternity of the mind in Part Five of the *Ethics*, a doctrine which, it might be argued, can only be understood in the light of the views of Maimonides and Gersonides.[12] In the philosophical literature on Spinoza throughout most of the last century, studies like those of

---

[12] Nadler 2001.

Strauss, Roth, Joël, and Wolfson remained the exception rather than the rule, and it was unusual to find a deep, systematic, and substantive study of Spinoza in relationship to his Jewish philosophical ancestors, and even rarer to find such a Judaic contextualizing discussion of the *Ethics*.[13]

In the second half of the twentieth century, great progress was made in understanding the Sephardic and Dutch-Jewish contexts of Spinoza's life. This was due in part to a number of studies that (thanks to some important archival discoveries) illuminated various aspects of the world of Amsterdam Jewry in the seventeenth century. We gained deeper insights into the Jewish dimensions of Spinoza's early biography and a better understanding of the personal and historical circumstances of his intellectual development. Among these studies are books and articles by the eminent historians I. S. Révah, Yosef Kaplan, Jonathan Israel, Richard Popkin, Henri Méchoulan, and Gabriel Albiac.[14]

All of this historical work was essential, of course. But it left untouched, in the post-Wolfson period, the more intricate philosophical task of identifying Jewish elements in Spinoza's thought, and doing so not impressionistically and haphazardly but with solid comparative analyses and arguments.[15] This project was not really initiated in a serious way until an important and influential 1984 article by Warren Zev Harvey, in which he attempts "to sketch a portrait of Spinoza as a Maimonidean, as the last major representative of a tradition that mightily dominated Jewish philosophy for almost five centuries following the appearance of the *Guide of the Perplexed*."[16] Harvey covers a limited number of topics on which the two thinkers can be fruitfully compared – the distinction between intellect and imagination, a shared contempt for anthropomorphism in the depiction of God, and the intellectual love of God as our *summum bonum* – and he really only outlines a program for further research. But Harvey nonetheless, fifty years after Wolfson, took seriously the spirit of the latter's program and

---

[13] I am concerned here mainly with the philosophical secondary literature on Spinoza and the way it addresses his relationship to earlier Jewish thought. By contrast, there has always been within the Jewish intellectual and literary tradition a tendency to recognize Spinoza as one of its own (although in very different ways throughout history). For an excellent review of this topic, see Schwartz 2012.

[14] Révah (1959) was extraordinarily important in this regard, although I am skeptical that De Prado played an important role in Spinoza's intellectual development. I should also mention the earlier groundbreaking work of Carl Gebhardt (especially Gebhardt 1922) and of A. M. Vaz Dias and W. G. Van der Tak (Vaz Dias and Van der Tak 1932).

[15] I should mention, however, Brykman 1972, which considers some Jewish themes she finds informing Spinoza's thought; and Levy 1972 and 1989.

[16] W. Harvey 1981.

began the process of looking closely at what could in fact be justifiably said about Spinoza's relationship to Maimonides (and, by implication, other medieval Jewish philosophers). While Wolfson's study was all over the place, throwing around passages helter-skelter (often without explanation), Harvey called for a more selective approach and more careful and critical scrutiny.

The situation when Harvey was writing was such that he could still say that portraying Spinoza as a Maimonidean "is admittedly controversial . . . it generally has not been held that there was a *distinctive* Maimonidean influence on Spinoza's philosophy."[17] It is hard to imagine anyone now being worried about making this kind of claim. In recent articles, Heidi Ravven,[18] Carlos Fraenkel,[19] Idit Dobbs-Weinstein,[20] and others have rightly taken it for granted that there is much to be gained by reading Spinoza in a Jewish philosophical context and have followed Harvey's lead by pursuing a deeper and more rigorous investigation of Spinoza's relationship to medieval Jewish rationalism on such topics as the nature of prophecy and the proper conception of God. Ravven, for example, has argued that while Spinoza certainly rejects Maimonides' view that the prophets were philosophers and that the Bible offers insights into central philosophical doctrines (particularly those of Aristotle), he nonetheless was greatly influenced by the Maimonidean account of the imaginative character and political utility of the prophetic writings in the Bible. And Fraenkel has drawn our attention to important parallels between Maimonides' God as "the *causa immanens* of all existents" and Spinoza's *Deus sive Natura*, despite Spinoza's apparent break (due to his monism) with central features of the conception of God in the medieval Jewish philosophical tradition. Meanwhile, volumes such as *Jewish Themes in Spinoza's Philosophy*[21] and the issue of *Studia Spinozana* devoted to the topic "Spinoza and Jewish identity" (2003) offer a wide range of studies by Spinoza experts and Jewish studies scholars on the relationship between Spinoza's metaphysics, epistemology, moral philosophy, and political thought, on the one hand, and, on the other hand, Jewish philosophical and religious thought – traditional and otherwise.

Over the last two decades, then, some elements of this (Jewish) part of the story of Spinoza's philosophy – as opposed to his biography – have begun to be filled in. We are beginning to get a fuller, if not necessarily simpler, picture of Spinoza's relationship to earlier Jewish thought. It thus seems a

---

[17] *Ibid.*   [18] Ravven 2001a and 2001b.   [19] Fraenkel 2006.
[20] Dobbs-Weinstein 1994 and 2004.   [21] Ravven and Goodman 2002.

good time to take stock and consider the state of things. Thus, in conceiving this volume I turned to a number of leading scholars and asked them to write essays in which they address some aspect or another of the relationship between Spinoza's philosophy and medieval Jewish philosophy.

There was never any assumption that this volume should be an exhaustive study of all the aspects of this relationship; the goal was not completeness. The invitation to participate specified only that the authors should focus on some specific problem and/or philosopher(s), and not concern themselves with grand overviews or comprehensive surveys. I gave no particular directions whatsoever as to what topic to address or whom to include. Part of the interest of the project would be to discover how these scholars would approach the issue. In this regard, the essays represent an exercise in contingency: upon whom would these experts in Spinoza's philosophy and Jewish thought call to illuminate which features of his metaphysics, epistemology, moral philosophy, religious thought, and political ideas?

Not surprisingly, given his stature in the history of Jewish philosophy and his obvious importance for Spinoza, most of the authors decided to focus on Maimonides. Thus, it may seem as if there is something of an imbalance in this volume. However, if the result of this is that we gain a deeper and more detailed understanding of the various dimensions and complexities of Spinoza's relationship to the twelfth-century rabbi, physician, and thinker who was the greatest of all Jewish philosophers, then the topical unevenness of the volume is something we should be able to live with.

Jacob Adler's "Mortality of the soul from Alexander of Aphrodisias to Spinoza" considers what he claims is a likely (and illuminating) source for Spinoza's heterodox views on the nature and fate of the soul, as well as for his "ratio of motion and rest" account of the individuation of body. He argues that Spinoza's denial of personal immortality, especially in the *Short Treatise*, bears a close resemblance to the theory of the "acquired intellect" in Alexander (that it is, in fact, "an Alexandrist theory of immortality"), and that Spinoza was likely influenced, directly or indirectly, by Alexander's doctrine. Adler thus considers various possible contemporary sources for Spinoza's acquaintance with Alexander's ancient theory, as well as what seems to be a change in doctrine in the *Ethics*.

In his chapter "Spinoza and the determinist tradition in medieval Jewish philosophy," Charles Manekin considers in particular the effect that Crescas's starkly deterministic position might have had on Spinoza's doctrine that "all things are determined ... not only to exist but also to exist and to act in a definite way" (*Ethics* Ip9d). He notes that there appear to be at least two fundamental differences between Crescas and Spinoza on the question of determinism and free will. First, Spinoza holds that "all things have been predetermined by God, not from freedom of the will, or absolute good pleasure but from God's absolute nature, or infinite power." Crescas, on the other hand, says that God wills the world into existence through beneficence and grace, taking pleasure in this activity. Second, although Crescas and Spinoza are both strict determinists, the former has generally been read by scholars as a *soft* determinist, i.e. one who holds that humans *deserve* divine reward and punishment when and only when they act voluntarily – even though all things, including human volitions, are determined. By contrast, Spinoza, a hard determinist, claims that notions like praise and blame arise from the illusory belief that humans possess free will. Manekin argues that the first difference, while real, is not as great as it seems, and that the second difference is no difference at all. His thesis is that Crescas is best read, like Spinoza, as a hard determinist who dispenses with the deservedness of divine reward and punishment, and in fact dispenses with a desert model of divine justice altogether.

Tamar Rudavsky's essay, "The science of Scripture: Abraham ibn Ezra and Spinoza on biblical bermeneutics," also focuses on the TTP. She compares Ibn Ezra's theory of Bible science with that of Spinoza. Her purpose is twofold: to emphasize the importance of science in their respective readings of Scripture, and to gauge the extent to which Spinoza radicalizes Ibn Ezra's readings of Scripture. She argues that both Ibn Ezra and Spinoza make use of scientific discourse in their analysis of the Bible; this application of scientific method to biblical hermeneutics attests to the attempts of both thinkers to render all intellectual enterprises rigorous and amenable to rational scrutiny.

Steven Frankel's essay, "Spinoza's rejection of Maimonideanism," approaches the complexities and apparent inconsistencies of Spinoza's relationship to Maimonides. He begins by examining the disagreement among contemporary scholars on this issue: some emphasize Spinoza's kinship with Maimonides, while others focus on the comprehensiveness of his critique. By examining the passages where Spinoza explicitly criticizes his great predecessor, Frankel argues that their minor differences over hermeneutical issues reveal a much more radical disagreement about the possibility of enlightening the multitude and making politics and religion more consistent with reason. He then explores how Spinoza's political project is shaped by his view that there is an unbridgeable chasm between, on the one hand, philosophy and, on the other hand, religion and politics.

Warren Zev Harvey, after noting some parallels between Maimonides' *Guide of the Perplexed* and Spinoza's *Ethics*, begins "'*Ishq, Ḥesheq,* and *amor Dei intellectualis*" with a puzzle that he finds in both texts: how can pleasure and love be attributed to the intellect when it has "no relation to the body." This "problem" leads him to an analysis of the connections between the Arabic '*ishq* and the Hebrew *ḥesheq* in Maimonides and the Latin *amor Dei intellectualis* in Spinoza. Harvey shows how Spinoza's use of the intellectual love of God in *Ethics*, Part Five, is indebted to Maimonides' discussion of the love of God in *Guide* III.51. As he traces the history of these terms from Al-Farabi, through Avicenna, Maimonides, and Gersonides, to Spinoza, Harvey shows how, in fact, the idea of intellectual passion goes back to Aristotle, for whom the idea is also problematic. If it seems more problematic in Spinoza, Harvey argues, it is only because he exerted the greatest effort to make philosophic sense of it.

Ken Seeskin, in "Monotheism at bay: the Gods of Maimonides and Spinoza," offers a comparative analysis of the theologies of the two philosophers. He looks especially at the anti-anthropomorphism that characterizes the Maimonidean and Spinozist conceptions of God. At the same time, he argues, there is an important difference between the thinkers on the question of the moral and theological value of humility. For Maimonides, Seeskin insists, humility is "the chief theological virtue," whereby one is "to bow one's head in the face of something too vast to understand." For Spinoza, on the other hand, humility is not a virtue; rather, its opposite, self-esteem, is what arises from the proper use of reason.

In "Moral agency without free will: Spinoza's naturalizing of moral psychology in a Maimonidean key," Heidi Ravven argues that in the *Ethics* Spinoza develops an account of moral agency that envisions a path of transformation toward ever greater and broader constitution of the individual in and with the environment. Hence Spinoza's theory cannot be considered to fall within compatibilist accounts of free will. According to Ravven, the power of the mind that Spinoza develops in the *Ethics* is its power to contextualize its own experience, its own embodied engagements and interrelations, within the infinite webs of nature. Thus the mind in furthering its knowledge always captures, reframes, and expands its initial and ongoing constitutive relations and relatedness, with a concomitant transformation in motivation, that is, in the scope and power of the *conatus*. She concludes by showing that Spinoza's account of moral agency reflects Maimonides' claim that coming to know, as far as humanly possible, God's attributes of action (i.e. the natural principles embodied in natural processes) through the theoretical study of nature is transformative not only of mind but of affect and motivation, because it brings the intellect into conformity with the divine reason underlying and informing nature. Hence the mind's ever increasing awareness of its universal natural constitution, and not some individual self-origination, is the source of its enhanced agency.

The essay by Steven Nadler, "Virtue, reason, and moral luck: Maimonides, Gersonides, Spinoza," examines the relationship between virtue (understood as the perfection of the intellect), rational understanding, and happiness in works such as Maimonides' *Guide of the Perplexed* and Levi ben Gershom's *Wars of the Lord*, and shows how these thinkers thereby deal with the problem of moral luck – that is, with the role that good or bad fortune may play in the achievement of human happiness and flourishing. Nadler then demonstrates how aspects of Spinoza's moral philosophy in Parts Four and Five of the *Ethics* represents a kind of radical but natural culmination of the medieval Jewish rationalist tradition on this topic.

The eternity of the mind is among the most notorious, difficult, and intriguing ideas in Spinoza's philosophy. "The human Mind cannot be absolutely destroyed with the Body," he writes enigmatically in *Ethics* Vp23, "but something of it remains which is eternal." According to Julie Klein, in her chapter "'Something of it remains': Spinoza and Gersonides on intellectual immortality," what remains after death, according to Spinoza, is purely intellectual and constitutes the "highest satisfaction" and "greatest joy" of the mind. Spinoza's position, she claims, reflects an influential position in the medieval Jewish tradition. She argues, on the basis of textual and conceptual parallels, that Spinoza drew on the work of Gersonides to articulate his position on the eternity of the mind and related metaphysical and epistemological issues.

In the final chapter, "Hasdai Crescas and Spinoza on actual infinity and the infinity of God's attributes," Yitzhak Melamed traces one thread in the development of the concept of the infinite. He examines Hasdai Crescas's argument against the Aristotelian (and Maimonidean) tradition that, in proving God's existence, relies on the impossibility of an actual infinite (in particular, the impossibility of an infinite regress of causes). He shows how Crescas's position must have influenced Spinoza's view (as detailed in the *Ethics* and the "Letter on the Infinite") on the real possibility of an actual infinite of effects following from a necessarily existing, infinite, simple cause. Melamed then turns to Spinoza's view that God, an infinite substance, must have infinite attributes and the precedent for this in Crescas.

Taken together, the essays in this volume – as selective as they are – present an illuminating if only partial overview the depth and complexity of Spinoza's relationship to his medieval Jewish philosophical forebears. There are, of course, many other dimensions to this relationship, and hopefully this collection will open new and suggestive pathways in Spinoza scholarship.

CHAPTER I

Mortality of the soul from Alexander of Aphrodisias to Spinoza

Jacob Adler

In Spinoza's *Short Treatise on God, Man, and His Well-Being*, we encounter the following remarkable passage:

1. Our soul is either a substance or a mode; not a substance, for we have already proven that there can be no limited substance in Nature. Therefore, a mode.

   . . .

6. This knowledge, Idea, etc., of each particular thing which comes to exist, is, we say, the soul of this particular thing.

7. Each and every particular thing that comes to exist becomes such through motion and rest. The same is true of all modes in the substantial extension we call body.

8. The differences [between one body and another] arise only from the different proportions of motion and rest, by which this one is so, and not so, is this and not that.

9. From this proportion of motion and rest, then, there comes to exist also this body of ours, of which . . . there must exist a knowledge, Idea, etc., in the thinking thing. This Idea, knowledge, etc., is also our soul.

   . . .

12. So if such a body has and preserves its proportion – say of 1 to 3 – the soul and the body will be like ours now are; they will, of course, be constantly subject to change, but not to such a great change that it

This chapter was written in part during an Off-Campus Duty Assignment from the University of Arkansas and a stint as Visiting Scholar at the Jewish Theological Seminary of America. I thank these institutions for their support. An early version of this chapter benefited from comments from Charlie Huenemann and the late Richard Popkin; naturally they bear no responsibility for my errors. For assistance of various sorts, I thank Ranon Katzoff, Menachem Kellner, Alan Mittleman, and Marc Saperstein. Finally, my sincere thanks to the staff of the Interlibrary Loan Department, Mullins Library, University of Arkansas, without whom this chapter would not have been possible.

goes beyond the limits of from 1 to 3; and as much as it changes, the
soul also changes each time.

. . .

14. But if other bodies act on ours with such force that the proportion of
motion [to rest] cannot remain 1 to 3, that is death, and a destruction of
the soul, insofar as it is only an Idea, knowledge, etc. of a body having
this proportion of motion and rest.[1]

This passage may well call forth puzzlement – indeed, may cause the reader
to stop fast. What in the world can Spinoza mean by a "proportion of
motion and rest," a proportion defined by a numerical ratio? And how can
such a proportion define our body or soul? In this chapter I propose to
explain this odd passage and relate it to texts with which Spinoza was likely
familiar. In particular, I shall argue that Spinoza was writing in the tradition
of the famous questioner of immortality, Alexander of Aphrodisias, and that
this connection helps place Spinoza in the history of philosophy as well as
in his contemporary setting.

For convenience, I shall refer to this proportion of motion and rest,
defined numerically, as the "essential ratio." Note that this concept of a
definitive numerical proportion is unique to the *Short Treatise*. In the *Ethics*,
we also read of a *ratio motus et quietis*, which might seem to amount to the
same thing, but in the *Ethics* there is no suggestion that this phrase refers to a
numerical ratio. Indeed, the Latin word *ratio*, has a great range of meanings,[2]
and, as I have argued elsewhere, the *ratio motus et quietis* as found in the
Ethics should be understand as a *configuration of motion and rest*, something
far more complex than a single numerical ratio.[3]

Alexander of Aphrodisias is now not the best known of philosophers.
Despite a recent resurgence in Alexander studies,[4] a person could spend
many years studying philosophy without encountering the name of
Alexander. Yet at one time he was a celebrated commentator on Aristotle
as well as an important Peripatetic philosopher in his own right. Until
supplanted by Averroës, Alexander was known as *the* commentator on
Aristotle. An earlier resurgence in Alexander studies was set off by the
publication in 1495 of Girolamo Donato's Latin translation of Alexander's
De Anima.[5] Alexander's views on immortality are not entirely clear. He

---

[1] KV Preface, note, Spinoza 1985, 95–96.
[2] See e.g. Gouldman 1664, s.v. *ratio*; Lewis and Short 1879, s.v. *ratio*, esp. sense B1c(a).
[3] Adler 1996.
[4] See Cohoe, forthcoming. Note also the large and increasing numbers of translations into English and
French, as well as the appearance of an issue of *Les Études philosophiques* (2008 (3)) devoted to Alexander.
[5] See the quotations assembled in Girsel 2012.

sometimes seems to say that the soul dies with the body; at other times, he seems to say that by achieving a certain level of intellectual attainment, a person's intellect gains a kind of permanence. But this permanent existence seems to be impersonal: so we may say that Alexander denies *personal* immortality. Either way, Alexander's views challenged the monotheistic tradition of belief in personal immortality.[6]

We will be looking at works that Spinoza read or knew or is likely to have read or known. A few words about this here at the beginning. Some scholars maintain a very strict standard, and will not admit that Spinoza was influenced by anything unless there is documentary evidence to that effect. Others assume that Spinoza was familiar with the whole body of previous philosophical literature.[7] I attempt to steer a middle course: I will not assume, without evidence or argument, that Spinoza knew or was influenced by a particular text. But the evidence or argument need not be conclusive; it is worth exploring possibilities that seem highly likely, though not absolutely certain.

Alexander in Amsterdam

Alexander was known in the Amsterdam Jewish community of Spinoza's time, at least among the more educated. We can point to two sources that confirm this.

Their tendency is epitomized by a quotation from Menasseh ben Israel's *Nishmat Ḥayyim* ("The Soul of Life"):

> Lo, Alexander of Aphrodisias defined the soul as a mere disposition and potential to receive the intelligibles in which it delights after death and achieves conjunction with the active intellect. And many were drawn after him, and they drank of these poisonous waters. And when I contemplated his words, I said to myself, "It is time to act for the Lord[8] and to remove from myself his heresy, which destroys the cornerstones and foundations of our Torah. Whoever does not breach [Alexander's] wall – may a snake bite him!"[9]

---

[6] For a useful brief summary, see Feldman 2010, 174–176.

[7] The most prominent practitioner of this second approach is Wolfson 1934.   [8] Psalms 119:126.

[9] *Nishmat Ḥayyim* II.1, Menasseh ben Israel 1995, 93. The phrase, "breach Alexander's wall" might also be translated, "reject Alexander's definition" or "throw off Alexander's yoke." The whole of this last sentence is based on Ecclesiastes 10:8b, "whoso breaketh through a wall, a serpent shall bite him." The key word here is *gader*, which originally means "fence" or "wall," but in philosophical Hebrew "definition." See Klatzkin 1926–1933, s.v. *gader*, especially the sub-entry for *gader paruts*. We shall have occasion later in the chapter to examine more closely the translation of this last sentence of Menasseh's.

Menasseh thus identifies Alexander as the champion denier of immortality, the well from which other deniers of immortality drew their water; and he states his concern in intemperate language.

Before Menasseh, we find another Amsterdam voice citing Alexander as the most important denier of immortality. Joseph Solomon Delmedigo – physician, astronomer, medical doctor, and rabbi – served as rabbi in Amsterdam in the late 1620s.[10] The exact dates of his time in Amsterdam are not clear: he had arrived by the summer of 1626[11] and departed in the winter of 1629–1630.[12] During his time there, Menasseh persuaded him to publish one of his two printed works, *Sefer 'Elim*, which emerged from the press of Menasseh in 1629. The publication of *'Elim* was a matter of scandal: the *deputados* of the Jewish community forbade the publication of eight major parts of the work.[13] J. d'Ancona attributes Delmedigo's departure from Amsterdam to the publication of this work, and Jeremy Pfeffer claims that the publication of *'Elim* made it impossible for Delmedigo ever again to get a rabbinical appointment.[14] These facts surrounding the publication of *'Elim* are of interest here. The book did not slip quietly from the press; it was evidently the sort of book that people might seek out and read to see what all the fuss is about.

Delmedigo likewise cites Alexander of Aphrodisias as the leading proponent of mortalism. He presents a detailed discussion of Alexander's view. (As a good physician, he also gives a nod to Galen, who likewise denies immortality.) Delmedigo himself rejects Alexander's view, and affirms immortality, but notes (as we shall have occasion to discuss further) that he nonetheless himself was accused of denying it.[15]

'Elim includes a letter from Delmedigo's disciple, Moses Metz, to Delmedigo's Karaite correspondent, Zeraḥ ben Natan. In this letter, Metz does not shrink from denying immortality. Again, he ascribes the denial of immortality to Alexander of Aphrodisias. He also describes the hostile reaction his view elicited: "Behold, I see that many have come forth against me with swords drawn, saying 'What shall we do for our sister,[16] our soul if she is nothing more than a temperament? Woe betide our latter end!'"[17] The inclusion of this letter from a disciple must have raised suspicions about the

---

[10] On J. S. Delmedigo see generally Barzilay 1974, supplemented by D'Ancona 1940. Barzilay seems to have been unaware of this important source on Delmedigo, perhaps because it is written in Dutch, perhaps also because it came out at an unfortunate time and place – the Netherlands in 1940.

[11] D'Ancona 1940, 123. Barzilay (1974, 78) gives the erroneous date of 1628; apparently he had not seen D'Ancona's article.

[12] Barzilay 1974, 78.   [13] D'Ancona 1940, 123–130.   [14] *Ibid.*, 130; Pfeffer 2010, 6.

[15] Delmedigo 1864, 89.   [16] Cf. Song of Songs 8:8.   [17] Metz in Delmedigo 1864, 53–54.

master. Indeed, Delmedigo's condemnation of youngsters who deny immortality – presumably including Metz – is rather weak. He essentially says, "Don't worry about them. They're just trying to shock you. When they grow up, they'll return to orthodoxy." [18]

It is of interest that Spinoza almost certainly owned a copy of *'Elim*, listed as *Een Rabbinsch Mathematisch boeck*, in the posthumous inventory of Spinoza's library.[19] As for Menasseh, there is no indication that Spinoza read his *Nishmat Ḥayyim*, nor is it likely that Menasseh was Spinoza's teacher in a formal sense, but it is reasonable to assume that Spinoza learned from Menasseh in an informal way, given that Menasseh was the most worldly of the Amsterdam rabbis.[20] I will proceed here on the assumption that Spinoza and Menasseh had some connection and that immortality, as a common interest, was among the subjects they discussed.

Who was this Alexander, and what was his teaching? Alexander was a prominent interpreter of Aristotle, active in the second and third centuries of the common era. In his *De Anima* he presented an interpretation of Aristotle's cryptic comments on the soul presented in the latter's *De Anima*, Book 3, Chapter 5. Alexander introduced terminology that set the terms for later discussions of the soul and its fate. The soul in its initial form is called the *material* (or *hylic*) intellect, which is no more than a disposition or potentiality to understand. Being merely a disposition, the material intellect perishes when the body perishes. This potentiality can only be actualized by something that is itself in act, namely, the *agent* (or *active*) *intellect*. If this intellectual potentiality becomes sufficiently developed, the person attains an *acquired intellect*, which is not subject to decay, and is thus immortal. For Alexander, it does this by achieving what is called conjunction with the agent intellect. Alexander himself identifies this agent intellect with God,[21] though others describe it otherwise: for Thomas Aquinas, it is part of the human soul; for Gersonides it is the separate intellect governing the sublunary realm.[22] This theory of the soul in its various manifestations came to be known as the theory of the acquired intellect.

---

[18] Delmedigo 1864, 85–86.   [19] Adler 1999; 2008; 2013.
[20] Nadler 1999, 93–100; Offenberg 1977, 30.
[21] Alexander 1495, fol. lir; 1887, 89; 1980, §3.27. Alexander says specifically that the agent intellect is identical with the first cause. I use triple citations of Alexander: the Latin translation of 1495 (reprinted many times in the sixteenth century), since this is the one Spinoza was most likely to have read; the Greek text of 1887, which is the standard way of citing Alexander; and (in most cases) Fotinis's English translation of 1980, since this is (so far) the only nearly complete English translation of the *De Anima*. In a few places I have used the newer translation by Victor Caston (Alexander 2012), which covers only part of the *De Anima* but is often clearer.
[22] Thomas Aquinas, *Quaestiones Disputatae de Anima*, Art. 5; Nadler 2001, 83.

We might spend considerable space explicating Alexander's view of the soul and its fate, but for the moment, the point of interest is what the Jewish sources of Spinoza's time thought about Alexander's view. The main doctrine they attributed to Alexander was the idea that the soul is a mere disposition (*hakhanah*) or potential (*koaḥ*), and therefore mortal.[23] Menasseh cites Moses of Narbonne (in his commentary on Maimonides' *Guide of the Perplexed*) and, above all, Isaac Arama, who again ascribe to Alexander the view that the soul is a disposition or potential.[24]

Surprisingly, perhaps, there is little mention of Gersonides. Gersonides presents the Alexandrist theory in great detail in Chapters 1 and 2 of his magnum opus, *The Wars of the Lord*.[25] One would have thought that this would be the natural source for those discussing Alexander, but in point of fact his his name is scarcely mentioned among the sources we have cited.[26] In another respect, it is not surprising. Though respected as a Bible commentator, Gersonides' philosophical works were roundly condemned by most of the Jewish writers who considered them. *The Wars of the Lord* was indeed often called *The Wars Against the Lord*, a pejorative title apparently already common by the time of its first publication.[27] A respected halakhic authority, Rabbi Isaac bar Sheshet (1326–1408), went so far as to rule that it was forbidden even to listen to his philosophical views:

> As for the sage, Rabbi Levi [ben Gershom], of blessed memory – even though he was a great sage in Talmud and wrote an excellent commentary on the Torah and the Prophetic books and followed in the footsteps of Maimonides – still, the [philosophical] sciences led his heart astray from following the true path, and he perverted some of the views of Maimonides . . . so that it is forbidden to listen to [his views on these subjects], and likewise with the immortality of the soul . . .[28]

By the seventeenth century, Gersonides' philosophical writings were hard to find and, with the decline of the Jewish philosophical tradition, difficult to understand.[29]

---

[23] *Nishmat Ḥayyim*, II.1, Menasseh ben Israel 1995, 93; *'Elim*, Delmedigo 1864, 89.

[24] *Nishmat Ḥayyim*, II.1–2, Menasseh ben Israel 1995, 96, 98.   [25] Levi ben Gershom 1984, 109–119.

[26] Menasseh writes, "And Gersonides spoke about it in Part 6, section 2 of his book, *The Wars of [the Lord]*" – this is Menasseh's complete discussion of Gersonides' theory of the soul. Menasseh erroneously cites Gersonides' book as *The Wars of God*. See *Nishmat Ḥayyim*, II.1, Menasseh ben Israel 1995, 96.

[27] Kellner 1976, 271; Jacob Marcaria in Levi ben Gershom 1560, 1b.

[28] *Responsa*, no. 45, Isaac bar Sheshet (n.d.), 20.

[29] Kellner 1976, 272; 2013, 284. Additional examples of the condemnation of Gersonides may be found in Broydé 1906, 32.

Rather it is Isaac Arama who comes in for criticism for following in the footsteps of Alexander. By contrast with Gersonides, Arama was a respected and influential author. His major work, the *'Akedat Yitsḥak* ("The Binding of Isaac") is described by one author as having a "tremendous influence on subsequent Jewish preaching."[30] *'Akedat Yitsḥak* consists of philosophical-homiletic sermons on the Torah. To a certain extent, it might be compared to present-day works that seek to present philosophy at a level accessible to the average educated person, though Arama's work was of course oriented to the Torah. In Menasseh's *Nishmat Ḥayyim* Arama's views on the soul form the subject of five chapters.[31] Menasseh again uses rather intemperate language: "When I had the leisure to investigate and examine [Arama's sixth sermon], I said to myself, 'Would that this gate[32] were closed and never opened, so that no one might enter it!' Our sages spoke well when they said, 'The greater the man, the greater the error.'"[33] Similarly, Saul Levi Mortera devoted much of his 1620 eulogy for Jacob Tirado to a critique of Arama's theory of the soul.[34] In a way, even if he knew about Gersonides, it made tactical sense to focus on Arama. Gersonides might be dismissed as a philosophical outlier: "What can you expect from one who wars against the Lord?" But Arama, as Menasseh suggests, was admired and influential. If even this great man could incline towards Alexander's view of the soul, it presented a real danger that must be repelled.

Arama discusses the soul in various places, but most intently in Sermon 6, whose scriptural starting point is Genesis 2:7: "[And the LORD God] ... breathed into his nostrils the breath of life; and man became a living soul." Arama does indeed describe the soul as a mere potential and disposition, a view which he frankly admits is the same as that of "some of the philosophers, such as Alexander and his supporters."[35] But in fact Arama pulls the sting from Alexander's theory by saying that if a person exercises this potential by philosophical speculation and by carrying out the divine commandments, then the person gains the acquired intellect,

---

[30] Kellner 1976, 273.   [31] *Nishmat Ḥayyim*, II.2, 3, 5, 6, 7, Menasseh ben Israel 1995.
[32] A play on words: *sha'ar* means both "gate" and "section of a book."
[33] *Nishmat Ḥayyim*, II.2, Menasseh ben Israel 1995, 98. The quotation attributed to the sages is found in a slightly different form in the Babylonian Talmud, *Bava' Metsi'a'* 96b.
[34] Saperstein 1991, 139. Time has not permitted me to consult the manuscript of this eulogy, whose text has never been published.
[35] *'Akedat Yitsḥak*, Sermon 6, Arama 1868, 1:66b, quoted also by Menasseh in *Nishmat Ḥayyim*, II.2, Menasseh ben Israel 1995, 98.

until this first potential becomes constituted as a substance[36] by means of [the] divine influx [*shefaʿ*] which is introduced into him in a great substantialization [*hitʿatsmut*]. It becomes stronger and stronger until it becomes a separate spiritual substance which does not at all decay when the body decays.[37]

There are two innovations here: first, the soul becomes "constituted as a substance"; immortality is not merely a matter of conjunction with the agent intellect (*à la* Alexander) or of attaining timeless truths (*à la* Gersonides). Second, it is not merely speculative knowledge but performance of the *mitzvot* that brings immortality.[38]

This first innovation is quite widespread. It goes back as least as far as the Hebrew translation of Averroës' commentary on Alexander's *De Anima*. This commentary is preserved in a work of Moses of Narbonne (thirteenth and fourteenth centuries), where we read that "the material intellect finally achieves conjunction with the separate intellect, wherein it is perfected and becomes constituted as a substance [*ve-yitʿatsem*]."[39] We find similar views in Ḥasdai Crescas, J. S. Delmedigo (both on his own account and attributed to Maimonides), and elsewhere.[40] It is not entirely clear that all these writers are referring to the same thing, but Arama leaves no doubt as to his view: the soul that studies and performs *mitzvot* is changed from a mere potential and disposition to a "separate, independent substance."[41] There is no worry that the soul may dissipate upon death, or that in immortality its individuality may be obliterated.

The second innovation obviates one of the elementary objections to the theory of the acquired intellect: if intellectual activity grants immortality, then a simple-minded pious person has no hope, whereas an evil genius gains eternal existence.[42]

Surprisingly, even this mitigated Alexandrism does not satisfy Menasseh and Mortera. Menasseh makes it clear that the only satisfactory view is one

---

[36] The phrase 'to become constituted as a substance' translates the Hebrew *hitʿatsem*. I adopt this translation from W. Harvey 1973, 434–435.

[37] *Ibid.*

[38] In addition to the quote from Sermon 6, see also Sermon 70, 3:155a–156a, where Arama clearly distinguishes his view. Moses Metz, Joseph Solomon Delmedigo's disciple, critiques this view by pointing out that it bestows no immortality upon those who have not learned of God or His commandments, a possibility which he sees as incompatible with the divine nature: see Delmedigo 1864, 54. Metz does not cite a source for this view, but it is likely drawn from Arama.

[39] Davidson 1988, 215; translation by the author.

[40] *'Or Hashem*, 2.6.1, Crescas 1990, 235 and elsewhere; Delmedigo 1864, 89; see citations in Klatzkin 1926–1933, s.vv. *hitʿatsmut, mitʿatsem*, and *ʿatsam*.

[41] *ʿEtsem nivdal ʿomed be-ʿatsmo*: *'Akedat Yitsḥak*, Sermon 32, Arama 1868, 1:276b.

[42] *Nishmat Ḥayyim*, II.1, Menasseh ben Israel 1995, 95.

that makes the soul immortal from the beginning – not just the beginning of the person, but from the beginning of creation for (says Menasseh) all souls were created during the six days of creation.[43] Delmedigo's experience also testifies to the unacceptability of mitigated Alexandrism:

> [I]n the days of my youth … I used to say that uneducated people [*'ame ha-'arets*] had no share in the world to come, for they had not become constituted as a substance from the intelligibles. And wicked, jealous people spread rumors about me on account of this so as to avenge themselves upon me, as if I had denied immortality. How could anyone with a conscience say such a thing? God forbid! That never crossed my mind.[44]

Although Delmedigo is referring to a time before he came to Amsterdam, his words still bear witness to the widespread rejection of Alexander's view that when a person begins life, his or her soul is a mere potential and disposition; this even though the advocates of this view affirm individual immortality.

How could these Amsterdam Jews have known about Alexander? They might have read Gersonides, despite the obstacles just mentioned. Menasseh and Delmedigo, as well as many ex-*conversos*, knew enough Latin to have read the Latin translation of Alexander; Delmedigo might even have read the original Greek. It is clear that Delmedigo read Alexander directly, for he correctly cites his *De Anima* (as well as John Philoponus' commentary on Aristotle's *De Anima*, where Alexander's views are presented).[45] Menasseh might well also have read Alexander, but his knowledge is less accurate,[46] so he may well have relied on secondary sources. In any case, as Guttmann and Ivry note, "Alexander's acquired intellect became a commonplace in Jewish philosophy."[47]

We shall have occasion to discuss the matter further.

Spinoza and Alexander

Spinoza thus found himself in a world where Alexander of Aphrodisias was a significant and controversial figure. Indeed, the whole subject of immortality, to which Alexander contributed so significantly, was a topic of great

---

[43] *Nishmat Ḥayyim*, II.4, Menasseh ben Israel 1995, 107.   [44] Delmedigo 1864, 89–90.

[45] *Ibid.*, 89.

[46] Menasseh criticizes Alexander for saying that one should achieve conjunction (in Hebrew, *lehidavek*, usually "cleave") with the agent intellect, whereas the Torah says that one should cleave to God. For Alexander, however, the agent intellect *is* God, so Menasseh's critique falls flat. Delmedigo, by contrast, is aware of the distinction: see Delmedigo 1629–1631, 17b–18a.

[47] Guttmann and Ivry 2007, 628.

concern. Steven Nadler has in fact argued persuasively that the denial of immortality was a major cause of Spinoza's excommunication.[48] It would seem natural that Spinoza would want to delve further into the views of the figure who was seen as the grandfather of mortalism.

If we can judge by the books in his library and the books that he cites, Spinoza had an interest in the theory of the acquired intellect, which in Alexander's version was perceived as the most threatening. We have already mentioned the discussion of Alexander found in Delmedigo's *Sefer 'Elim.* However, Maimonides' discussion of Alexander is more important for our purposes, given Spinoza's interest in this greatest of Jewish philosophers. Maimonides' views on the soul are not presented all in one place, and not with perfect clarity.[49] It is clear, however, that he accepted some form of the theory of the acquired intellect. It would seem that his more traditional-sounding statements on the soul were intended to mollify the more conventional among his readers, while allowing the elite to see through the camouflage.[50] This tactic seems to have been successful. The elite did indeed see through the camouflage and what they saw was a person who had followed in the footsteps of Alexander. Maimonides' recommendation of Alexander is well known: in a letter to his translator, Samuel ibn Tibbon, Alexander is the first name that appears in a short list of worthwhile commentators on Aristotle,[51] but Maimonides' references to Alexander are exceedingly few. He does not mention Alexander in connection with his discussion of the nature of the soul and immortality, but among the commentators on the *Guide of the Perplexed* some describe his view as Alexandrist. Moses of Narbonne, Isaac Abravanel, and Shem Tov ben Joseph ibn Shem Tov all ascribe to Maimonides an Alexandrist theory of soul.[52] The claim of Alexandrism is also made by Abravanel in his commentary on Genesis.[53] As a devoted student of Maimonides, Spinoza is likely to have read some of these commentaries on the *Guide.* His copy of the *Guide* included the commentary of Shem Tov ben Joseph ibn Shem Tov, so we can presume that

---

[48] Nadler 2001, 157–184.
[49] Maimonides' views on the soul can be best sought in the secondary sources, whose authors have gleaned the relevant passages from Maimonides' works. See, for example, Ivry 2009, 51–60 and Rudavsky 2010, 85–109.
[50] On this particular point see Ivry 2009, 57.   [51] Marx 1935, 378.
[52] *Commentary on the Guide,* I.68, Moses of Narbonne 1852, 13b; *Commentary on the Guide,* I.1, Isaac Abravanel in Maimonides 1872, 13; *Commentary on the Guide,* I.1, Shem Tov ben Joseph ibn Shem Tov in Maimonides 1872, 12.
[53] Abravanel 1993, 67.

he consulted at least that one.[54] As a devoted student of Torah, Spinoza is likely to have seen Abravanel's commentary. Maimonides, we might add, was so successful in disguising his views that Menasseh ben Israel refused to believe that he advocated the theory of the acquired intellect, regarding the claims of Alexander's influence as slanderous.[55]

Other books that Spinoza consulted might have informed him about the theory of the acquired intellect. Joseph ben Shem Tov ibn Shem Tov's *Kevod 'Elohim* and Ḥasdai Crescas's *'Or Hashem* both contain careful presentations of the theory. These two works are among the very few that Spinoza cites by author and title.[56] Delmedigo's *Novelot Ḥokhmah*, found among the books in Spinoza's library, also contains an extensive exposition of the theory.[57] The *Diálogos de Amor* of Judah Abravanel (also known as León Hebreo) were also to be found on Spinoza's bookshelf. In the first dialogue, Judah Abravanel supports a version of the theory very close to that of Alexander. Judah, like Alexander, but unlike most Jewish advocates of the theory, holds that the agent intellect is God Himself.[58] We may also assume that Spinoza discussed these issues with Menasseh, who inveighed so vehemently against the Alexandrist view of Isaac Arama. Spinoza could well have learned about Alexander from Gersonides' *Wars of the Lord*, and indeed it is highly likely that he read that work. He refers to Gersonides as "a man of great learning," though his only explicit reference is to Gersonides' commentary on the prophetic books, not to the *Wars of the Lord*.[59]

Of course, aside from these books by Crescas and Ibn Shem Tov, we cannot be sure that Spinoza actually read the works mentioned above, or that he read them in time for them to influence the writing of the *Short Treatise*. But given the number of them, it seems most likely that Spinoza knew and considered seriously the theory of the acquired intellect. Delmedigo's *Sefer 'Elim* in particular seems a good candidate for such a role; his influence can be detected already in the *Short Treatise* and the *Treatise on the Emendation of the Intellect*.[60]

---

[54] Freudenthal 1899, 276, says that Spinoza's copy of the *Guide* was the Venice 1551 edition, which includes the commentaries of Shem Tov ben Joseph ibn Shem Tov and Profiat Duran.

[55] *Nishmat Ḥayyim* II.1, Menasseh ben Israel 1995, 93.

[56] Joseph ben Shem Tov ibn Shem Tov 1555, fol. 22b – 71a; *'Or Hashem*, II.6.1, Crescas 1990, 226–251; English translation in W. Harvey 1973, 407–476. Spinoza references Ibn Shem Tov in Chapter 5 of the TTP, Spinoza 2002, 443. He references Crescas in Ep 12, Spinoza 1985, 205.

[57] Delmedigo 1629–1631, 15b–24a. *Novelot Ḥokhmah* ("Fallen Fruit of Wisdom") constitutes volume 2 of Delmedigo's *Ta'alumot Ḥokhmah*, which is listed as no. 56 in the list of books in Spinoza's library, found in Freudenthal 1899, 161.

[58] Feldman 1997, 53–54; León Hebreo 1937, 40–50.

[59] TTP, note 16 to Chapter 9, Spinoza 2002, 576–577.   [60] See Adler 1999.

Given this background, it would seem natural for Spinoza to go to the source and read what Alexander actually had to say, especially if he became aware of the fragmentary and inaccurate presentations of Alexander's views. A copy of the *De Anima* would not be too hard to obtain. By the time of Spinoza's birth, there had been seven editions and printings of the Latin version.[61] Examining Alexander's *De Anima*, we find that there are significant parallels between it and Spinoza's *Short Treatise*.

First, Alexander and Spinoza both deny that the soul is a substance.[62] This assertion, bland though it may seem to anyone living after Locke,[63] was at the time a shocking proposition.

Second, Alexander says that the soul perishes with the body, if it is related only to the body:

> Soul is therefore form of the body ... Because a form of this sort is inseparable from its body, it must consequently perish along with its body – that part of it, at least, which is form of a corruptible body.[64]

Likewise Spinoza:

> If [the soul] is united with the body only, and the body perishes, then it must also perish...[65]

Third, the soul, according to both Alexander and Spinoza, can achieve a kind of immortality by acquiring the highest kind of knowledge by uniting with the supreme and eternal intellect of God. Alexander calls this "conjunction with the agent intellect":

> At the moment when [our] intellect comprehends this supreme intellect in its act of intellective vision ... it becomes in some way that supreme intellect ... [A]n intelligible of this sort is impervious to destruction ... [T]he intellect too which has this intelligible as the object of its intellective act is also incorruptible.[66]

And Spinoza:

> [I]f [the soul] is united with another thing, which is, and remains, immutable, then ... it will have to remain immutable also. For through what would it then be possible that it should be able to perish?[67]

[61] The Latin translation of Alexander's *De Anima* was published 1495, 1502, 1520, 1535, 1538, 1549, and 1559. The 1520 publication is erroneously described as Alexander's commentary on Aristotle's *De Anima*, a work that has been lost.
[62] Alexander 1495, f. c2v; 1887, 17; 1980, §1.34; KV II, Preface, note §1, Spinoza 1985, 94.
[63] *Essay Concerning Human Understanding*, II.27.10–15, Locke 1877, 247–251.
[64] Alexander 1495, fol. c6v; 1887, 21; 1980, §1.46.   [65] KV II.23, §2, Spinoza 1985, 141.
[66] Alexander 1495, fol. l1v–l2r; 1887, 89–90; 1980, §3.28–29. Bracketed word added by Fotinis.
[67] KV II.23, §2, Spinoza 1985, 141.

[B]ecause it is a mode in the thinking substance, it has been able to know and love this [substance] also, as well as that of extension; and uniting itself with these substances. . . it has been able to make itself eternal.[68]

Fourth, in the *Short Treatise* Spinoza says that the intellect is passive:

[T]he intellect is wholly passive . . . So it is never we who affirm or deny something of the thing; it is the thing itself that affirms or denies something of itself in us.[69]

In the *Ethics*, he subsequently rejects this doctrine.[70] Alexander similarly says that in the act of understanding, the soul is passive: he compares the soul to a blank writing tablet, which passively receives the marks inscribed upon it. (He nicely distinguishes soul from the intellect, which as a mere potential or disposition cannot be acted upon.)[71]

Now, these parallels by themselves are probably shared by many sources. But there is one parallel that stands out uniquely. We read in Alexander:

[T]he soul is not a particular kind of blend [*temperamento*] of bodies – which is what a harmony is – but a power that emerges above a particular kind of blend [*temperamento*] of bodies, analogous to the powers of medicinal drugs, which are assembled from a blend [*immixtione*] of many [ingredients]. For in their case too, the mixture, composition and proportion of drugs – such that one of them, it might turn out is 2:1, another 1:2, and another 3:2 – bear some analogy to a harmony. The power, however, which emerges from the blend of drugs exhibiting this harmony and proportion is not likewise a harmony too . . . The soul is also of this sort. For the soul is the power and form that supervenes on the blend [*temperamento*] of bodies in a particular proportion, not the proportion or composition of the blend [*temperamenti*].[72]

Here we see a remarkable similarity: the soul comes to be when the elements composing the body are mixed in a certain quantitative proportion. It is this detail which provides the strongest evidence that Spinoza was following Alexander. For Alexander, the mixture is the temperament of the body. It must be conceded that Alexander subsequently rejects this view, saying that the elements involved in the temperament do not remain constant;[73] but

---

[68] KV II, Preface, note, §15; Spinoza 1985, 96. In this early work, Spinoza sometimes refers to distinct substances, rather than what he would later call attributes of one substance.

[69] KV II.16, §5, Spinoza 1985, 124.   [70] *Ethics* IIIp1 and its demonstration, Spinoza 1985, 493–494.

[71] Alexander 1495, fol. k4v–k5r; 1887, 84–85; 1980, §3.12.

[72] Alexander 1495, fol. d1v; 1887, 24–25; 2012, 51. The interpolated Latin words are taken from Alexander 1495, whose Latin text Spinoza is most likely to have seen. I have here used the more recent translation by Caston, since it in this case is much clearer than Fotinis's version.

[73] Alexander 1495 fol. d2v; 1887, 26; 1980, §1.57.

this apparent inconsistency should not let us dismiss the fact that Alexander does in one place evidently endorse the view. This view of the soul seems to be unprecedented. One might call to mind Plato's *Timaeus*, where the soul is described in mathematical terms, but here the soul arises *before* the body, rather than emerging from the constitution of the body; and in any case the account seems more mystical than scientific.[74] One can also see in Aristotle the view to which Alexander was reacting: Aristotle rejects – one might say ridicules – the view that the soul is a harmony, defined by a proportion determining the mixture of elements. But no actual examples of a mathematical proportion are given, and Aristotle in any case seems hardly to take the view seriously. I thus endorse a suggestion mooted but ultimately rejected by Alan Gabbey, that the ratio of motion and rest is "possibly an ingenious neo-Cartesian reformulation of the traditional Galenic medical doctrine of humoral balance . . ."[75]

The essential ratio as temperament

The concept of temperament was central to the Galenic school medicine, which played an exceedingly important role in Western medicine from Galen's own time until the seventeenth century, when it began to decline. The temperament – also called complexion or *crasis* – is the controlling mixture of the four primary qualities constituting a physical object: cold, hot, moist, and dry. In the case of a human being or other animal, it can also be considered as the mixture of the four humors: blood, phlegm, yellow bile, and black bile (with the corresponding temperaments: sanguine, phlegmatic, choleric, and melancholic). This doctrine can be found in the classic Galenic sources, such as Galen himself and Avicenna, but also had a prominent place in the theories of important physicians of Spinoza's era, such as Lazare Rivière, Daniel Sennert, Johan van Heurne, as well as Spinoza's correspondent, Lambert van Velthuysen.[76] In Galenic medicine, temperament plays an important role in the functioning of body and mind;

---

[74] Plato, *Timaeus*, 35a–37c.   [75] Gabbey 1996, 168.

[76] The classic sources on the subject of temperament are Galen and Avicenna. On Galen, see Siegel 1968, 205 ff., and citations there. Avicenna's views will be found in the *Canon of Medicine* I.1.3 (Avicenna 1507–1964, fol. 2r–4v; English translation: Avicenna 1930, 57–75). I cite Gruner's translation because it generally translates Latin terms by their English cognates, unlike the more recent translation by Mazhar H. Shah (Avicenna 1966), which is in other respects superior. On temperament see also Klibansky *et al.* 1964, Chapters 1–2, and Temkin 1973, 17–20.

On the theory of temperaments as it existed in Spinoza's time, see King 1970, 15–36; as well as primary sources such as Rivière 1656, 4–17; Heurne 1609, 6–17; Sennert, *Institutes of Medicine*, I.1.4, Sennert 1641, 250–257; Velthuysen 1657, 25, 34, 52, 89, 92, 132, 156, 187, and elsewhere. A copy of this

if not identical with the soul, it is at least an important constituent of a person's identity. Avicenna indeed claims that "[E]very individual person has a temperament unique to himself, and it is impossible for any other person to have an identical temperament, or even to approximate thereto," a statement accurately cited by Menasseh.[77]

One unique feature of Alexander's discussion of temperament is his use of a quantitative ratio to describe it. This detail is particularly significant, since temperament theorists, for various reasons, rarely thought of the temperament as a quantitative ratio. As Lester S. King notes, most of the Galenic theorists thought of a temperament as involving a mixture of elements in "due proportion." "But what constitutes the due proportion is not made explicit. There is no numerical expression. Indeed, the need for quantitative determination was not felt."[78] One does sometimes find ordinal rankings – one creature may be hotter or moister than another – but cardinal numbers seem not to be applied to temperaments, except in the cited passage from Alexander. It was sometimes said that there could be no such cardinal measurements because the elements are, literally, imponderables – they cannot be weighed; hence it makes no sense to speak of a mixture of some particular ratio. And even if the elements could be weighed, the process of combining causes some of them to be dominated and diminished by the others, so the initial ratio would no longer exist in the mixture.[79] Perhaps also the lack of quantification was due to the inability of pre-modern medicine to measure the quantities in question; after all, how can one make cardinal measurements of heat and cold without a thermometer, a device not invented until the seventeenth century?[80]

The agreement between the two philosophers is thus remarkable. One is even tempted to speculate that between the second and seventeenth centuries, no one else held this precise combination of views.

But can we really understand Spinoza's essential ratio as a temperament? Three considerations suggest that we can.

First, it is now known, on the basis of the writings of Niels Stensen, that Spinoza attended lectures and anatomical dissections at the University of Leiden; Stensen mentions associating familiarly with Spinoza at the

---

last book was in Spinoza's library: see Freudenthal 1899, 163, item (122). Rivière's book was published in the Netherlands in 1657, 1662, and 1663; Heurne's in Leiden in 1627, 1638, and 1666. On the choice of these books, see King 1970, 15–17; 1974, 8; Müller 1991, 36–52; Suringar 1864, 163.

[77] *Canon of Medicine* I.1.3, Avicenna 1930, 61; *Nishmat Ḥayyim* III.2, Menasseh ben Israel 1995, 186.

[78] King 1970, 19–20.

[79] Both reasons are given in Petrus de Abano 1523, 26r. The section in question (*Differentia* 18, 25v–27r) is perhaps as good a source as any on this topic.

[80] Middleton 1966.

university, and, since Stensen was studying medicine, it seems likely that Spinoza attended the same lectures. Spinoza thus had the medical knowledge to make use of this concept.[81]

Second, by interpreting the concept of temperament in terms of Spinoza's physical concepts, we get the essential ratio. The believers in temperament base it on four primary qualities: hot, cold, moist, and dry. Spinoza has only two: motion and rest. We must first consider what *these* are. Motion, evidently, is pretty much what we mean in English by motion. Of course, for Spinoza, every physical object has a certain (non-zero) quantity of motion, even if the object is stationary:[82] the motion he speaks of is evidently that of the invisible particles that make up the object.[83] But how do we measure the quantity of motion? And how can we even speak of, let alone measure, a "quantity of rest"? The most plausible response relies on what Spinoza says in his reworking of Descartes's physics: thus "quantity of motion" means what we would now call *momentum*, and "quantity of rest" means what we would now call *inertial mass*, i.e. the power of remaining at rest, or resisting motion.[84] So to determine an object's essential ratio, we add up the momenta of its particles and divide this sum by the mass of the whole object.[85] What we have then is a measure of the object's temperature – not, of course, as we would now measure it, but still, what we have is a quantity that increases as the temperature of the object increases, and decreases as the latter decreases. Thus Spinoza writes in the appendix to the *Short Treatise*:

> The human body, then, is nothing but a certain proportion of motion and rest . . . [I]f the rest happens to increase, and the motion to decrease, the pain or sadness we call *cold* is thereby produced. On the other hand, if this [increase] occurs in the motion, then the pain we call *heat* is thereby produced.[86]

So much for heat and cold. How would Spinoza deal with moisture and dryness? "Moisture" is ambiguous: it can refer to the fluidity of water or to its power of wetting things.[87] The latter seems unpromising as a

---

[81] Totaro 2002, 31.   [82] KV App, II.14, Spinoza 1985, 155.   [83] Ep 6; Spinoza 1985, 178–179.

[84] PPC IIp21–22 and corollaries, Spinoza 1985, 281–283.

[85] This interpretation of the essential ratio follows what Alexandre Matheron calls "formula F": see Matheron 1969, 39–40.

[86] KV App, II.14–15, Spinoza 1985, 155; emphasis and bracketed word supplied by the translator.

[87] Both interpretations are found in the work of Aristotelian-Galenic theorists and are noted by Robert Boyle, in a work read by Spinoza. See Aristotle, *De Generatione et Corruptione* II.2, 329b–330a; Rivière 1656, 8; *Philosophia Naturalis*, Chapter 5, thesis 45, Heereboord 1665, 47; Boyle 1772, 1.319. Spinoza's comments on this work of Boyle's are found in Ep 6, Spinoza 1985, 173–188.

fundamental quantity; fluidity, then, seems to be the better choice. Dryness, correspondingly, gets interpreted as solidity (or "firmness," as Robert Boyle calls it). Spinoza's letter 6 confirms this view: the underlying reality of things we call "fluid" is that they have a high "proportion of motion to mass" of the minute particles constituting the fluid, whereas "solidity" presumably corresponds to a low proportion.[88] The four ancient qualities thus reduce to two. Though it might seem odd that fluidity and heat are equated, it is not really strange: it is the motion called heat which results in solid bodies liquefying, and the relative lack of motion called cold that results in their solidifying.

The temperament, then – the essential balance of hot, cold, moist, and dry – reduces to the essential ratio.

Third, there is another equivalence between the temperament and the essential ratio, namely, their functional equivalence. In Galenic medicine, the temperament plays a threefold role: it explains somatic events, explains psychic events, and is a constituent of personal identity. We find that the essential ration fills these same three roles.

First, the ratio plays a causal role in the functioning of the body. Most egregiously, if the proportion of motion to rest cannot be maintained, death results.[89]

Second, the ratio plays a causal role in psychic events by way of the Spinozistic parallelism of soul-mind and body.[90] The ratio is responsible for sensation:

> And this change [in the ratio], which arises from the fact that other bodies act on ours, cannot occur without the soul's becoming aware of it . . . And this change is what we call sensation.[91]

And also for emotion, pleasure and pain:[92]

> [I]t is easy to infer. . . the principal causes of the passions. For regarding the body, and its effects, Motion and Rest, they. . . make themselves known to it

---

[88] Ep 6, Spinoza 1985, 181–182. I follow Shirley in translating *moles* as "mass," rather than "bulk," as in Curley's translation: see Spinoza 2002, 773. See PPC IIp25–27 (Spinoza 1985, 284–287), where it is clear that *moles* refers to inertial mass.

[89] KV II, Preface, note §14, Spinoza 1985, 96.

[90] In the KV the strict parallelism is not always affirmed. See, for example, KV II.19.8–9, Spinoza 1985, 131–132.

[91] KV II, Preface, note, §13, Spinoza 1985, 96.

[92] KV II.19.15 and note thereto. The quotation from the body of the text appears in Spinoza 1985, 133–134; the translation of the note is taken from Wolf's translation of the *Short Treatise* (Spinoza 1910, 123–124), which seems in this case to provide a better reproduction of the meaning of the passage. Bracketed interpolations are by the translator.

as objects. And according to the appearances they present to it, whether good or bad, so the soul is also affected.

Those [objects] by which we are affected most harmoniously (as regards the proportion of Motion and rest, of which they consist) are most agreeable to us, and as they depart more and more from this [harmonious proportion, they tend to be] most disagreeable.[93]

There is one more functional equivalence – a matter of detail, but quite telling. Spinoza writes:

So if a body has and preserves its proportion. . . the soul and body will be like ours now are; they will, of course, be constantly subject to change, but not to such a great change that it goes beyond the limits of from 1 to 3; and as much as it changes, so also the soul changes each time.[94]

What are "the limits of from 1 to 3"? The very phrase seems ungrammatical and the concept paradoxical. After all, either the ratio is 1 to 3 or it isn't. But, on the current hypothesis, Spinoza is merely reproducing an aspect of the temperament: although a person has a certain precise temperament, the actual constitution of the person's body may vary within a certain range called the "latitude."[95] The ratio-temperament thesis enables us easily to explain this otherwise rather mysterious comment of Spinoza's.

With this one more piece of the Alexander–Spinoza relationship falls in place. Both say that the soul is something – not a substance – that arises when the constitution of the body can be characterized by a certain numerical proportion. The soul as such is mortal and dies with the body, unless one has received the influx of the divine intellect and thus achieved conjunction with God.

The temperament among Spinoza's contemporaries

Would Spinoza's contemporaries have recognized this essential ratio as a reformulation of the concept of temperament? It is likely that they would. For one thing, many of Spinoza's friends and correspondents were medical practitioners. Franciscus van den Enden, Juan de Prado, Dirck Kerckring, Adriaan Koerbagh, Lodewijk Meijer, Jacob Ostens, Nicolaus Steno, Lambert van Velthuysen, Georg Hermann Schuller, Johannes

---

[93] KV App, II.15–16, Spinoza 1985, 155.   [94] KV II, Preface, note, §12, Spinoza 1985, 96.
[95] See e.g. Avicenna, *Canon*, I.1.3: "[There is a] temperament peculiar to each separate person, in that he is alive and also in health. It shows a range between two extremes – upper and lower" (Avicenna 1930, 60–61). The latitude is also mentioned, e.g. by Daniel Sennert: *Institutes of Medicine* I.1.3, Sennert 1641, 250.

Bouwmeester, Johannes Hudde (known more for his mathematical works), Burchard de Volder, and Henri Morelli were all medical doctors; Ehrenfried Walther von Tschirnhaus, probably Spinoza's most acute correspondent, studied medicine at Leiden and was what we would now call a practitioner of alternative medicine.[96] Among these, Lodewijk Meijer, a close friend of Spinoza's, has a special affinity. In two dissertations – philosophical and medical – Meijer outlines a theory of two temperaments expressed in mechanical terms much like Spinoza's. In the philosophical dissertation, Meijer agrees with Spinoza in saying that the basic constituents of matter are motion and rest, and physical objects are characterized by what he calls a *contemperatio motus et quietis*, which is a quantitative proportion. (It is significant that the word *contemperatio* is a synonym of *temperamentum*.) The quantity of rest is, as I have suggested for Spinoza, what we would now call the object's inertial mass.[97] In the medical dissertation, Meijer outlines, *inter alia*, a temperamental theory that has only two temperaments, phlegmatic (*constitution pituitosa*) and choleric (*constitution biliosa*). We may omit the physiological details of each temperament, but to be brief, the phlegmatic temperament is characterized by a low ratio of motion to rest, and the choleric by a high one.[98] These medical practitioners, and most especially Meijer, would have been inclined to understand Spinoza's essential ratio as a reworking of the temperament concept. In the writings of Spinoza's correspondent, Lambert van Velthuysen, we have some evidence that Spinoza did in fact work with a theory of temperament. Velthuysen had frequent conversations with Spinoza, so his statements bear considerable weight.[99] Velthuysen ascribes to Spinoza the view that "people do not arm themselves with swords or resort to violence for the sake of revenge: but rather [they do so] because they are brought to it by the temperament and motion of the spirits and blood," and that "when you understand that the temperament or motion of the spirits have changed, or there is a change or deletion of the impressions in the brain which the mind uses in imagining, then the person's judgments, feelings, and ways of being will change."[100] Granted, these words were written long after the composition of the *Short Treatise*, and Spinoza's views had changed in the meantime, but it is of interest that Velthuysen sees him as using the temperament concept.

---

[96] Adler forthcoming; Coert 1938; Fischer 1921.
[97] *Disputatio Philosophica*, §§ 41, 10, 16, Meijer 1660a, fol. A6r, A3r, A3v.
[98] *Disputatio Medica*, Theses 32–36, Meijer 1660b, fol. a4r–v.   [99] Klever 1991.
[100] Velthuysen 1680, 1466–1467.

It seems, then, that Spinoza's friends would understand the essential ratio as a reworking of the concept of temperament in the terms of the mechanical philosophy, and Spinoza knew that they would so understand it.

Meanwhile, Back in Amsterdam

We have made the case that Spinoza wrote the *Short Treatise* under the influence of Alexander of Aphrodisias, and in particular that the *Short Treatise* presents an Alexandrist theory of immortality. Spinoza does here use the word *onsterfelijk* ("immortal"), and not simply "eternal," as in the *Ethics*.[101] Although it seems most likely that Spinoza had in mind an impersonal form of immortality or, if personal, one not involving consciousness, still (as we have seen in Arama) it is possible to understand Spinoza's theory as providing personal immortality by the stratagem of saying that the soul becomes constituted as a substance out of the intelligibles.

How does this view square with the claim put forward by Steven Nadler that Spinoza's theory of the eternity of the mind reflects the influence of Gersonides?[102] The similarities between Gersonides' views and those expressed in the *Ethics* are too striking to be dismissed, and Nadler's arguments are cogent. The most likely explanation is simply change over time: the *Short Treatise* differs in many ways from the *Ethics*. In particular, the Alexandrist concept of a numerical ratio of motion and rest is replaced by a very different concept bearing the same name,[103] and (as we have noted) the thinking mind is no longer described as passive. So at least two important Alexandrist principles are gone. What then are we to make of the testimony that Spinoza was denying the immortality of the soul even before he was put under the ban, and soon afterwards?[104] The simple answer is that an Alexandrist, even a mitigated Alexandrist like Arama, would be likely to say that the *soul* is mortal, but that the *intellect* of those who develop it properly is immortal.

Indeed, it seems that in the Amsterdam of Spinoza's time, it was not enough to say that a person could achieve immortality. One had to say that the soul was *intrinsically* immortal. Historically speaking, this is a strange requirement. As Nadler notes, it is strange that denial of immortality was

---

[101] Spinoza 1869, 114.
[102] Nadler 2001, 94–131. Nadler notes with some surprise that there is little discussion of the question of Gersonides' influence on Spinoza's views on this subject (see Nadler 2001, 194n2). To the sources mentioned there, we might add a brief but telling discussion in Dobbs-Weinstein 1998, 211–213.
[103] Adler 1996, 267–272.   [104] Lucas 1863; Nadler 2001, 155–156; Révah 1959, 64.

unacceptable in the Jewish Amsterdam of the seventeenth century, when it had been acceptable in earlier times.[105] How much stranger that it was unacceptable even to say that immortality was possible, but had to be achieved. This view was expressed not only by philosophers, but is found even in the Zoharic literature, particularly in the *Midrash ha-Ne'elam* (The "Mystical" or "Hidden Midrash"), which Arama cites in support of his view.[106]

The passage cited by Arama is just one of a number of such passages. The Zohar speaks, as one might expect, in slightly mystified language, but the view is clear enough. One might point out in particular the passage designated in the Hebrew edition as "The Discourse on the Intellectual Soul and the Rational Soul,"[107] where we read,

> Rabbi Judah asked Rabbi Dostai, "The soul in a human being that is called *intellectual*, what kind of soul is it and where is its seat?" He said to him, "...[W]hen [a person] grows up and sees the affairs of the world and looks into his heart,[108] he on his own draws upon himself this soul."[109]

Or an extract from the passage quoted by Arama:

> Rabbi Isaac quoted Rabbi Aha, who said, "Whoever devotes himself to Torah acquires the soul [*neshamah*] on his own, as we have learned, 'If one comes to purify himself, they help him' [Babylonian Talmud Shabbat 104a]. Woe to the wicked, who cleave to the power of the earth, which is called the living soul [*nefesh ḥayah*][110] that is created from the earth, on account of which they will come to an end forever and ever and ever."[111]

The implication is clear: a person comes into the world with a mortal soul, which is made immortal only if the person devotes himself or herself to Torah. As a result we have the problem raised by Moses Metz, mentioned above: if immortality is acquired by Torah study, non-Jews have no immortality, a conclusion that the *Midrash ha-Ne'elam* likewise affirms.[112]

---

[105] Nadler 2001, 156–181.

[106] *'Akedat Yitsḥak*, Sermon 6, Arama 1868, 67b–68a; citing *Midrash ha-Ne'elam* 10c–11c, to be found in *Zohar* 1974–1975, 17:151–161; *Zohar* 1981, 1:540–548.

[107] *Ma'amar Nefesh ha-Sikhlit ve-Nefesh ha-Medaberet*.

[108] The heart is here considered the seat of the intellect as well as of the emotions.

[109] *Midrash ha-Ne'elam* 6d, *Zohar* 1974–1975, 123, § 316; *Zohar* 1981, 519, my translation. *Zohar* 1981 is the French translation; no English translation has yet been published.

[110] This might also be translated as "animal soul."

[111] *Midrash ha-Ne'elam* 11a, *Zohar* 1974–1975, 155, §432; *Zohar* 1981, 543. It is of interest that this view is attributed in one passage to a certain "Rabbi Alexandrai," whom some later scholars have identified as Alexander of Aphrodisias: see Rapoport 1885–1886, 6–7; Werblowsky 1959, 134; Zweifel 1856, 83–84, n.3.

[112] *Midrash ha-Ne'elam* 10c; *Zohar* 1974–1975, 151, §414; *Zohar* 1981, 539–540.

Menasseh had to somehow rescue the Zohar, which he did by reinter-
preting the passage quoted by Arama and by citing other passages that
support the view of intrinsic immortality.[113] Maimonides, as we have seen,
had to be rehabilitated, a trend already found in the works of Abraham
Shalom (Spain, fifteenth century).[114] Gersonides is tougher to repaint as a
supporter of personal immortality, but Shalom does not shirk the task. He
takes the path mentioned above, by saying that the material intellect is
constituted as a substance by the intelligibles that it acquires.[115]

Why this opposition to the theory of the acquired intellect, when
(suitably modified, as in Arama) it does affirm personal immortality for
those who learn Torah and perform *mitzvot*? We can only speculate. Most
likely it is the dilemma posed by Metz. If immortality is achieved by
intellectual accomplishment alone, then simple pious people are doomed
to extinction, whereas wicked intellectuals gain eternal life. And if immortality can be achieved by studying the Torah and performing *mitzvot*, then
non-Jews are doomed to extinction.[116] The first alternative makes a mockery
of reward and punishment, as if life were a philosophy test, with the prize of
eternal life going to those who garner the high grades. The second alternative would be uncomfortable for a community looking over its shoulder
to discern what the Dutch authorities might be thinking. After all, the
provincial assembly of Holland had in 1619 set guidelines for the admission
of the Jews to the cities of Holland, among which was that the Jews must
affirm that "there is a life after death in which good people will receive their
recompense and wicked people their punishment."[117] It would surely not
please the Dutch authorities if the Jews said, "*We* have immortality; *you*
don't." The theory would also seem to have troubling consequences for the
Jews still living in Spain and Portugal, forced to conceal their identity. If
immortality is achieved by Torah study and performance of *mitzvot*, they
have little hope of attaining it.

One might point out that the theory could not have been so unacceptable, since Delmedigo published his book, *'Elim*, with the approval of the
Jewish communal authorities. Let us recall that *'Elim* contains an out-and-
out denial of immortality by Moses Metz. If he could get away with
publishing such a book, why couldn't Spinoza get by with something less
extreme? But the publication of *'Elim* was probably the cause of
Delmedigo's leaving Amsterdam.[118] Though he was not put under the

---

[113] *Nishmat Ḥayyim* II.2, Menasseh ben Israel 1995, 100–102.   [114] Shalom 1575, 125a–b.
[115] *Ibid.*, 122a–b.   [116] Metz in Delmedigo 1864, 54.   [117] Quoted in Nadler 2001, 180.
[118] D'Ancona 1940, 123–130.

ban, a recently discovered manuscript – the last known writing from Delmedigo's hand – shows that Delmedigo was ostracized and suffered a life of poverty and alienation. His words are moving even today:

> I am exiled from my city, from my palace on high, my mansion . . . The light of my eyes, my books, they too are not with me . . . And I dwell in a foreign land with the children of the Diaspora, and there is neither food nor fine clothes in my home . . . For I have killed a man with my book, as with a sharp threshing-sledge. . . and my wound should silence every foul-speaking mouth.

The man that he killed was, of course, himself, and the book with which he killed himself was presumably *'Elim*. He was never again able to obtain a rabbinical position. The last phrase quoted above served as a warning (too late for Spinoza) that one should watch one's words.[119]

In any case, the affirmation of such a theory – even if it included a belief that personal immortality could be attained – would have got Spinoza into trouble, just as it did when the young Delmedigo affirmed it. And we have a bit of evidence in the saying of Menasseh, quoted near the beginning of this chapter: "Whoever does not reject Alexander's definition, may a snake bite him!" It was intimated above that this saying has another meaning. The word *naḥash* – "snake" in Hebrew – is also an acronym for *niduy, ḥerem, shamta'*, a commonly used abbreviation.[120] Taking it in this sense, Menasseh may be taken to say, "Whoever does not reject Alexander's definition – let him be excommunicated!" Spinoza did not reject Alexander's definition; the consequences are well known.

---

[119] Pfeffer 2010, 6. Ellipses as in the original.

[120] *Niduy, ḥerem*, and *shamta'* are the three levels of the Jewish ban (or excommunication), in increasing order of severity. The abbreviation is most frequently referenced in invoking the prohibition against reading private mail: see www.chidusheitorah.com/sites/default/files/Heb%206%20Shabtai%20Atlow.pdf, accessed 27 November 2013. For citations of the abbreviation, including numerous instances from Spinoza's time and before, see www.responsa.co.il/search/"נדוי%20חרם%20שמתא".aspx, accessed 27 November 2013.

CHAPTER 2

Spinoza and the determinist tradition in medieval Jewish philosophy

Charles H. Manekin

Historians of Jewish philosophy have suggested for some time that Spinoza's acceptance of determinism and rejection of free will were influenced by the philosophy of Hasdai Crescas.[1] Since Spinoza mentions Crescas approvingly in another context, it may indeed be that Crescas's starkly deterministic position had an effect on Spinoza's doctrine that "all things are determined . . . not only to exist but also to exist and to act in a definite way."[2]

But there appear to be at least two fundamental differences between Crescas and Spinoza on the question of determinism and free will. First, Spinoza holds that "all things have been predetermined by God, not from freedom of the will, or absolute good pleasure but from God's absolute nature, or infinite power." According to Crescas, on the other hand, God wills the world into existence through beneficence and grace, taking pleasure in this activity – perhaps the very "absolute good pleasure" that Spinoza denies.[3]

Second, although Crescas and Spinoza are both strict determinists, the former has generally been read by scholars as a *soft* determinist, i.e. one who holds that humans *deserve* divine reward and punishment when and only when they act voluntarily – even though all things, including human volitions, are determined.[4] By contrast, Spinoza claims that notions like praise and blame arise from the illusory belief that humans possess free will. Since the will is not free but rather determined, it is proper to excuse vicious behavior rather than blame its subject for it. Whether Spinoza completely rejects moral responsibility is a matter of scholarly dispute.[5] I assume that

---

[1] Joël 1866, 54–57; Waxman 1920, 124–138. For others, see Feldman 1984, 25n.16.

[2] *Ethics* Ip29dem, Spinoza 1925, II.71; 1985, 134. Crescas is mentioned in Ep 12, Spinoza 1925, IV.62; 1985, 205. Cf. Wolfson 1934, s.v. Crescas, and Waxman 1920, 130–138.

[3] *Ethics* Iapp, Spinoza 1925, II.77; 1985, 439; *Light of the Lord* 2.6.1, Crescas 1990, 242.

[4] Feldman 1984, esp. 17–32; W. Harvey 1998, 137–158; and Waxman 1920, 129.

[5] *Ethics* Iapp is the *locus classicus* for the view that "praise and blame, sin and merit" arise on the mistaken view that men think themselves free. Cf. *Ethics* IIp48 and IIIp2s for the denial of free will. Recently

Spinoza is best read as a hard determinist, i.e. one who rejects the deservedness of reward and punishment and does not connect desert to the volun-
tariness or uncompelled nature of actions. Spinoza does hold that humans
can achieve a measure of freedom in a deterministic world, but Spinozistic
freedom is not the same as compatibilist free will. And so his determinism
appears to differ from that of Crescas.

The first difference, while real, is not as great as it seems, and the second
difference is no difference at all. The first difference is not as great as it seems
when one examines Crescas's views on God's will and creative agency. With
respect to the second difference, I will argue that Crescas is best read, like
Spinoza, as a hard determinist who dispenses with the deservedness of
divine reward and punishment, and in fact dispenses with a desert model
of divine justice altogether.

Needless to say, applying contemporary terminology and concepts such
as "compatibilist" or "hard" and "soft determinist" to past thinkers is tricky
business. Even the concept of "free will" is problematic. Julius Guttmann,
for example, considered Crescas to be different from all previous medieval
Jewish philosophers in deciding in favor of determinism rather than freedom of the will.[6] But this assumes that freedom of the will is an unambig-
uous concept that can be applied to medieval Jewish thinkers.[7] To my
knowledge, the phrase 'free will' does not appear in pre-modern Hebrew
philosophical texts, whereas 'free choice' does not appear in those texts prior
to the fifteenth century.[8] Jewish philosophers in the Middle Ages spoke
primarily of 'choice' (*behirah*) or 'will' (*ratzon*), and their main question was
not whether the will was free, but rather whether human choice was effica-
cious, i.e. whether humans have the ability to choose and act, uncompelled
or unconstrained by external physical causal factors, and in such a way as to
produce effects.

Moreover, Guttmann's claim that Crescas was unique among Jewish
philosophers in his acceptance of determinism ignores the presence of a
tradition, or at least a strong current, of determinism in fourteenth-century

---

scholars have argued in various ways that a notion of moral responsibility can be extracted from
Spinoza. See Della Rocca 2008, 140; Garrett 1996; Kisner 2011, 67. For Spinoza as a hard determinist
see Pereboom 2001, xviii; Slote 1990.

[6] Guttmann 1973, 270.

[7] Frede 2011, 1–18, considers this assumption's difficulty with respect to Aristotle, but similar difficulties
continue throughout the Middle Ages, especially in Arabic and Hebrew philosophy

[8] In Abner of Burgos's *Ofrenda de zelos* (*A Jealousy Offering*), which appears to be a Spanish translation of
a fourteenth-century Hebrew work entitled *Minḥat Qena'ot*, we find the phrase *la libertad del alvedrio*,
but the Hebrew original may simply be *behirah*, "choice." In any event, the phrase refers to a statement
of Baḥya ibn Paquda, which makes no mention of free will. See Alfonso de Valladolid (Abner of
Burgos) 1990, 56.

Spanish Jewish philosophy that appears to have been influenced by Avicennian determinism. In what follows I offer a preliminary sketch of that tradition. Spinoza's direct knowledge of Avicenna is unlikely, but an Avicennian tradition of determinism could have reached him through his acquaintance with the Spanish Jewish philosophical tradition.

Avicennian determinism

Establishing an undercurrent of Avicennian determinism in late medieval Spanish Jewish philosophy will help us explain why defenses of causal determinism begin to appear among the Jews during this period, and why it met with such stiff resistance by Jewish Aristotelians such as Isaac Albalag, Isaac Polgar, and Moses of Narbonne.[9] Avicenna viewed himself as part of the Aristotelian tradition, but his Aristotelianism was tempered by Neoplatonist and, perhaps, Stoic elements that were more conducive to a stronger causal determinism than straight Aristotelianism. The Jewish Aristotelians emphasized those elements in Aristotle's thought – accidental causality, chance, future contingency, the importance of unconstrained choice – that resisted deterministic conclusions. Indeed, Avicenna's use of such concepts, as well as his acceptance of the apparent unknowability of future contingents and unpredictability of matter, have led various scholars to argue that he wavered on his commitment to determinism.[10] But Catarina Belo has recently argued that these concepts should be understood within his overall deterministic framework, and, as she points out, most scholars read Avicenna as a hard determinist.[11]

Let us first focus on three related doctrines where Avicenna's metaphysical determinism is explicit and pronounced. The first is his understanding of the division of existents into what is "necessary of existence" and what is "possible of existence." That which is necessary of existence is understood as that existent which, considered in itself, must possess existence, whereas that which is possible of existence is understood as that existent which, considered in itself, need not possess existence. Sometimes Avicenna understands this distinction in light of his distinction between a thing's essence and its existence: where a thing's essence entails its existence, then the thing is necessary of existence; where it does not, then it is possible of existence.

---

[9] For anti-determinism texts of Albalag and Moses of Narbonne, see Manekin 2007, 140–152; cf. Sirat 1985, 308–322.

[10] Cf. Ivry 1984; Janssens 1996.

[11] Belo 2007, 120: "It is my conviction that Avicenna's system should be ranked alongside that of the Stoics and of Spinoza as a paradigm of classical metaphysical determinism."

Avicenna derives from these notions the metaphysical consequences that what is necessary of existence has no cause for its existence, for its essence is sufficient for its existence, whereas what is possible of existence has a cause for its existence.[12]

Were Avicenna to claim merely that whatever exists that is not causally self-sufficient has an external cause for its existence, then this in itself would not imply determinism. For most Aristotelians claim, for example, that all things have causes and that effects are necessary *relative* to their causes.[13] But they deny that all things have always been necessary, for *inter alia* there are things that come about by accident or by chance. Avicenna, by contrast, maintains that whatever is possible of existence with respect to itself is necessary of existence through another, when it exists. This means for him not only that the possible, when it actually exists, has a necessary connection to its cause, but also that it is rendered necessarily existent through its cause. Whatever exists does so of necessity, either by virtue of itself or by virtue of its cause. And yet, though the latter exists of necessity when it exists, it also retains its possible character – not because at some time of the future it could cease to exist, which is what more orthodox Aristotelians often say, but because even when it exists it is not ontologically self-sufficient.

Another source of Avicenna's determinism, and what points him away from the Aristotelian tradition, is his doctrine of the world emanating necessarily from God, who alone is the "necessary of existence" in itself. This process is an eternal process that is not carried out successively in time. On the contrary, God and the various intermediate causes throughout the system are viewed as essential efficient causes which coexist with their effects. Even in our world of generation and destruction, the essential efficient cause is not seen as preceding its effect, but as coexisting with, producing, and necessitating it.[14]

Avicenna's emanationism is related to a third doctrine with deterministic implications, namely, that God's self-knowledge is the cause that produces/necessitates the world to be as it is. In an eternal act of self-intellection, God intellectually cognizes Himself as the cause of all other existents, and this cognition entails both the existence of those effects and God's knowledge of them. God intellects Himself as the cause of all other existents, both of their essences and of their actual existence, and His knowledge is of the

---

[12] *Shifā: Metaphysics* I.6, Avicenna 2004, 30; cf. Hourani 1972.
[13] See Sorabji 1980, 7–23, for this reading of Aristotle's *Metaphysics* VI.3. Cf. Moses of Narbonne's arguments in Manekin 2007, 145–148.
[14] *Shifā: Metaphysics*, VI.1, Avicenna 2004, 198–199.

intelligible forms of reality that emanate from Him. Since the intelligible forms are instantiated in matter as particulars, God is said to know particulars insofar as He knows their constituent properties, or as Avicenna puts it, God knows particulars "in a universal way."[15] This knowledge is not temporal knowledge, nor does God's knowledge change when an event passes from future to present to past.[16]

All things are in principle knowable/explicable through their causes. This is the case not only for future necessary events such as eclipses,[17] but even chance events like finding a treasure, for chance events are necessitated.[18] In Al-Ghazali's *Opinions of the Philosophers*, a very popular text in fourteenth- and fifteenth-century Jewish philosophy, God's knowledge is likened to that of an astrologer in some sense, who predicts human future through knowledge of causal astral influences. This analogy was attributed to Al-Ghazali by orthodox Aristotelians such as Isaac Albalag and Isaac Polgar, who criticized him for it.[19]

Having adopted this rigid deterministic picture of the world, in which all essences and existents are necessitated by God's eternal self-intellection, and in which the world in its finest detail is necessitated to be the way it is according to the divine plan, Avicenna is obliged to explain several philosophical and religious problems, notably, the existence of evil,[20] the nature of divine reward and punishment, and divine justice. If everything is determined by the divine decree (*al-qadar*), then what is the point of divine punishment? This is a question to which Avicenna returns in several writings, most notably in his *Pointers and Indications*, and in a short essay called *The Secret of Destiny*. In the former he states that punishments are not directly meted out by a principle external to nature, and consequently, they need not be justified by any independent purpose. They are merely the consequences of the soul's actions, just as the consequences of gluttony are illness. If one, however, wishes to view punishments as arising from an external principle, then the fear of divine punishment is beneficial, for the most part, because it motivates individuals not to sin.[21] If a particular individual goes ahead and sins anyway because of the causes arising from the divine decree, assent (to this belief) exists for the sake of the general

---

[15] See Adamson 2005.   [16] *Shifā: Metaphysics*, VIII.6, Avicenna 2004, 288.   [17] *Ibid.*, 288–290.
[18] See *Dānish Nāmai 'alā'i*, secs. 31–32, Avicenna 1973, 63–65. This Persian work was not translated into Hebrew, but many of its doctrines appear in Al-Ghazali's popular *Opinions of the Philosophers*.
[19] For Albalag, see Manekin 2007, 142; Polgar refers to Albalag's response to Al-Ghazali in *'Ezer ha-Dat* 3, Polgar 1984, 118–119.
[20] *Shifā: Metaphysics*, IX.6, Avicenna 2004, 337–339.
[21] *Pointers* 7.22–33, Avicenna 1892, 188–189; Avicenna 1951, 463–465.

intention, even though punishment is not appropriate for this individual and not necessary for the Merciful and the One who Chooses.[22]

In the *Secret of Destiny* Avicenna considers the purpose of God's requiring or forbidding, praising or blaming, rewarding or punishing certain actions, if everything is subject to divine "control, determination, knowledge, and will." His answer is that commandments and prohibitions serve as incentives for cognizant beings to perform good actions and refrain from bad ones. Without knowledge of the commandment they would not desire to perform the mandated act; without knowledge of the prohibition they would not be afraid to perform the forbidden act. The purpose of praise and blame is to lead such knowledgeable beings to repeat, or to avoid repeating, praiseworthy or blameworthy acts. The purpose of the punishments prescribed by the religious Law is to restrain the cognizant being from such transgression, or from repeating it. The theologians are wrong to think that God punishes out of anger or enmity, for God wills that the being who models himself on Him should refrain from wrongful acts.[23] God does not punish out of hostility or a sense of being aggrieved; punishment is not retribution. Nowhere does Avicenna say explicitly what is the secret of Destiny, or why it is secret. But given his criticism of the theologians' view of divine punishment, the secret appears to be associated with his hard deterministic views, perhaps the idea that "reward" and "punishment" are not meted out by a divine judge who assesses responsibility for human actions but rather are the necessary consequences of a causal order. The *Secret of Destiny* is not mentioned in subsequent Jewish philosophy, but the "secret" of causal determinism is, as we shall presently see.

To sum up: Avicenna presents us with a clear precedent of a philosophical determinist who deals with core issues in religious philosophy such as divine reward and punishment, the purpose of the religious commandments, the nature of the soul's final reward, and the causative power of divine knowledge. Although he sometimes does this under the rubric of the traditional Muslim belief in divine predestination, his philosophical interpretation is anything but traditional. The traditionalists portray God as decreeing, through his inscrutable will, the course of each and every state-of-affairs within world history before He creates the world, whereas for Avicenna God is the Necessary of Existence, who through self-intellection,

---

[22] Although belief in external punishment has no benefit in this particular case, such a belief is useful for the most part.

[23] Hourani 1966, 27–33.

necessarily and eternally imposes His most perfect plan on the world through a series of intermediary causes, themselves eternal. The traditional interpretation views God as personal, voluntaristic, and supernatural, whereas Avicenna's God is an impersonal agent acting through an eternal unchanging will that unfolds an expression of the necessity of the divine nature. With respect to possibility and voluntary agency, Avicenna is a compatibilist, i.e. he holds that they are compatible with the necessitarian world-view he describes, but he does not hold that will is compatible with moral desert, unlike soft determinists. He is particularly interested in showing that his determinism can be squared with divine reward and punishment, which he interprets as the natural consequences of actions, and not as part of a desert-based conception of justice.

Although few of Avicenna's philosophical writings were translated into Hebrew, his doctrines had a considerable influence on late medieval Jewish philosophy, a phenomenon recently dubbed "Avicennian knowledge without Avicenna."[24] Moreover, there are thirteenth- and fourteenth-century Spanish-Jewish philosophers, writing in Arabic and Hebrew, who refer explicitly to Avicenna's writings and are influenced by Avicennian doctrines, such as Joseph ibn Waqar, Moses ha-Lawi of Saville, and Abner of Burgos. The last two are relevant to our sketch of the history of Avicennian determinism among Spanish-Jewish philosophers.[25]

Moses ha-Lawi of Seville

Joseph ibn Waqar's fourteenth-century treatise on the reconciliation of philosophy and religion includes a collection of *Metaphysical Aphorisms* by Moses ben Joseph ha-Lawi of Seville, a thirteenth-century thinker who was considered an important philosopher and mathematician by Spanish Jews in the late thirteenth and fourteenth centuries.[26] In one of his aphorisms, Moses defends Avicenna's view that God knows particulars not *qua* particulars but rather "in a universal manner":

> God (may He be praised) knows particulars, and he rewards and punishes according to merits and transgressions. But he knows all this in a universal manner, to the extent that His Knowledge (may He be praised) encompasses all existents and their circumstances, without any new knowledge being originated in Him. This is so because God, when knowing His essence,

---

[24] Freudenthal and Zonta 2012.   [25] See Vajda 1955; for Ibn Waqar, see Sirat 1985, 381.

[26] Cf. *Light of the Lord* 1.3.3, Crescas 1990, 113, where Crescas states that his view accords with that of the "great philosophers" such as Al-Farabi, Avicenna, Averroës, and Moses ha-Lawi.

knows the rest of existents in the manner we explained. Now this is clear with respect to universal existents. But God is above the apprehension of particulars *qua* particulars, [i.e.] as sometimes existing and sometimes not existing. For the knowledge of a thing's existence is not the knowledge of its nonexistence, and the knowledge of one who knows things from this aspect is undoubtedly originated. God is above apprehending things from this aspect.[27]

God knows particulars in a general or universal fashion, that is, as universal types rather than as concrete particulars. This characteristically Avicennian view appears briefly in Abraham ibn Ezra, and versions of it surface in Abner of Burgos and Gersonides.

Moses explains in the next aphorism how people can be rewarded and punished for their merits and transgressions if God knows particulars in a universal manner:

> So that you may understand how knowledge is of particulars, while reward and punishment for merits and transgressions are in a universal manner, imagine that you have been appointed to govern a certain city. Your knowledge encompasses all kinds of good and bad actions, and you have prepared the proper recompense for each and every action. The inhabitants of the city fulfill [the laws] by virtue of the general charge that proceeded from you. Do you not see that through your acting justly with the inhabitants of the city you have combined knowledge of the circumstances of the city, the circumstances and actions of its inhabitants, with your removing of what is proper for you to remove yourself from? For not one of the particular actions is excluded from your general knowledge. Or perhaps you consider your knowledge and governance deficient because you do not know whether Zaid committed a transgression at a certain time and a certain place in the city?[28]

According to Moses' thought experiment, the governor knows all the sorts of actions that the inhabitants can perform, and he arranges matters such that the various actions bring about the appropriate consequences. Although he is not acquainted directly with individual inhabitants, he knows that that a certain type of individual will behave wickedly under certain types of circumstance, and he creates laws and institutions so that this type of behavior carries with it the appropriate punishment. In a similar fashion, God governs the world, and the fact that he is not directly acquainted with individuals *qua* individuals does not constitute a deficiency in his knowledge or his providence.

[27] Vajda 1955, 164–165   [28] *Ibid.*, 165.

Up to this point Moses' naturalistic theory of divine reward and punishment could be found in Aristotelians like Maimonides. However, the continuation suggests something more deterministic:

> The inhabitants' carrying out of the law by mutual compensation designates the reward and punishment in this world. (Our discussion of [reward and punishment in] the next world will be deferred to its proper place.) The manner of this fulfillment should be discussed at more length than is possible for this short treatment, in addition to the consideration that this is a gate of knowledge upon which the multitude are not allowed to knock.
>
> Yet if you, dear reader, are one of those who have advanced beyond their level, then it suffices for you to know that God (may He be praised) has implanted within the nature of most people the love of goods and the fear of evils, as well as the readiness and continual preparedness regarding the reward and punishment in the next world. Now these are consequent upon obedience and rebellion, just as the body's benefit is consequent upon beneficial behavior and its harm consequent upon harmful behavior. Praised be to He who combines the majesty of existence and the occupation with particulars in a manner appropriate to His Essence, so that good works are not set aside by him.[29]

How does God know that there are individuals who act in accordance with his plan if he is not directly acquainted with them? Moses' answer is that God implants within the nature of most people "the love of goods and the fear of evils" so that they are determined to act according to their divinely bestowed natures; reward and punishment in this world are nothing more than the natural consequences of their actions. This veiled reference to Avicenna's determinism is reinforced when, in the parable of the city, the inhabitants are said to obey the laws by virtue of the "general charge" that proceeds from the leader. Moses calls this subject "a gate of knowledge upon which the multitude are not allowed to knock" – perhaps because they would confuse causal determinism with the fatalistic claim that they will be rewarded and punished no matter what they do, or that God is unjust.

Abner of Burgos

The most thoroughgoing hard determinist among medieval Jewish thinkers was Abner of Burgos (c. 1270–c. 1347). One of the most distinguished savants of his generation, according to Moses of Narbonne, Abner converted later in life to Christianity and under his new name, Alfonso de Valladolid, wrote some anti-Jewish polemics and continued his

[29] *Ibid.*, 166.

scientific work. Yet when he was a young man, decades before he converted, he defended strict causal determinism in a book entitled *The Secret of Recompense*. Though the work is no longer extant, references contained in later writings give us a glimpse into its doctrines, and portions of it apparently were incorporated in Abner/Alfonso's *A Jealousy Offering*, the third and last of his defenses of determinism, and the only one extant.

Some of the themes of the lost *Secret of Recompense* can be inferred from references in later writings: God's eternal knowledge causally necessitates, via the instrumentality of the heavenly bodies, the temporal existence of individual substances and accidents. Since human volitions are accidents, they too are necessitated, but this does not make them any less volitional in character. For agents are said to will something, in so far as they accord, desire, and choose it, even if this comes as a result of compulsion, *a fortiori* if the compulsion is not felt. Divine recompense is nothing more than the natural consequence of the Law's observance or abrogation, which itself is causally determined. This causal determinism is the "secret of recompense" that should be hidden from the multitude, because, Abner implies, they would erroneously confuse causal determinism with fatalism and conclude that since everything is decreed, human endeavor is futile. In fact, human endeavor is *not* futile because it forms an essential link in the chain of causes that necessitates the preordained outcome.[30]

There is no evidence that *The Secret of Recompense* provoked any reaction initially, and it was not until years later, after Abner had converted and begun to write anti-Jewish polemical treatises, and after he had written another defense of astral determinism called *The Tower of Strength*, that a response came in the form of a letter entitled *The Refutation of Astrology*. (Neither work is extant.) The letter was composed by Isaac Polgar, his former student, who circulated it with two other letters attacking Abner's religious and philosophical views. Judging from later sources, Polgar's letters amounted to a defense of the "mainstream" philosophical interpretation of Judaism of the period, an interpretation that was heavily indebted to Maimonides and to Averroes. It appears that the main thesis of the *Refutation of Astrology* was that astrology is both false and harmful to religion: false because it has no scientific basis and actually contradicts Aristotelian science; harmful to religion because those who accept it place their faith in astrologers rather than God. To the

---

[30] The historical reconstruction of the lost treatise in this and subsequent paragraphs is based on Abner's *Jealousy Offering*, Isaac Polgar's *Support of Religion*, and Moses of Narbonne's *Treatise on Choice*.

traditional arguments against determinism Isaac added three new ones, which we will examine below, and challenged his former teacher to refute his arguments.

Abner responded to the challenge immediately with *A Jealousy Offering*, in which he continues his polemic with Polgar. This work, extant in medieval Spanish, and probably a translation from the original Hebrew composed under Abner's direction, is the main source of our knowledge of Abner's determinism. In the introduction, Abner portrays his former student Isaac as a heretic who denies divine knowledge of particulars, and hence, divine reward and punishment, because he denies the knowability of future possibles. Abner claims that all the prophets, sages, and the philosophers of all the gentiles, including Aristotle and Averroes, believed that God watches over all things in a particular manner with His eternal knowledge. It was to answer Isaac's "evil and hideous heresy" that Abner decided to interrupt his scientific pursuits and to take up his cudgel a third time in defense of astral determinism.

Yet although Abner portrays himself here and elsewhere as a defender of orthodoxy, his own view of how God knows particulars appears anything but traditional. He cites approvingly Avicenna's view that God knows particulars in their universal aspect, i.e. as ideal types rather than as concrete spatio-temporally instantiated particulars. He also cites approvingly Avicenna's and Al-Ghazali's doctrine that God knows future events through knowledge of their necessitating causes, which is how the astrologers know them; except that, unlike the astrologers, God's knowledge is perfect because He knows *all* the causes.[31] For Abner, as for Avicenna, God's Eternal Knowledge entails that particulars exist at a given time and place, but unlike Crescas, Abner does not say that God knows particulars in their particular aspect.

What enables Abner to preserve metaphysical possibility in a deterministic universe is Avicenna's distinction between the "divine existence" of essences or general natures and concrete material individuals, whose individuality is due to their particular natures. "Substances and essences, which are the subjects of philosophy, only have existence in the eternal divine existence, and the individuals, in so far as they are individuals, exist only in temporal existence, as Avicenna proved in his *Metaphysics*."[32] The causal

---

[31] *A Jealousy Offering*, Chapter 7, Alfonso de Valladolid (Abner of Burgos) 1990, 40. (References are to this edition since it is more readily available than that of Sainz de la Maza Vicioso 1990.)

[32] *A Jealousy Offering*, Chapter 4, Alfonso de Valladolid (Abner of Burgos) 1990, 25. The reference appears to be to *Shifā: Metaphysics*, V.I, Avicenna 2004, 156, where Avicenna speaks of the divine existence. It does not appear in Avicenna's *Najāt*, parts of which were translated into Hebrew. This is

necessitation of individual substances and accidents eliminates possibility with respect to their temporal existence, but not with respect to their eternal existence, where possibility remains. Abner uses the example of a piece of wax, which necessarily has a particular form at each and every instant (depending upon its causes), yet by its very nature retains the eternal capacity to receive new forms. Material individuals are at once necessary and possible: as concrete, temporally designate individuals they are necessary because they are causally necessitated to be what they are at a certain time. Yet they are also possible because they possess the "eternal possibility which is in eternal existence," the possibility possessed by essences. Hence they possess possibility in themselves (in eternal existence, in essence), and necessity through another (in temporal existence). According to Abner, it is Polgar's failure to distinguish between temporal and eternal existence that underlies most of his arguments against determinism.

Having established that metaphysical possibility is compatible with determinism Abner attempts to do the same for voluntary agency. Like Polgar, he accepts the Aristotelian notion that the will has (or is) a capacity for effecting opposites equally. But master and student view this capacity differently. Polgar, according to Abner, locates it in an individual agent's ability to act without an external cause necessitating the action. For if the will were determined to effect one of the opposites by an "external necessitant," argues Polgar, then it would lack, in effect, the capacity for effecting two opposites equally, and hence voluntary agency would be no different from natural agency.[33] Abner, by contrast, locates the capacity in the very nature or essence of will. A voluntary agent has the capacity to act or to refrain from acting, depending on what she desires. As long as the act is a consequence of will, it is considered to be voluntary. But each individual act – and the preceding volition – is necessitated by its causes. He describes the process culminating with an action as follows: first there is perception of an object by the senses, which is produced by causes that ultimately stretch back to the movement of the sphere. When there is accord between the imaginative and appetitive faculties, the appetitive faculty moves the natural heat, which moves its limbs of necessity, and an action is performed. Will is nothing more than the originated accord or assent to perform an action. Abner refers to Aristotle's *Book of the Soul,* by which he means Averroes' *Middle Commentary* on the same, where the point is not how will is

only one of several passages that shows Abner's knowledge of Avicenna, though how this knowledge reached him needs to be examined further (cf. Szpiech 2010). I intend to discuss this in a separate article.
[33] Alfonso de Valladolid (Abner of Burgos) 1990, 28–29.

determined, but rather what are the necessary and sufficient conditions for animal movement originated by soul.[34]

Abner does not consider the place of reason or deliberation in human action, and this is a significant omission. Aristotelians of a libertarian bent accepted that the will does not have an autonomous power over its actions; Aristotle had already argued that when the process of deliberation has taken place and the agent is ready to act in accordance with it, the action necessarily follows.[35] Polgar himself holds that actions follow necessarily from the accord between inner and external causes, but he considered the external causes to be *inclining* rather than *determining*, a position Abner finds absurd. Rational deliberation and intellect are considered so essential to Aristotelian versions of libertarianism that it is a pity that Abner does not meet their challenge head on.

Had he done so he probably would have argued that the rational deliberation that precedes action is *itself* astrally determined and hence cannot serve as the locus for indeterminism. This emerges from his defense against Polgar's third line of argumentation against astral determinism, namely, that since the intellect is separate from matter, and hence cannot be acted upon by the heavenly bodies, it follows that voluntary action cannot be determined by the heavenly bodies. This argument, which appears to have its sources in astrological literature, is not an uncommon one in Jewish philosophy.[36] Abner counters that insofar as the soul origi-nates action and movement it is *not* separate from matter, nor is the disposition to receive the universal truths and concepts, namely, the poten-tial or material intellect. Polgar finds it astounding that Abner can make the material intellect subject to the influence of the stars. Abner does concede that the acquired intellect is exempt from celestial causality, but he holds, appealing to Averroës, that the acquired intellect is none other than the active intellect as conjoined to man. Hence no part of *human* intellect is exempt from celestial causality.[37]

Once Abner allows that even acts in which compulsion is felt by the agent are nevertheless voluntary, it is not surprising that he does not adopt the compatibilist strategy of distinguishing between actions that are merely causally determined, for which we are morally responsible, and those that are compelled, for which we are not. If one performs a commandment

---

[34] *Middle Commentary on the Book of the Soul*, Averroës 2002, 125–127. This understanding of will as the accord between the appetitive and imaginative faculties, which is also in Crescas, clearly refers to animal and not Divine will.

[35] Knuuttila 1993, 26.   [36] Manekin 1997, 196–197.

[37] Alfonso de Valladolid (Abner of Burgos) 1990, 30

inadvertently, or against one's will, the benefit will still be forthcoming, just as a patient who is forced to take medicine will get well in spite of herself. On Abner's explanation of divine recompense, a sinner no more deserves the evil consequences of his actions than a person deserves weight loss if he goes on a diet. The whole issue of desert is irrelevant to divine recompense, because divine justice is fundamentally different from human ("political") justice, where bad actions are excused only if they are performed unintentionally. A violation of divine law, intended or not, carries with it dire consequences. Once recompense is made the necessary consequence of certain actions, then the distinction between intentional and inadvertent becomes otiose, according to Abner.

Still, as in Avicenna and Moses ha-Lawi, all this is a secret that should be kept from the multitude, who conceive of divine action in terms of human justice, and hence who require laws and a system of rewards and punishments to motivate their behavior. The belief that free will is not divinely determined is necessary for the multitude:

> For the benefit in concealment is that people will labor and endeavor, and will not be idle or lazy, in their occupations, or in their performance of the commandments, or in their refraining from trangressions, all of which follows from their weak understanding of the doctrine of free will [*libre alvedrio*]. This alone rendered it necessary for God to give them the Law, so that they would merit receiving recompense on account of it, just as it is the practice of people to thank someone who benefits them of his own volition and choice, and not to thank someone who does it without his volition and choice. They likewise impute guilt and disgrace to someone who harms them of his own volition and choice, and they do not impute blame or disgrace to someone who harms them without his volition and choice. For they liken and consider equivalent God's ways and thoughts with their own ways and thoughts.[38]

Unless the people thought somehow that they were *meriting* their reward and punishment by performing commandments of their own free will, they would not actually perform the commandments.

According to Abner, the notion that it is just to reward or punish intentional actions, and that it is unjust to reward or punish unintentional or inadvertent actions, arises from the expectations of human social intercourse, which are governed by the principle of reciprocity. If Peter will not compensate Paul for the good Paul is about to bestow upon him, then Paul will not go ahead and bestow that good. But Peter will only compensate

---

[38] *Ibid.*, 70.

Paul if he believes that the good is bestowed by Paul knowingly and intentionally. Abner claims that this model of recompense is entirely irrelevant with respect to God and man. True, the Bible speaks of God requiting good for good, and evil for evil. But this is merely a manner of speaking, since no good or harm can be done to God. Rather God's judgments, like His laws, are eternal truths that are necessarily instantiated in the temporal world by human actions with their consequences:

> Recompense does not come from God for the sake of an anticipated benefit, or the semblance of a benefit, as is the case of the recompense provided by men for each other. Rather, it is entailed by the wisdom of God, which is the pure truth, and not the semblance of truth. [The demonstrated truth of divine determinism] reinforces man's need to labor as much as is within his power at learning, teaching, and the deliberate actions that intend toward the good.[39]

Citing Naḥmanides, Abner claims that "the commandments were legislated for the good of human creatures, so that they conduct themselves with uprightness and righteousness." Thus divine justice, unlike human justice, reflects God's concern with His creatures. On a desert model of punishment, a person who is compelled to place his hand near a fire is unjustly punished when his hand is burned. But on a paternalistic model, when the intention is to teach somebody a lesson about the dangerous consequences of being too close to fire, such compelled actions may indeed be appropriate.

Crescas

Avicennian hard determinism could have reached Crescas through various channels, but Abner's influence on Crescas is attested already by his student, Joseph ben Shem Tov ibn Shem Tov, who writes:

> And the righteous rabbi [Hasdai], of blessed memory, was drawn after the apostate Abner, the author of a book that he called the *The Secret of Recompense*, all of it replete with evil sophistries, powerful falsehoods and lies.[40]

Since Joseph ibn Shem Tov refers to Abner's earlier work and not the later *A Jealousy Offering*, one should be careful in drawing the lines too closely

---

[39] *Ibid.*, 75.
[40] Joseph ibn Shem Tov, *Commentary on the Ethics*, Oxford Bodley Mich. 404 (Ol. 197) [Neub. 1431] fol. 56b.

between *A Jealousy Offering* and Crescas's *Light of the Lord*. Still, Abner's later work appears to incorporate material from the former, so it is of clear relevance, especially when one notes how much Crescas has appropriated from Abner.[41]

We saw above that Abner posits an interpretation of divine justice that undermines the distinction between compelled and uncompelled acts. Since reward and punishment are the necessary consequences of actions the issue of compulsion appears to be moot; swallowing medicine will produce an effect whether one takes it willingly or under compulsion. While Crescas appears to endorse this position in an earlier part of the section on choice,[42] he later explicitly requires that acts and mental states come about without felt coercion or compulsion for them to be justly requited by God.[43] This suggests that he has "softened" Abner's hard determinism, i.e. that he has found a place for what we could call moral responsibility for voluntary actions in a deterministic universe. On closer examination, however, Crescas does not abandon hard determinism but rather accounts for the voluntary/involuntary distinction within the framework of an Abnerian conception of divine justice. Even what scholars consider to be the more voluntaristic stratum of the thesis need not detract from this hard determinism.

Crescas begins his section on choice by claiming that choice is a cornerstone of the Torah, that the term 'commandment' does not pertain to one who is compelled and coerced to do a certain act, that the simple will must be able to choose one of opposing courses of action, and that the nature of the possible underlies choice. While initially sounding libertarian, Crescas provides interpretations of 'choice,' 'will,' and 'possibility' that are compatible with strict determinism (but *not* with the deservedness of reward and punishment). He first presents the arguments of those who believe that the nature of the possible exists (Chapter 1) and then the arguments of those who believe that the nature of the possible does not exist (Chapter 2). Framing the discussion in this matter is historically inaccurate, since none of his determinist predecessors claimed that the nature of the possible did not exist; rather it was their opponents, Isaac Polgar and Moses Narbonne, who accused them of denying the existence of the possible. Still, it serves Crescas's purpose to frame the dispute as one concerning whether the

---

[41] Y. Baer was the first scholar in modern times to show this dependence, and for years his incomplete Hebrew translation of the medieval Spanish text (in Baer 1940) was used by historians of Jewish philosophy instead of the Spanish. Needless to say, judgments of Abner's influence should now be made on the basis of comparing all the known texts.

[42] *Light* 2.5.3, Crescas 1990, 213.   [43] *Ibid.*, 213–224.

nature of the possible exists or not, so that he can come up with his own compatibilist solution, which owes much to the compatibilist solutions of Abner and Avicenna.

Crescas's own compatibilist solution rests on the Avicennian claim that existing things other than God are possible in themselves but necessitated by their causes. In a deterministic universe, the will is the capacity to effect one of two opposing alternatives; human choices are effective; the possible *per se* exists; chance events occur; diligence and effort are not futile; and divine commandments motivate people to achieve, through their diligence and effort, the desired results. Reward and punishment are not unjust because they are the necessary consequences of worship and transgression, as effects are necessitated from causes:

> Thus, divine wisdom consigned them, i.e., the commandments and the prohibitions, to be intermediate movers and powerful causes to direct human beings towards human happiness. His beneficence and simple grace is responsible for this. And this is the divine equity that is alluded to in the verse: "God disciplines you just as a man disciplines his son" [Deut. 8:5]. It is well known that a father does not discipline his son with the intent to exact revenge, nor to render justice, but for the benefit of the son. So too when God disciplines human beings, His intention is not to exact revenge from them, nor to render political equity, which is only appropriate when human [actions] are completely volitional, without any compulsion or coercion. Rather, His intention is for the good of the entire nation, and this is what He intends by [the discipline.] Consequently, [the discipline] is appropriate even if [one] is necessitated with respect to his cause, because it is good for man.[44]

Divine equity, unlike political equity, does not require that human actions be "completely volitional, without any compulsion or coercion." On the contrary, "if reward and punishment are necessitated from worship and transgression as effects are necessitated from causes, they are not considered unjust, just as it is not unjust for one who comes close to a fire to be burned, even if his approach was involuntary." Crescas refers his reader to his discussion of reward and punishment in the third treatise, where he cites Deuteronomy 8:5 as the proof text for his claim that the essential intention of rewards and punishment promised in Scripture is divine beneficence, grace, and the bestowal of perfection. And this is consistent with speculation, "for it has been demonstrated of God that He is the true good, and that it is appropriate that He, on account of His perfection, causes his

---

[44] *Ibid.*, 214.

beneficence to flow, since it has been demonstrated indubitably that He has the ability to do so."

So far Crescas hews fairly closely to the paternalistic theory of divine justice that we found in Abner. But his next move appears to contradict what he has just written, since he claims that:

> the necessitation of the [punishing and rewarding] is appropriate when the agent does not feel coerced or compelled, which is the foundation of choice and will. But, when humans act under coercion and compulsion and not through their wills, the coerced and compelled actions are not acts of their souls, because they do not act with the accordance between their appetitive faculty and imaginative faculty. Thus, it is not appropriate that a punishment should follow.[45]

Recent Crescas scholarship has used Crescas's distinction between coerced and uncoerced actions to give his theory of divine justice a desert-based reading, i.e. that humans deserve reward and punishment when their actions are not coerced and compelled, but rather are voluntary acts of their soul.[46] But there are several problems with this reading. First, it flies in the face of Crescas's general view that the primary intention of Divine reward and punishment is to benefit humans; second, it ignores Crescas's distinction between divine and human justice; third, it is difficult to reconcile with some of Crescas's examples, such as the person who is burnt even though his closeness to a fire is involuntary, or David and the Israelites, who are punished for deeds for which they are unsuited, according to the Talmudic rabbis.[47]

Indeed, the force of Crescas's distinction between coerced and uncoerced actions is not to indicate which recompense is *deserved*, but rather which is *appropriate*. Given a paternalistic model of justice, where reward and punishment are for the person's benefit, it is generally inappropriate to punish wrongdoing that is compelled, e.g. where no lesson can be derived from it. As Crescas puts it, "punishment for a compelled transgression does not belong to divine justice, for what good will proceed from it?" Crescas's appeal to the voluntary/involuntary distinction is entirely within the

---

[45] *Ibid.*, 215.

[46] See W. Harvey 1998, 143: "Here Crescas clarifies that divine punishment, no different from human punishment, is justified only with regard to voluntary acts"; cf. Feldman 1984: "[For Crescas] compulsory acts are indeed excusable; but a merely motivated act is not" (27).

[47] *Light* 2.5.4, Crescas 1990, 219: "'David was not suited to do that deed, nor was Israel suited to do that deed' [B. T. *Avodah Zarah*, 4b–5a]. Despite their being unsuited for the deed, they were punished. And this [difficulty] can only be solved according to the approach that we have chosen." Most of the scriptural and rabbinic proof texts adduced by Crescas in this chapter are already found in Abner. Some are not cited in Baer 1940.

framework of a divine, paternalistic system of justice, where reward and punishment for the performance or transgression of commandments are part of a regimen for the benefit of creatures. The distinction does not appear in Abner and, to be sure, it appears to contradict Abner's view that since recompense follows from actions as effects follow from causes, there is no ground for distinguishing between compelled and uncompelled actions. But Crescas's introduction of the distinction is entirely compatible with hard determinism and represents a refinement of Abner's view rather than a rejection.

Once Crescas introduces the distinction, however, he has to account for the appropriateness of rewarding and punishing beliefs which are not subject to will and, in some cases, are compelled by reason. Clearly there is no question of such reward and punishment being deserved, but how can it even be appropriate as a training regimen when beliefs are not subject to will? Crescas answers this question by first arguing that the purpose of the acts of worship and good deeds is the feeling of desire and joy, "which is nothing other than the pleasure of will in doing good." It is through this feeling that one conjoins with God, who creates the world through love, joy, and beneficence. So it is certainly appropriate that the conjunction with God follows necessarily from the mental state as the effect follows the cause. And while beliefs are not subject to will, the possession of beliefs may be accompanied by a feeling of the pleasure and joy "that we experience when *God grants us His belief, and the diligence to apprehend its truth* ... The arousal of Joy and the effort in comprehending the beliefs' truth are matters that are consequent upon will and joy."[48] It is not the possession of the belief *per se* that is God's intent, but rather the affective attitude that one is motivated to take toward attaining the belief and which accompanies it. Crescas then extends this to actions: what is most meaningful is not the actual performance of the commanded action (though this, too, carries with it necessary recompense), but rather the will and desire to perform the action.

The upshot of Crescas's argument is to devalue the possession of the intellectual beliefs *per se* and to value the expression of love and desire that underlies the acquiring and contemplation of those beliefs. In this he both opposes the view of the Jewish Aristotelians that the acquisition and contemplation of true beliefs are the goal of the commandments, and adopts their view that the performance of commandments is essentially instrumental for inculcating the correct mental states – for them, intellectual

---

[48] *Light* 2.5.5, Crescas 1990, 222.

beliefs; for Crescas, affective attitudes of joy and the good will. Some of Crescas's anti-intellectualism may stem from Abner and from an earlier tradition of Spanish-Jewish traditionalism, but his replacement of the primacy of intellect with the primacy of will does not appear in Abner's extant writings, and may suggest some awareness of the new-found scholastic emphasis on will.[49] Nevertheless, this emphasis is perfectly compatible with hard determinism, although publicizing this to the multitude is dangerous, since they will use it to excuse evildoers.[50]

To sum up: divine "reward" and "punishment" are the necessary consequences/concomitants of actions and beliefs that are causally necessitated through the decree of God for the benefit of humankind. This paternalistic conception of Divine justice does not require positing human free will, even compatibilist free will, any more than rewarding and punishing beloved pets require the assumption that they *deserve* to be rewarded and punished. On the contrary, we reward pets for obedience and punish them for disobedience, not because we hold them morally responsible for their actions, but in order to train them to be good pets. Reward and punishment, like praise and blame, are appropriate in the absence of moral responsibility – appropriate, but not deserved.

Spinoza

Something like the above, albeit with regard to punishment, appears in Spinoza's letter to his friend Oldenberg:

> "But," you urge, "if men sin from the necessity of their nature, they are therefore excusable." You do not explain what conclusion you wish to draw from this. Is it that God cannot be angry with them, or is it that they are worthy of blessedness, that is, the knowledge and love of God? If you say the former, I entirely agree that God is not angry, and that all things happen in accordance with His will; but I deny that on that account all men ought to be blessed; for men may be excusable but nevertheless be without blessedness and afflicted in many ways. A horse is excusable, for being a horse and not a man; but, nevertheless, he must needs be a horse and not a man. He who goes mad from the bite of a dog is indeed to be excused, yet he is rightly suffocated. Finally, he who cannot control his desires, and keep them in check through fear of the laws, although he is also to be excused for his weakness, nevertheless

---

[49] Ravitzky 1988, 39–48. For a healthy dose of skepticism concerning Crescas's direct acquaintance with Scholastic writings see Feldman 2012.

[50] *Light* 2.5.3, Crescas 1990, 214.

cannot enjoy tranquility of mind and the knowledge and love of God, but of necessity he is lost.[51]

People who behave badly are to be excused for their actions because they do so out of the weakness of the nature, but that does not mean that they do not suffer and hence are not "punished." What it means is that this punishment does not proceed from an offended God who holds them morally accountable for their actions, but rather is nothing else than the natural consequence of their bad behavior. It is possible to read Spinoza's remark that "God cannot be angry with them" simply as his denial of a personal God or as an expression of the view that emotions cannot be attributed to God, with which he would have been familiar from Maimonides.[52] But given the context of the assumption that God cannot be angry with one who sins "from the necessity of his nature," Spinoza's point appears to be a specific one about the inappropriateness of anger or other reactive attitudes in this situation. God is not angry, nor is *anybody* angry who understands that the behavior is necessitated, that free will is an illusion, and hence that punishment, while appropriate, is not deserved.

God does not act out of anger, but according to Spinoza, neither does he act out of love. And this brings us to what appears to be the big difference between Spinoza and medievals such as Abner and Crescas. S. D. Luzzatto expressed it as follows:

> On the one hand it is clear that Spinoza's theory is close to that of R' Ḥasdai, in so far as both deny the nature of the possible, and view connectedness and necessity in every thing. The difference between them is that according to Spinoza, every thing is determined with a predetermination without a principle, whereas according to R' Ḥasdai, everything is determined, but the determination has a principle, i.e., the will of God.[53]

Luzzatto's comment is reminiscent of Leibniz's comment in the *Theodicy* that:

> Spinoza went further: he appears to have explicitly taught a blind necessity, having denied to the Author of Things understanding and will, and assuming that good and perfection relate to us only, and not to him. It is true that Spinoza's opinion on this subject is somewhat obscure: for he grants God thought, after having divested him of understanding, *cogitationem, non intellectum concedit Deo* ... Nevertheless, as far as one can understand him,

---

[51] Ep 78, Spinoza 2002, 952.
[52] See *Ethics* Vp17, Spinoza 1925, II.291; Spinoza 1985, 604. According to Kisner 2011 (65n.16), the point is merely Spinoza's rejection of a personal God.
[53] Luzzatto 1970, 120

he acknowledges no goodness in God, properly speaking, and he teaches that all things exist through the necessity of the divine nature, without any act of choice by God. We will not waste time here in refuting an opinion so bad, and indeed so inexplicable.[54]

Luzzatto claims that Spinoza's determinism lacks a principle, whereas Leibniz calls it blind because, according to Spinoza, the world does not proceed from an agent that has intellect and will and chooses the best of all possible worlds. But even conceding that Spinoza's God or Nature does not act through intelligence and will for a purpose, this does not imply that this determination is "blind," certainly not in the sense that it is inexplicable or unintelligible. On the contrary, it has been argued that Spinoza's determinism derives from the principle of sufficient reason,[55] the idea that each thing that exists and does not exist has a sufficient reason/explanation why it exists and why it does not exist, respectively. The fact that this explanation does not appeal to God's intelligent design but rather to His nature (or Nature) does not reduce in the slightest the rationality of the system as a whole. (It seems odd to call "blind" the derivations of the theorems of Euclidean geometry.) On the contrary, since God's nature is most perfect, things have been produced by God with the highest perfection.[56]

In any event, what distinguishes Spinoza from Crescas (and Leibniz) is not the maximal rationality or perfection of the world but whether it is the product of an intelligent, voluntary agent. According to Leibniz this means that the necessity of the actual world is relative to God's choosing it over other possible worlds; according to Spinoza, the necessity of the actual world is not relative but absolute since there are no other possible worlds. As for Crescas, while he uses the language of divine voluntary agency, there are at least two reasons to consider his position closer to Spinoza's than that of Leibniz.

First, Crescas does not embrace the notion that God chooses this world over other possible worlds; in fact, God is not described as choosing to create a world at a certain instant at all. Although the manuscripts are not consistent on this point,[57] one can read his position as suggesting that God wills eternally an infinite successive number of actual worlds in a sort of perpetual creation. Even the manuscript version that presents this sort of creation as one of several options does not imply that God chooses this option over others, only that we are unable to determine which of the options is correct, since the doors of rational inquiry are locked at this point.

---

[54] Leibniz 1985, 238. [55] See Della Rocca 2008, 75.
[56] See *Ethics* Ip33s2 Spinoza 1925, II.74; Spinoza 1985, 436. [57] See W. Harvey 1998, 41–42 and 41n.2.

There is no suggestion that he accepts anything remotely like a possible-world model, or that, like Maimonides, he exempts God from the Aristotelian principle of plenitude.[58] On the contrary, he explicitly includes God within the principle when he writes:

> Since all of existence is good . . . it is appropriate that the divine beneficence – which is appropriately the most perfect beneficence conceivable – not diminish bringing into existence any good that possibly exists.[59]

The notion that God eternally brings into existence all possible existence sounds a lot like Spinoza's remark that "no truly sound reason can persuade us to believe that God did not will to create all the things that are in his intellect, with that same perfection with which he understands them."[60]

Second, Crescas follows Gersonides in claiming that God creates the world not for any advantage to Himself but out of beneficence and grace. But unlike Gersonides, who claims that the deficiency of matter requires that the world be created at an instant through the bestowal of form on eternal formless matter, Crescas argues that an eternal will emanates eternally the good, and because this emanation is a product of will rather than natural necessity, in a process of continual creation from nothing, then the many can follow from the one. Indeed, God can be the agent of miracles, through His beneficence and grace, because there are no impediments to His will.[61] This is what Crescas calls "necessitation of the world from God, in the manner of bestowing good." Throughout this discussion, there is no hint of the sorts of worries raised by Maimonides and Al-Ghazali concerning the neo-Aristotelian concept of God eternally willing the emanation of the world. For Maimonides the essence of will is to will and not to will; whereas for Crescas, "the will for a certain thing is nothing but its love of the thing willed."[62] This sort of active will differs from a Spinozistic notion of infinite will;[63] and, although God lacks for nothing, it appears to inject final causality into the divine action. Divine love for Crescas seems to be other directed; its object is the thing willed, and not God himself. This appears to be a crucial difference between Crescas's account and that of Spinoza (and Avicenna). Still, all three reject the concept of a creator God that freely chooses the actual world out of a set of possibilities, infinite or otherwise.

---

[58] See Manekin 1988.   [59] *Light* 2.6.4, Crescas 1990, 267.
[60] See *Ethics* Ip33s2, Spinoza 1925, II.76; 1985, 438.   [61] *Light* 3.1.1.5, Crescas 1990, 315.
[62] *Guide* II.21, Maimonides 1963, 314–315; *Light* 2.2.4, Crescas 1990, 170.
[63] See *Ethics* Ip32dem, Spinoza 1925, II.72; 1985, 435. See also Feldman 2008.

CHAPTER 3

The science of Scripture: Abraham ibn Ezra and Spinoza on biblical hermeneutics

T. M. Rudavsky

Introduction

That Spinoza was influenced by Ibn Ezra in his own theory of biblical hermeneutics is not news. Recent scholars have traced the trajectory of biblical hermeneutics from Ibn Ezra to Spinoza, while Noel Malcolm has discussed in particular the probable importance of both Isaac la Peyrère and Hobbes.[1] Ibn Ezra's Bible commentaries unleashed many supercommentaries, but perhaps his most famous commentator was Spinoza, who in his TTP enlisted "Ibn Ezra, a man of enlightened mind and considerable learning" in support of his own contention that Moses could not have written the Pentateuch.[2] In this chapter I compare Ibn Ezra's theory of Bible science with that of Spinoza. My purpose is twofold. I first focus on the importance of science in their respective readings of Scripture. In conjunction with the first, my second purpose is to gauge the extent to which Spinoza radicalizes Ibn Ezra's reading. As I argue below, both Ibn Ezra and Spinoza make use of scientific discourse in their analysis of the Bible; this application of scientific method to biblical hermeneutics attests to the attempts of both thinkers to render all intellectual enterprises rigorous and amenable to rational scrutiny. For Ibn Ezra, biblical interpretation itself becomes a science, leading to the "astrologization of Scripture," whereas in the case of Spinoza it leads to a tightly constructed philological method based on the methods of "Nature."

Both Ibn Ezra and Spinoza were preoccupied with the philological aspects of the Hebrew language and both emphasized the importance of being able to embark upon a philological examination of the scriptural texts. Another way of making this point is in terms of the standard exegetical distinction between *peshat*, the plain straightforward reading of Scripture,

---

[1] See Curley 1994 and Curley forthcoming; W. Harvey 2010a; James 2012; Malcolm 2002; Nadler 2011; Popkin 1996.
[2] TTP 8, Spinoza 2001, 105.

and *derash*, which is associated with a homiletical reading.[3] We shall see that Ibn Ezra and Spinoza have little patience for *derash* inasmuch as they both see it as obfuscating the philological reading and leading the reader farther from the "original" meaning of Scripture. The emphasis on *peshat* is evident in Spinoza's description of how to study Scripture, which "should inform us of the nature and properties of the language in which the Bible was written and which its authors were accustomed to speak ... a study of the Hebrew language must undoubtedly be a prime requisite."[4] We shall return to the importance of *peshat* in the context of grammatical and philological study below.

Following upon Curley's point that "it was in the extension of the scientific outlook and scientific methods to the study of historical texts that Spinoza was innovative and influential,"[5] I shall demonstrate that this extension is adumbrated already in Ibn Ezra, who was a bit of a radical. In the first part of the chapter I discuss briefly the importance of science and scientific method to both thinkers. In the second part, I look at the application of scientific method to the art of biblical interpretation. Part three examines the implications of this application, turning first to their dismissal of miracle, and second to their respective rejection of Moses' authorship of the Pentateuch.

The importance of science

Ibn Ezra and the science of astrology

Born in Tudela in *c*. 1089, Abraham ibn Ezra was a poet, grammarian, biblical exegete, philosopher, astronomer, astrologer, and physician. His life falls into two periods: until 1140 he lived in Spain where he was a friend of Ibn Tzaddik, Ibn Daud, Moses ibn Ezra, and Judah Halevi. The second period dates from 1140 when he left Spain for a time of extensive wandering in Lucca, Mantua, Verona, Provence, London, Narbonne, and finally Rome. It was during this period that most of his works were composed. His wanderings forced him to write in Hebrew as well as Latin, a fact that perhaps saved his works from oblivion. He died in *c*. 1167 in either Rome or possibly Palestine.

---

[3] For a detailed explanation of the four ways and levels of reading Scripture – *peshat, remez, derash*, and *sōd*, associated with the exegetical notion of (PaRDeS), see Talmage 1999. In this chapter we shall be primarily concerned with *peshat* and *derash*, although *sod* (secret) will play a role as well.

[4] TTP 7, Spinoza 2001, 88.   [5] Curley 1990, 65. See also Savan 1986, 95–124.

Although Ibn Ezra did not write any specifically philosophical works, he was strongly influenced by the Jewish Neoplatonist philosopher Solomon ibn Gabirol, and his works contain much Neoplatonic material. For example, he accepts Ibn Gabirol's doctrine that intelligible substances are composed of matter and form, and he uses Ibn Gabirol's descriptions of God as the source from which everything flows. Recent scholars have focused upon Ibn Ezra's equation of "The One" with "The All," as reflected in the following passages: "God is all, His glory fills all, from Him is all"[6] and "For God is all, and all comes from Him."[7] Whether or not Spinoza was influenced by these passages in his own identification of God with everything (*Deus sive Natura*) is not clear.[8]

More importantly for our purposes, however, Ibn Ezra was totally ensconced in the scientific literature and thought of his time. Because Ibn Ezra was one of the first Hebrew scholars to write on scientific subjects in Hebrew, he had to invent many Hebrew terms to represent the technical terminology of Arabic. For example he introduced terms for the center of a circle, for sine, and for the diagonal of a rectangle. His own research he describes as *hakmei ha-mazzalot* (science of the zodiacal signs), a term he uses often to refer to a number of branches of science: astrology, mathematics, astronomy, and regulation of the calendar. Sela has argued that Ibn Ezra's scientific treatises are all cross-referenced, suggesting that they represent a single body of texts designed to deal with the different branches of *hokhmat ha-mazzalot*.[9] Inasmuch as the purpose of these works was primarily to educate and introduce scientific findings to a lay audience, they serve as an excellent source for learning about scientific texts available in twelfth-century Spain.

One of Ibn Ezra's main aims was to convey the basic features of Ptolemaic science, astronomical as well as astrological, as they were transformed by the Arabic sciences.[10] Thus, for example, his best-known work *Beginning of Wisdom* (*Reshit Hokhma*) functions as an introductory astrological text book and deals with the zodiac constellations and planets, their astrological characteristics, and more technical aspects of astrology. Ibn Ezra's star list appears as a section of his work *The Astrolabe*. The list is

---

[6] Commentary on Exodus 33:21, Ibn Ezra 1988b, 704.
[7] Commentary on Exodus 23:21, Ibn Ezra 1988b, 511. See also Genesis 1:26.
[8] See for example *Ethics* Ip15: "Whatever is, is in God, and without God nothing can be, or be conceived." For further discussion of this point, see Jospe 2009, 211; Kreisel 1994, 29–66.
[9] Sela and Freudenthal 2006, 163.
[10] *Ibid.*, 168. That astrology was considered one of the sciences as well as astronomy is discussed in Sela 1999 and Thorndike 1955.

given in the form of a paragraph, in which the coordinates are given in Hebrew alphabetic numerals, and the Arabic names are transliterated into Hebrew characters. As Goldstein has pointed out, many of the discrepancies between Ibn Ezra's star positions and those in the Greek text of the *Almagest* can be traced to the Arabic versions of the *Almagest*.[11]

In addition to works in astrology, Ibn Ezra wrote several books on Hebrew grammar, including *Moznaim*, written in Rome, which contained a detailed review of the works of previous grammarians, and *Sefer ha-Yesod*, in which he tells the reader that he will reveal all the secrets of the Hebrew language. Scholars have noted the scientific methodology and precision of *Sefer ha-Yesod*.[12] In contrast to many scholars who do not see Ibn Ezra as an original thinker, and who consider his grammatical works to be primarily "study books," Charlap emphasizes Ibn Ezra's original innovations: according to Charlap, "Ibn Ezra's uniqueness is expressed primarily by his eclecticism and his application of scientific standards of thorough examination, research and implementation, which resulted in a unique study of various issues in Hebrew grammar."[13] A third work of grammar, *Sfat Yeter*, was most likely written at the end of his stay in Italy. In the introduction to this work, Ibn Ezra states that trying to understand the biblical text without a solid grounding in grammar is "like banging your head against a brick wall."[14] He informs the reader that there is one true meaning to Scripture, and that a biblical text should not be interpreted in ways that obfuscate that meaning. We shall return to the importance of this point below.

Spinoza and the "New Science"

Like Ibn Ezra, Spinoza was focused upon the importance of science, even in the interpretation of Scripture. Whereas Ibn Ezra was influenced by the astrological theories derived from Ptolemy, Spinoza is influenced by the larger scientific and mathematical world-view in which the new Copernican astronomy was embedded. Spinoza thus advocates a methodological program of natural science that, rooted in a mathematical view of nature, is then applied to Scripture. In the TTP, which was published anonymously in 1670 but probably commenced much earlier, Spinoza forces the issue of biblical hermeneutics against the backdrop of a theory of demonstrative certainty attained by the New Science. Writing at the forefront of revolutionary changes in natural philosophy, methodology, and science, Spinoza

[11] Goldstein 1996, 12.   [12] For details of Ibn Ezra's grammar, see Charlap 2001; Lancaster 2003.
[13] Charlap 2001, 80.   [14] Ibn Ezra 1984, 85, ll. 10–11.

will claim that religion and science occupy different domains: religion is concerned primarily with the moral sphere, while science pertains to the domain of truth. We shall return to this point below.

Recent discussion has centered on the extent to which Spinoza was interested in the New Science. While Maul suggests that Spinoza was estranged philosophically from experimental science,[15] others have argued that Spinoza was indeed taking part in the so-called rise of modern science.[16] Even a cursory look at his correspondence confirms Spinoza's interest in the New Science. While it is true that Spinoza did not carry out original research in the physical or mathematical sciences, he did have a sound knowledge of optics and the current physics of light. A similar interest can be traced to Spinoza's interest in astronomy and optics, as attested by many references in his letters.[17] In fact, as I argue below, his very appropriation of scientific method to biblical hermeneutics attests to his attempt to render all intellectual enterprises scientific.

I have discussed elsewhere the importance of a "mathematized" methodology for Spinoza's scientific outlook, and the appropriation of this mathematical schema to human experience.[18] As Spinoza states in the *Ethics*, mathematics, "which is concerned not with ends but only with the essence and properties of figures, had not shown men another standard of truth."[19] By eliminating the quest for final causes, mathematics reintroduces a model of proper order against which other objects can be studied. In his preface to Part Three of the *Ethics*, Spinoza says that he will "consider human actions and appetites just as if I were considering lines, planes, or bodies."[20] Here the proper method of study of human action, including human emotions, is Euclidean geometry.

But what do we do in situations that appear to be impervious not only to the mathematical certitude exemplified by geometry, but also to the entire domain of natural science? In particular, how do we approach the truths of religion, which utilize their own measure of certitude independent of scientific method? According to Spinoza, herein lies the source of the conflict between science and religion. Spinoza recognizes the difficulties inherent in understanding religious statements and dogmas. The certainty

[15] See Maull 1986, 3: "[Spinoza's] philosophy was strikingly disconnected from the shifting and interrogating science that went on around him . . . he was as remote from elementary 'doing' of science and especially from the idea of learning by experience as Plato was."

[16] For discussion of this point, see Curley 1994, 65–99; Siebrand 1986, 62.

[17] See Ep 26 (Spinoza 1995, 175–176); Ep 32 (*ibid.*, 192–198); Ep 36 (*ibid.*, 206–210); Ep 39 (*ibid.*, 215– 221); Ep 40 (*ibid.*, 217–220); Ep 46 (*ibid.*, 247–248).

[18] See Rudavsky 2001.   [19] *Ethics* Iapp; Spinoza 1985, 441.   [20] Spinoza 1985, 492.

reflected in prophecy itself is based on the imaginative and not the rational faculty, he argues, and so does not carry the sort of certainty reflected by metaphysics and ontology: "the certainty afforded by prophecy was not a mathematical certainty, but only a moral certainty."[21] The methods of science, which aspire toward the certitude represented by mathematical geometry, are thus pitted against the constraints of biblical interpretation and give rise to the antagonism of Spinoza's audiences. As with Ibn Ezra, the techniques used by Spinoza to analyze Scripture are a direct result of the challenges posed by the sciences of the day.

The science of biblical hermeneutics

Astrological and philological secrets: Ibn Ezra

It is clear that Ibn Ezra and Spinoza not only shared a deep interest in the scientific developments of their respective ages, but that both incorporated this interest into their reading and critical analysis of Scripture. Ibn Ezra was careful not to state his positions too boldly, and because of his constantly alluding to "secrets" in these commentaries, based on both astrological and philological considerations, his works inspired numerous supercommentaries. Ibn Ezra himself claimed that only the individual schooled in astrology, astronomy, or mathematics will be in a position to understand his own commentaries properly.[22] As we shall see below, this emphasis upon reading Scripture through the eyes of scientific discourse adumbrates Spinoza's own method.

Ibn Ezra is best known for his biblical commentaries, which are written in an elegant Hebrew, replete with puns and word plays. These commentaries were commenced in Rome when Ibn Ezra was already sixty-four, and incorporate much astrological material. In the introduction to his standard (long) commentary on the Pentateuch, Ibn Ezra summarizes his exegetical method as follows:

> This *Book of Jashar*, composed by Abraham the poet
> is bound by ropes of grammar
> the eyes of the intelligent will find it fit.
> All who take hold of it will be glad.[23]

Ibn Ezra describes his method as satisfying both meticulous philology ("ropes of grammar") and strict rational plausibility ("eyes of the intelligent"). In this

---

[21] TTP 2, Spinoza 2001, 22.   [22] Sela and Freudenthal 2006, 166.
[23] Commentary on Genesis, Introduction, Ibn Ezra 1988a, 1.

way, much of his commentary is devoted to precise linguistic clarifications, grounded in the Hebrew philology of the time.[24] As we shall see below, Ibn Ezra makes ample use of astrology in his interpretation of biblical passages, providing his readership with a unique combination of astrological science tempered with philological and grammatical hermeneutics.

Reminiscent of Maimonides' celebrated parable of the palace, Ibn Ezra construes truth as residing in the center of a circle, with each of five interpretive methodologies standing somewhere in relation to that center.[25] The first group he claims (associated with the Babylonian academies, Jews living in the Islamic East) strays far from the original text; "if truth be likened to a dot within a circle then this approach can be compared to the periphery of the circle, which goes round about only to return to its starting point."[26] These commentators tend to be prolix, wordy, and often extrapolate from unfounded scientific theories.[27] The second group of commentators (including primarily the Karaites) interpret verses as they see fit and "are ignorant of the form of Hebrew and therefore err even in grammar."[28] Groups three (Christian scholars) and four (Jewish scholars living in the Christian West) are similarly excluded; the former "invent secret explanations for everything in Scripture . . . [and] believe that the laws and statutes of the Torah are riddles," while the latter rely not on grammar but on Midrashic exegesis. These Midrashic interpretations are not "in keeping with the literal meaning of the text," and deter readers from analyzing the text from a grammatical point of view.[29] In short, Ibn Ezra tells us, the Midrashic interpretations of these four groups "are like clothes to the naked body,"[30] the naked body obviously referring to the literal meaning of a biblical verse.

Only his own method, Ibn Ezra tells us, avoids the errors of the other four, in that it is based on scientific philology and is focused on grammatical analysis: "I will, to the utmost of my ability, try to understand grammatically every word and then do my best to explain it. Every word whose meaning the reader desires to know will be found explained the first time the word is encountered."[31] If the other commentators provide ill-fitting

---

[24] Simon and Jospe 2007.
[25] For detailed analysis of the palace motif in medieval Jewish (and Christian) thought, see Talmage 1999.
[26] Commentary on Genesis, Introduction, Ibn Ezra 1988a, 1.
[27] Anybody who has worked through Ibn Ezra's commentaries can but smile at this description, inasmuch as his own comments tend to be prolix indeed, and often stray far from the original point at hand!
[28] Commentary on Genesis, Introduction, Ibn Ezra 1988a, 3.   [29] *Ibid.*, 10–11.   [30] *Ibid.*, 15.
[31] *Ibid.*, 17.

clothes inasmuch as they are all guilty of ignorance of science, philology, linguistics and grammar, only Ibn Ezra's clothes "fit."

Let me make this point another way. Unlike many other medieval exegetes, Ibn Ezra was primarily interested in *peshat* (plain, surface meaning) rather than *derash* (homiletical meaning), *remez* (allegorical meanings), or *sōd* (esoteric, secret meaning).[32] Ibn Ezra's focus upon *peshat* is reflected in this emphasis upon the linguistic, or grammatical meaning of the text. In this preoccupation with the plain meaning of Scripture, Ibn Ezra's analysis resembles modern scientific exegesis and in particular the "Higher Criticism," which is concerned with questions of the origin and authorship of the text.[33] Ibn Ezra was thus viewed (by his near peers as well as by modern scholars) as one of the forerunners of "natural" scriptural interpretation; his emphasis upon *peshat* led ultimately to the diminished importance of rabbinic *derash*. We shall return to this point below when we visit Spinoza's own abhorrence of *derash*.

Ibn Ezra's method of adjudicating conflicting meanings in Scripture is moderately straightforward. With verses having to do with laws, statutes, and regulations, he will defer to the reading of the rabbinic sages, even if an alternative reading is possible; he thus rejects the view of the Sadducees who claimed that rabbinic readings often contradicted "the literal meaning of Scripture and the rules of grammar."[34] But are there instances in which *peshat* is not appropriate? Ibn Ezra suggests in his introduction that we should engage in non-literal interpretation of Scripture only in those cases when *peshat* contradicts what we know through reason or experience; as Jospe puts it, it is reason that guides us to a correct, scientific understanding of Scripture.[35]

In addition to his adherence to a "plain" interpretation of Scripture, Ibn Ezra was the first Jewish author to interpret a significant number of biblical events in the context of astrological theory, as well as to explain certain commandments as defenses against the pernicious influence of the stars. And so what we have is a curious melding of philological analysis coupled with astrology. Reflecting the doctrine of climatology found in Ptolemy's *Tetrabiblos* II, Ibn Ezra argues that individuals having similar horoscopes, but living in different climates, or having different nationalities, will meet a different fate. In a number of texts Ibn Ezra claims that climate is a strong

---

[32] See the comments pertaining to *peshat* and *derash* at the start of this chapter.
[33] Jospe 2009, 182. Jospe further argues (*ibid.*, 185) that Ibn Ezra's "higher criticism is a logical development of his rationalist philosophy and reading of Scripture."
[34] Commentary on Genesis, Introduction, Ibn Ezra 1988a, 19.   [35] Jospe 2009, 189.

variable in the determination of astrological forecasts.[36] The only exception to strict astrological determination occurs in the case of divine intervention. As an example of intervention on the part of divine providence, Ibn Ezra gives the example of a river destined (by the stars) to overflow and destroy the inhabitants of a certain town. If the people in that town turn to God with all their hearts, God might "put it into their hearts" to leave the city on the very day that the river overflowed "as is its nature." The river flooded the city, but the people were saved. In this case, "Now God's decree was not altered and He saved them."[37] And so Ibn Ezra maintains that astrological determinism can work in conjunction with providence to avert an evil decree.

Further, in the midst of an extended commentary to Exodus 3:15 which has to do with the meaning of the proper names of God,[38] Ibn Ezra uses the verse as an opportunity to put forward a concise description not only of Hebrew philology and grammar, but of an elaborate cosmological scheme as well, suggesting that understanding the name of God requires knowledge of these systems. Adhering to the standard medieval distinction between three worlds (the lower world, middle world, and upper world), he focuses upon the celestial objects in the middle world: the five ministering stars (Mercury, Venus, Mars, Jupiter, and Saturn), the sun and moon, and the stars that make up the constellations, which are a level above the five planetary objects. Ibn Ezra then turns to the astrological component of this cosmology: he describes the order of the constellations and then maintains that "the inhabitants of the lower world are affected by them in accordance with their makeup."[39] Given that there are 120 possible conjunctions in each one of the 360 degrees, it is due to the irregular movements of the planets that "different things happen to man's body and certainly to his fortune in this lower world."[40] Further, a human being's soul receives power as well "from above in accordance to the arrangement of the ministers, that is, the arrangement of each 'minister' vis à vis the great hosts at the time of a person's birth."[41] In other words, an individual's body and soul are both influenced by the astrological powers accruing from the constellations and planets. Far from being just an exegetical detour, Ibn Ezra's point is that language, cosmology, and astrology all play an important role in adjudicating God's name "I am what I am": the "what" of God is explicated in terms of both philology and astrology.

---

[36] E.g. Ecclesiastes 1:12; Psalms 87:5–6; Exodus 25:40.

[37] Commentary on Exodus 33:21, Ibn Ezra 1988b, 701.

[38] Commentary on Exodus, 3:15; Ibn Ezra 1988b, 64. This verse follows the famous passage in Exodus 3:14 in which God reveals himself to Moses as "I am . . . that I am" (*eheyeh asher eheyeh*).

[39] *Ibid.*, 89.   [40] *Ibid.*   [41] *Ibid.*, 90.

Spinoza's biblical hermeneutics

Like Ibn Ezra, Spinoza too is focused upon the literary and grammatical dimensions of Scripture. As noted by Strauss, the foundation for understanding Scripture is, according to Spinoza, "knowledge of the character of the Hebrew language. The whole range of possible meanings in each single utterance occurring in Scripture is to be defined by knowledge of ordinary usage of the Hebrew language."[42] Understanding the underlying grammar of Scripture, coupled with the methods of natural science, will provide Spinoza with the tools to carry out his project. Noting that "neither dictionary nor grammar nor textbook on rhetoric" has remained from Hebrew speakers of old, Spinoza in Chapter 7 of TTP embarks upon a preliminary study of the unique vagaries of Hebrew as a language, listing many peculiar features and anomalies associated with the Hebrew of Scripture.[43] Not surprisingly given his preoccupation with the Hebrew language, Spinoza, like Ibn Ezra, prepared a Hebrew grammar. Entitled *Compendium Grammatices Linguae Hebraeae*, this work was prepared for acquaintances who, having read the TTP, wanted to learn Hebrew. Spinoza's purpose in this work, as related by Nadler, was to provide a secularized Hebrew for those who wanted to speak it rather than approach it as a "holy tongue."[44] The work remained incomplete, however, and was not nearly as detailed as were the grammars of Ibn Ezra.

To what extent is Spinoza's radical critique reflective of motifs we have seen in Ibn Ezra? In a letter to Oldenberg, written in 1665, Spinoza states two explicit aims of the TTP: to enable ordinary humans to engage in philosophical thinking by freeing them from the errors and prejudices of the theologians; and to free philosophy itself from the shackles and authority of religious authorities.[45] These purposes are clearly articulated in the TTP as well. Spinoza claims that as long as exegetes stick to his method, they will be

---

[42] Strauss 1997, 259.   [43] TTP 7, Spinoza 2001, 94.

[44] For details on Spinoza's grammar, see Nadler 1999, 324–326. As Nadler notes, Spinoza's work is fairly idiosyncratic, but he does in fact try to secularize Hebrew. In this respect, Spinoza adumbrated Eliezer ben Yehudah's attempts in the nineteenth century to both secularize and modernize a "holy" tongue.

[45] Spinoza summarizes his intentions as follows: "I am now writing a Treatise on my views regarding Scripture. The reasons that move me to do so are these: 1. The prejudices of theologians. For I know that these are the main obstacles which prevent men from giving their minds to philosophy. So I apply myself to exposing such prejudices and removing them from the minds of sensible people. 2. The opinion of me held by the common people, who constantly accuse me of atheism. I am driven to avert this accusation, too, as far as I can. 3. The freedom to philosophise and to say what we think. This I want to vindicate completely, for here it is in every way suppressed by the excessive authority and egotism of preachers." See Ep 31, Spinoza 1995, 185–186.

able to uncover the teachings of the Bible.[46] Spinoza takes on what he calls "theological prejudices" in order to provide a more proper understanding of theology, offering three distinct stages. The first stage consists in discussing the authorship of the various books of the Bible. Spinoza will argue that the Pentateuch is a compilation, written by several individuals, and assembled during the era of the Maccabees. His underlying argument is that each book must be considered on its own merits.[47] The second stage is to dismiss the incorruptibility of the Bible, while the third stage concerns the marginal notes in the Masoretic text. Spinoza will argue that the Masoretic marginalia do not indicate divine mysteries concealed in the main body of the text, as thought by certain commentators.[48]

In order to achieve his aims, Spinoza sees as his task the development of a biblical hermeneutic that can allow for a new understanding of Scripture that does not enslave philosophy or would-be philosophers. In the preface to the TTP, Spinoza rails against those who "do not even glimpse the divine nature of Scripture, and the more enthusiastic their admiration of these mysteries, the more clearly they reveal that their attitude to Scripture is one of abject servility rather than belief."[49] Because of their anti-intellectual attitude toward Scripture, nothing is left of the old religion but "the outward form."[50] Therefore Spinoza resolves to "examine Scripture afresh, conscientiously and freely, and to admit nothing as its teaching which I did not most clearly derive from it."[51]

In order to distill the teachings of Scripture, Spinoza thus needed to develop a proper methodology, one that included knowledge of biblical grammar as well as full understanding of the author of Scripture. In a manner reminiscent of Ibn Ezra, Spinoza presents a methodology, rooted in a philological study of the biblical text, based on a distinction between the *meaning* of a text as opposed to its *truth*. Spinoza is clear as to the importance of seeking the *meaning* of a text, which is derived "simply from linguistic usage" in contradistinction to its *truth*, which is embedded in history, authorial intention, etc.[52] Spinoza uses as an example Moses' description of God as "God is fire," and emphasizes the importance of uncovering the literal meaning of the term "fire" in this context. If, Spinoza argues, the term is "not found from linguistic usage to have any other meaning," then it should not be reinterpreted or analogized to suit the understanding of the reader.[53] As with Ibn Ezra, Spinoza rejects a homiletical reading of Scripture (*derash*) in favor of *peshat*; only a straightforward

---

[46] James 2012, 161.   [47] TTP 10.   [48] TTP 11.   [49] TTP, preface, Spinoza 2001, 5.   [50] *Ibid.*
[51] *Ibid.*   [52] TTP 7, Spinoza 2001, 89.   [53] *Ibid.*

peshat will yield the meaning of a scriptural verse or passage. The meaning of a text thus consists of a correct account of the thought processes, assumptions, and intended meanings of its author; it requires careful reconstruction of the historical and linguistic circumstances in which the text was written. But textual meaning may have little to do with truth of fact.

For Spinoza, truth of fact represents an absolute reality grounded on the laws of philosophy and science. Just as we use the laws of nature to study and understand nature itself, so too we use the internal history of Scripture to understand the meaning of scriptural passages. Based on this methodology, Spinoza proceeds to show that many statements in Scripture are factually false. By removing theology from the domain of truth-functionality, Spinoza paves the way for the independence of philosophical (and scientific) truth on the one hand, and religious doctrine on the other. Note that this move allows for denying "truth" in the religious sphere altogether. The only truths to be found in Scripture are moral verities, which should be distinguished from objective, scientific truths.[54] Interestingly, this separation of meaning from truth has led modern literary theorists to claim Spinoza as a forerunner of modern hermeneutics and contemporary literary theory. Norris does a credible job of debunking this overly glib embrace of Spinoza, pointing out that Spinoza never abandoned a theory of adequate truth; Spinoza's point in the TTP is simply that Scripture does not reflect this truth, not that there *is* no objective truth.[55] Truth is associated with reason, with philosophical reflection, and does not pertain to what we find in Scripture, which as noted above, is associated with the imaginative sphere.[56]

How then does Spinoza approach the process of reading Scripture? Just as Ibn Ezra used the methods of contemporary science to inform his reading of Scripture, so too is Spinoza's method rooted in the New Science. If, as noted above, the Bible carries no canonical status different from other works, then God has provided us with two sources for knowledge: the book of the Law, and the book of nature. In order to ascertain the meaning of Scripture, the biblical scholar must approach the text much like a scientist approaches nature; just as the natural scientist collects and orders data, so too must the

---

[54] See TTP 13, Spinoza 2001, 153–157.　　[55] See Norris 1991.

[56] In the *Ethics*, Spinoza returns to the notion of truth in more detail, and elaborates three distinct epistemic levels of truth, which he articulates in terms of imagination, reason, and intuitive science. According to Spinoza, knowledge of the first kind (imagination) is the cause of falsity, whereas knowledge of the second and third orders is necessarily true. Spinoza goes on to argue in the demonstration to *Ethics* IIp41 that the first kind of knowledge concerns all those ideas that are inadequate and confused.

Bible scholar collect and order the data contained in Scripture and interpret it in light of historical, social, cultural, and linguistic contexts taken from Scripture. Spinoza claims that Scripture must be read literally and not allegorized, claiming that there must be a clear understanding of the nature and properties of the language in which the text was written and in which the authors spoke.

It is important to note Spinoza's insistence that scientific method should be used exclusively for understanding both books. In the TTP, Spinoza articulates his method as follows:

> Now to put it briefly, I hold that the method of interpreting Scripture is no different from the method of interpreting Nature, and is in fact in complete accord with it. For the method of interpreting Nature consists essentially in composing a detailed study of Nature from which, as being the source of our assured data, we can deduce the definitions of the things of Nature. Now in exactly the same way the task of Scriptural interpretation required us to make a straightforward history of Scripture and from this, as the source of our fixed data and principles, to deduce by logical inference the meaning of the authors of Scripture.[57]

In other words, Spinoza reiterates that both nature and Scripture should be amenable to a similar methodology: just as we apply the laws of nature to deduce the interpretation and understanding of nature, so too we must deduce the meaning of Scripture from its laws and history. By "nature" Spinoza means the causal nexus of the universe (a view that is amplified in the *Ethics*), and which leaves no room for supernatural causation. How then does Spinoza account for miracles, which presumably violate the causal nexus? We turn now to this final issue.

Applying science to scripture

On miracles in Scripture

Nowhere is the application of scientific method more effective than in the treatment of miracles. In their respective examination of the relation between science and Scripture, both Ibn Ezra and Spinoza use Joshua 10:12–14 as proof text to support their scriptural hermeneutics. One of the most pressing problems centered around how to interpret the miracle expressed in Joshua 10:12–14. By denying the alleged miracle of the sun standing still in the sky, one ran the risk of denying God's intervention in

---

[57] TTP 7, Spinoza 2001, 87.

the natural world, leaving no room for divine intervention and presence in
the natural order. But acknowledging the event in the face of reason and
prior experience threatened to undermine the natural order.[58] The text itself
reads as follows. Joshua and his men are worried that there will not be
sufficient time to defeat the five Amorite kings, and so Joshua prays to God
to extend the day:

> Joshua addressed the Lord; he said in the presence of the Israelites: "Stand still,
> O sun, at Gibeon, O moon, in the Valley of Ajalon!" and the sun stood still
> and the moon halted, while a nation wreaked judgment on its foes . . . thus the
> sun halted in mid-heaven, and did not press on to set, for a whole day.[59]

Both Ibn Ezra and Spinoza use this miracle as an opportunity to reinforce a
scientifically based understanding of Scripture. Unfortunately Ibn Ezra's
commentary on Joshua has been lost, but it is clear from the following
exegesis of Deuteronomy 32:4 that according to Ibn Ezra, the laws of nature
are fixed and stable; the sun's standing still for Joshua does not and cannot
contradict this principle. Ibn Ezra explained Deuteronomy 32:4 "The
Rock – His deeds are perfect, yea, all His ways are justice/law" in the
context of the Joshua miracle:

> "For All His ways are Justice" His ways do not change. On the contrary, they
> follow one law. This is the praise of God . . . The standing still of the sun is
> no argument to the contrary because, as I explained in its place, its secret is
> clear, from the clause "And thou, Moon in the valley of Aijalon (Ibid.)."[60]

What are we to make of this "secret"? Ibn Ezra returns to the example in his
astrological work *Sefer ha-'Ibbūr*. In that work he notes first, that reason
is the ultimate judge of the reality of a phenomenon, and not the senses;
second, that a prophet will never produce a sign or omen contrary to sense
perception or to reason; and finally, that a miracle cannot involve an inner
contradiction. Do these three imply that the sun in fact stood still at
Gibeon? Ibn Ezra tells us that:

> Perhaps you might think of the signs and wonders performed by the
> prophets, that they are contrary to the senses and contrary to reason.
> Heaven forfend that they be so, rather, the signs are the opposite of nature.
> Even the standstill of the sun – it is not incompatible with reason that the sun
> should stand still, for as we know, the fact that the Lord moves [the sun] is a
> secret, so He might also make it stand still as a secret.[61]

---

[58] See Vermij 2002, 241–242.   [59] Joshua 10:12–13.
[60] Commentary on Exodus 32:4, Ibn Ezra 1988b, 236.
[61] Ibn Ezra 1874, 11a; the English translation can be found in Schwartz 2005, 80.

Now one might interpret this passage in two ways: either that the sun actually did stand still, the reality of the miracle being without doubt; or second, that the sun might not have stood still although it appeared to do so, this being a "secret" known only to a few. As Schwartz notes, many rationalist super-commentators on Ibn Ezra "devised entirely natural explanations as to why the sun had stood still," hence rejecting altogether any supernatural or miraculous explanation of the event.[62] But other commentators say that Ibn Ezra denied that the sun stood still.[63] Gersonides for example took Ibn Ezra to be saying the latter, namely that the sun never stood still.[64]

Spinoza is more radical than Ibn Ezra in his use of the Joshua account, using it to bring home his rejection of supernatural miracles altogether. Within his new mechanistic philosophy, Spinoza argues first that every event falls within a comprehensive system of causal laws (there can be no random events), and second that these causal laws possess the same kind of necessity as the laws of mathematics and logic. He then shows how biblical miracles can be explained in naturalistic terms. In the TTP, Spinoza uses Joshua 10:12–13 as an example of how to rule out supernatural miracles.[65]

All the commentators, says Spinoza, try to demonstrate that the prophets knew everything attainable by human intellect. In fact, however, there are many things that the prophets simply do not know. Take Joshua, for example. Spinoza's conclusion is that we cannot expect scientific knowledge of the prophets. According to Spinoza, Joshua was a simple prophet who, confronted with an unusual natural phenomenon, namely "excessive cold-ness of the atmosphere," attributed to this phenomenon a supernatural explanation. Joshua had no knowledge of astronomy, nor should we attrib-ute to him such knowledge; he believed, as did the others in his time, that "the sun goes round the earth and the earth does not move, and that the sun stood still for a time."[66] Spinoza has no patience for those who, having learned to philosophize and recognize that the earth moves rather than the sun and that the sun does not move around the earth, make every effort to bend science to Scripture:

> Do we have to believe that the soldier Joshua was a skilled astronomer, that a miracle could not be revealed to him, or that the sun's light could not remain above the horizon for longer than usual without Joshua's understanding the cause? Both alternatives seem to me ridiculous.[67]

---

[62] For details on these naturalistic interpretations, see Schwartz 2005, 103.   [63] See *ibid.*, 102–105.

[64] In his *Wars of the Lord*, Gersonides argued that the miracle in question was that the Israelites defeated their enemies while the sun seemed to maintain the same altitude; he adds that miracles do not involve the abrogation of natural law. See Levi ben Gershom 1999, 491.

[65] See TTP, preface, Spinoza 2001, 53.   [66] TTP 2, Spinoza 2001, 26.   [67] *Ibid.*

Scientific knowledge, Spinoza reminds us, should not be expected of prophets. In fact, on Spinoza's reading, Joshua was totally ignorant of the scientific explanation for this event; Spinoza's own explanation, reflecting his knowledge of optics, drew upon yet another natural phenomenon, namely refraction as a result of large hailstones. As we shall see below, either the biblical text is compatible with our rational conceptions or it is not; and if it is not, it must be rejected. Once again, *derash* has been rejected in favor of *peshat*, an exegetical move that Ibn Ezra would have applauded.

In Chapter 6, Spinoza returns to the topic of Joshua in the context of his naturalization of miracles. Why does Spinoza return a second time to the miracle of Joshua? Strauss points out that "it is not a matter of chance that the only example that Spinoza treats in the context of his critique of miracles should be one that demonstrates a clash between natural science and Scripture."[68] In this passage, Spinoza gives a socially contextual explanation of why Joshua might have offered the explanation we find in Joshua 10, arguing that the Hebrews adapted their description of the event in question in order to persuade the gentiles "who worshipped visible Gods" that the sun answers to a higher order than just natural law, namely that the movement of the sun was "changeable and under the command of an invisible God."[69] For this reason, the Hebrews "conceived and related this event quite differently from the way it could really have come about."[70]

Although Ibn Ezra and Gersonides had laid the groundwork for the naturalization of miracles, Spinoza's reading of the biblical miracles is even more radical in his categorical denial of supernatural occurrences, including both magic and miracles. Spinoza is clear that "no event can occur to contravene Nature, which preserves an eternal fixed and immutable order."[71] More specifically, nothing happens in nature "to contravene [Nature's] universal laws."[72] Not even God can contravene these laws, since God/Nature observes those laws. Thus any apparent miracle, according to Spinoza, is simply an event the causes of which are unknown to our intellect. It is in this context that Spinoza's elaboration of the Joshua example must be understood.

The most secret of secrets: Ibn Ezra and Spinoza on the authorship of Scripture

We turn finally to the most radical topic of all, namely the authorship of Scripture. Ibn Ezra's enigmatic suggestions regarding the authorship of

---

[68] Strauss 1997, 137.   [69] TTP 6, Spinoza 2001, 81.   [70] *Ibid.*, 81.   [71] *Ibid.*, 73.   [72] *Ibid.*, 73.

Scripture, derived from application of his philological-exegetical method-ology, were the result of what he took to be anachronistic passages imper-vious to *peshat*. For example in his remarks on Genesis 12.6, "And the Canaanite was then in the land," Ibn Ezra suggests that "it is possible that the Canaanites seized the land of Canaan from some other tribe at that time. Should this interpretation be incorrect, then there is a secret meaning to the text. Let the one who understands it remain silent."[73] This secret alludes to the fact that when this verse was written, the Canaanites had already been expelled by the Israelites; thus the verse must have been written at least a generation after Moses. In Genesis 22:14, commenting upon the phrase "In the mount where the Lord is seen," Ibn Ezra refers the reader to Deuteronomy 1:2, suggesting obliquely that certain phrases in the Pentateuch, among them this one, were added later.[74] More specifically, Ibn Ezra speculates on what these words might mean (since we know that Moses never actually crossed the Jordan River) and suggests that "If you understand the secret of the twelve . . . then you will recognize the truth."[75] Ibn Ezra mentions Deuteronomy 31:22, Genesis 12:6, Genesis 22:14, and Deuteronomy 3:11 as further support for his "secret," namely that just as the last twelve verses of Deuteronomy, which describe the death of Moses, could not have been written by Moses, so too these other verses contain information that Moses could not have known or written.[76]

Ibn Ezra thus, at the very least, opened the door to the possibility that Moses was not the author of the entire Pentateuch and his comments regarding Moses' authorship were revisited by subsequent generations of Jewish and Christian exegetes. The trajectory from Ibn Ezra through the late medieval period up to the mid-seventeenth century has been traced admirably by others. Suffice it to mention Malcolm's detailed history of biblical interpretation prior to and including both Hobbes and Spinoza. Malcolm traces Ibn Ezra's works down to the fifteenth-century Hebraist Alfonso Tostado Ribera de Madrigal (Tostatus 1400–1455), whose works were extremely influential in the sixteenth and seventeenth centuries.[77] Subsequent scholars extrapolated from Ibn Ezra and Tostatus, arguing that it was the scribe Ezra who had compiled the books of Joshua, Judges,

---

[73] Commentary on Genesis, 12:6, Ibn Ezra 1988a, 151.

[74] Commentary on Genesis, 22:14, Ibn Ezra 1988a, 226.

[75] Commenatry on Deuteronomy, 1:1, Ibn Ezra 1988c, 3. For detailed commentary upon Ibn Ezra's "Secret of the Twelve," see W. Harvey 2010a.

[76] The entire question of Ibn Ezra's own beliefs regarding the authorship of the Torah is itself problematic, and scholars have interpreted him differently, in part reflecting their own views. See Strickman's summary of these interpretations in Ibn Ezra 1988a, "Foreword."

[77] For details of this trajectory, see James 2012; Malcolm 2002, 404–407; Nadler 2011.

and Kings.[78] This line of thought was further developed by Isaac la Peyrère and Thomas Hobbes, culminating finally with Spinoza.[79] What these authors were doing was:

> "to take some theories that were widely available and set them off in a new direction; as so often seems to be the case in the history of ideas, the advance of radical heterodoxy came about not by means of a frontal assault on the orthodox tradition, but through a more complicated and opportunistic judo-like manoeuvre."[80]

In particular, Malcolm notes that in the case of Spinoza, all his arguments pertaining to biblical authorship, with but one minor exception, could be found in the standard commentaries.

Given, then, the historical trajectory from the twelfth to the seventeenth centuries, what do we make of Spinoza's appropriation of Ibn Ezra's hints and "secrets"? Spinoza follows Ibn Ezra's suggestion that Moses did not write all of the Torah, and emphasizes the significance of this claim for how one is to approach and read Scripture. Clearly Ibn Ezra enabled Spinoza to think through the details of exegesis. Harvey notes that in the six instances in which Spinoza mentioned Ibn Ezra explicitly, his "interpretation of Ibn Ezra's esoteric teaching is thus mostly accurate."[81] Spinoza, however, goes even farther than Ibn Ezra, and suggests that the surviving texts of the Pentateuch were written not by Moses, but rather by the scribe Ezra:[82]

> Since then, there is no evidence that Moses wrote any other books but these, and he gave no instructions for any other book but this book of the Law together with the Canticle to be preserved religiously for posterity, and finally, since there are many passages in the Pentateuch that could not have been written by Moses, it follows that there are no grounds for holding Moses to be the author of the Pentateuch, and that such an opinion is quite contrary to reason.[83]

---

[78] Malcolm 2002, 407–409.

[79] For discussion of La Peyrère, see in particular Malcolm 2002; Popkin 1996; 1987. Hobbes had argued in *Leviathan* that Scripture is not uniformly the word of God, but rather that God conveyed His word to the prophets through revelation. He maintains that Moses wrote very little, if any, of the Pentateuch. See Nadler 2011, 116 for discussion of Hobbes.

[80] Malcolm 2002, 411. See also, at 431: "Modern biblical criticism grew out of this tradition; it was not 'founded' by Hobbes or Spinoza, even though it may have been stimulated in some ways by their writings."

[81] W. Harvey 2010a, 47.

[82] It should be noted that according to Jewish tradition, Ezra the scribe recovered the content of Moses' original books (under divine guidance) but produced the surviving Masoretic text and fixed the canon with the help of a Grand Synagogue.

[83] TTP 8, Spinoza 2001, 110.

But if in fact we accept the claim that Ibn Ezra had already questioned Moses' authorship of parts of the Torah, what makes Spinoza's point so contentious? James makes the point that unlike his predecessors, Spinoza shifts the burden of proof, arguing that "unless the surviving text explicitly indicates that Moses *did* write a particular book, we cannot legitimately conclude that he was its author."[84] But even more contentious is the conclusion that for Spinoza, "If the Bible is a historical and thus natural document, then it should be treated like any other work of nature."[85] In other words, the Scriptures are no different from any other text: there is no domain of truth unique to Scripture that is not shared by other intellectual disciplines. By removing the unique, unassailable quality of biblical statements, Spinoza paves the way for the independence of philosophical (and scientific) truth on the one hand, and religious belief on the other.

Conclusion

Throughout the history of Jewish thought, Jewish philosophers addressed theoretical issues against the backdrop of their intellectual neighbors: the works of Ibn Ezra and Maimonides incorporated the theories of their Islamic peers; Crescas and Albo reflected influences of Christian scholasticism; and sixteenth-century thinkers evinced the effects of the rise of the New Science. This cultural interaction affected the interpretation of Scripture as well. In this chapter I have demonstrated the ways in which scientific advance and learning influenced both Ibn Ezra and Spinoza. Both thinkers were consummate scientists, and adapted the rigorous methods of science to their reading of Scripture. In the case of Ibn Ezra we see an emphasis upon philological analysis, whereas in the case of Spinoza we see an emphasis upon rigorous internal reading based as well upon grammar and language. Ibn Ezra's method suggested that Moses was not the author of the entire Pentateuch, whereas Spinoza's adherence to the importance of using scientific method in approaching Scripture forced him to reject divine authorship of the Torah altogether. But Spinoza's more radical move was to deny that Scripture had any philosophical or scientific veracity. Unlike Ibn Ezra, who tried to read the Scriptures in light of modern philosophical and astrological scientific teachings, Spinoza denied the tenability of this entire enterprise.

According to Spinoza, Scripture cannot be accommodated to the new sciences. Scripture cannot be regarded as a source of knowledge; and

---

[84] James 2012, 167. [85] See Nadler 1999, 278.

because it is neither a philosophical nor a scientific work, Scripture cannot provide scientific or mathematical truths; Scripture provides only moral guidance and piety. By pushing the views of his predecessor to their logical extreme, Spinoza thus exposes the implications of Ibn Ezra's carefully constructed hermeneutic methodology. Carlos Fraenkel has argued that the TTP marks the end of classical Jewish philosophy, in that it destroys the traditional of religion as a whole insofar as it is grounded on the truth of revelation.[86] Drawing upon Fraenkel's assessment, my claim is that Ibn Ezra provided the fertile seeds for this destruction.

---

[86] Fraenkel 2007.

CHAPTER 4

Spinoza's rejection of Maimonideanism

Steven Frankel

According to the prevailing view among contemporary scholars, Maimonides and Spinoza share so much in common that in order to understand Spinoza, one must first recognize his debt to Maimonides. Spinoza's profound kinship with Maimonides is revealed by his adoption of the terms of medieval theology (form, essence, mode, attribute, substance, etc.), and also its goals (*amor Dei intellectualis*).[1] Spinoza, according to this view, simply carried the arguments of Maimonides to their logical conclusions.[2] At first glance, this is surprising since Maimonides presents himself as a defender of revelation, while Spinoza launches a devastating critique of Scripture and its defenders, particularly Maimonides. But according to contemporary scholars, such differences can be explained as the result of political accommodations to their respective audiences.[3] Thus, Zev Harvey argues that Spinoza "was a Maimonidean in the sense that fundamental elements of Maimonides' philosophy recur as fundamental elements of his philosophy."[4] Their kinship is obscured because Maimonides addresses a Jewish audience while Spinoza addresses a

I wish to thanks Timothy Sean Quinn and Marc Cohen for their helpful comments and criticisms.

[1] For more on Spinoza's debt to the Jewish tradition, see Nadler 1999, 114ff.

[2] The attempt to assimilate the views of Maimonides with those of Spinoza generally takes the form of the claim that "Spinoza's position is a logical outcome of Maimonides or that Maimonides at least leaves the door open for Spinoza" (Batniksky 2003–2004, 517). Steven Nadler suggests that Spinoza's denial of personal immortality is "simply the logical culmination" of Maimonides' view of the soul (Nadler 2001, 95, 130).

[3] "Made of sterner stuff and living a few centuries later, Spinoza would have perhaps demanded the overthrow of the old order with its effete institutions so as to build upon its ruins a new society . . . But being what he was and living at a time when belief in the potency of reformation had not yet been shaken by doubt, he chose to follow in the footsteps of rationalizers throughout history. The story of this rationalization is the story of his TTP" (see Wolfson 1934, 333). Wolfson asserts that Spinoza's "reputed God-intoxication was really nothing but a hang-over of an earlier religious jag" (348). Richard McKeon treats Spinoza as the last of the scholastics (McKeon 1928).

[4] See W. Harvey 1981, 172. Similarly, Shlomo Pines asserts that Spinoza "does Maimonides the honour, rarely or never vouchsafed to him in modern times, to disprove him . . . [H]e is able to do this because he is prepared to adopt some of the presuppositions of Maimonides. He also pays [Maimonides] the, in a sense, greater compliment of adapting some of his ideas" (Pines 1968, 3).

Christian one. David Biale offers an interesting variation on this theme. He argues that Spinoza generally follows Maimonides though he is not concerned with the juridical deficiencies of the rabbinic tradition; nonetheless, Spinoza – whom Biale refers to as "Maimonides' stepson" – built his rational faith on Maimonidean foundations.[5] Spinoza thought he was breaking radically from the Jewish tradition. In hindsight, we can see what Spinoza could not, namely that his "arguments are squarely in the Maimonidean tradition."[6]

But there is also reason to be skeptical of such claims. For one thing, Spinoza may have had his own reasons for overstating his kinship with Maimonides. He may have wished, for example, to adopt the appearance of a pious heir to the medieval tradition to distract readers from the overall effect of his analysis, which is to undermine revelation. As Martin Yaffe suggests, Spinoza puts "new wine in old bottles that still bear their original labels along with traces of the original contents."[7] Hobbes too was struck by the boldness of Spinoza's critique of religion rather than his debt to medieval philosophy or Maimonides.[8] According to Leo Strauss, Spinoza's appropriation of Maimonides to advance his own very different theological-political program was "amazingly unscrupulous" and ruthlessly Machiavellian.[9] Along these same lines, Joshua Parens argues, as the title of his book *Maimonides and Spinoza: Their Conflicting Views of Human Nature* suggests, that the "main value to be derived from studying Maimonides is to gain distance from our own world and viewpoint, which has been so deeply shaped by the thought of Spinoza."[10]

The goal of this chapter is to show that the causes of this scholarly disagreement and the difficulty in assessing the relation between Spinoza and Maimonides reflect Spinoza's own contradictory treatment of Maimonides. In Chapter 5 of the TTP he criticizes Maimonides for giving too much authority to the Bible at the expense of reason; in Chapter 7, he criticizes Maimonides for giving too much authority to reason. The contradiction is exacerbated by the fact that Spinoza seems guilty of espousing the very position that he criticizes: he appears to give too much authority to the Bible when he offers a set of theological dogmas and insists that all decent men (*honestos*) submit to them.[11] On the other hand, he insists in his

---

[5] Biale 2011, 29.   [6] *Ibid.*, 25.   [7] Spinoza 2004, 253.
[8] For a discussion of Aubrey's famous account of Hobbes and his reaction to the TTP, see Curley 1992.
[9] See Strauss 1968, 244: "Spinoza's critique is directed against the whole body of authoritative teachings and rules known in Spinoza's time as Judaism" (253).
[10] See Parens 2012, 1.   [11] TTP 14, Spinoza 1925, III.177; 2004, 164.

critique of miracles (in Chapter 6) that the Bible's teaching reflects a profound ignorance of nature and can be safely put aside. As we shall see, Spinoza adopts a novel view of the relation between reason and revelation that explains this contradiction and exposes his estrangement from Maimonides.

Spinoza's critique(s) of Maimonides

Spinoza examines Maimonides' position at length, quoting him twice in the TTP in Chapters 5 and 7. The first quote comes from Maimonides' popular text, the *Mishneh Torah* (*Hilkhot Melachim*), to the effect that the decision to submit to the Noahide laws, and more generally to revelation, is valid only on the grounds that they are commanded by God.[12] A person who accepts them because they are consistent with reason, according to Maimonides,[13] is neither pious nor has a share in the world to come. The laws of Noah resemble natural law inasmuch as they apply to all mankind ("the children of Noah"). But unlike natural law, their force comes from a covenant with God reported in Genesis 9, and not from reason's recognition of their truth. Even though reason and revelation point to the same universal law, they arrive at this law in different ways and this difference is decisive: faith and salvation involve obedience to the divine law; reason does not obey any law but consents only to what it understands. (Spinoza presents a similar argument on behalf of the separation of reason and revelation in Chapter 15 of the TTP.) As we shall see, when we turn to the context of this critique, the substance of the disagreement virtually disappears altogether.[14]

Spinoza prefaces his remarks on Maimonides with a sketch of his political teaching: men need to live in communities for the sake of security and comfort, and were they fully rational, they would recognize this necessity and act in accordance with it. Unfortunately, "human nature is constituted quite otherwise. All men do seek their own advantage, but hardly on the basis of the dictates of sound reason."[15] The purpose of government, therefore, is to check men's passions and compel them to behave peacefully.

---

[12] It is important to keep in mind that Spinoza's primary audience is not the Jewish community, but rather the Protestant community as he encountered it in Holland. Maimonides can be read as a less provocative stand-in for scriptural interpreters such as Ludwig Meyer; see Preus 2001, 37.

[13] According to Joseph Caro, the passage expresses not only Maimonides' personal opinion but also that of the Jewish tradition; see Strauss 1968, 248–249.

[14] Spinoza's use of this passage infuriated the neo-Kantian Hermann Cohen, who wished to establish the universalism of Jewish ethics. For a fuller discussion of Cohen's position see *ibid*.

[15] TTP 5, Spinoza 1925, III.73; 2004, 59.

Spinoza also explains that the role of government is not to educate men and make them more reasonable. Although the exertion of power by government is necessary and even beneficial, men resent such compulsion.[16] This is the case "least of all," Spinoza writes, when they are "serving their equals and being regulated by them."[17] Men do not resent all authority, for example, if they are persuaded of the superiority of the sovereign. But for irrational men, only miracle workers or prophets are capable of persuading the multitude of their superiority.[18] Short of such "demonstrations," resentment will throw a state into perpetual turmoil, with its subjects rooting for its downfall.

Spinoza introduces his own political theology to dramatize the problem and suggest a solution. The Israelites did not resent the authority of Moses because it was rooted in compelling claims about the divine and promises of reward, which kept the Israelites in awe of Moses' political power. Moses astutely perceived the political backwardness of this nation – "a people incapable of self-rule" – and prescribed a fitting system of law which eliminated all freedom of thought and choice. He crafted a law so that every action and decision "admonished them to obedience always" and, thanks to a ceremonial law, even their "own decree" would not be free.[19]

In contrast to the Mosaic regime, the Gospels teach that Christ frees all nations from the Mosaic law in favor of another divine law, the hallmark of which is the free or voluntary submission to its authority:

> Paul concludes that, since God is the God of all nations, that is, is equally propitious to all, and since all men equally live under the law and under sin, therefore God sent his Christ to all nations, to free all men equally from the slavery of the law, so that they might no longer act by the command of the law, but by the steadfast decree of the spirit. Accordingly Paul teaches precisely what we mean.[20]

The essence of a living faith is freedom, that is, the decision to obey the divine law enumerated in Scripture according to one's "free will."[21] While Judaism is

---

[16] See Gilden 1973, 377–387.   [17] TTP 5, Spinoza 1925, III.74; 2004, 59.

[18] "Men in general judge more by their eyes than by their hands, because seeing is given to everyone, touching to few. Everyone sees how you appear, few touch what you are; and these few dare not to oppose the opinion of the many, who have the majesty of the state to defend them" (in Machiavelli 1998, 71). Spinoza's emphasis on freedom throughout the TTP refers to political freedom, that is, the ability to pursue one's passions and desires and not action in accord with reason.

[19] TTP 5, Spinoza 1925, III.76; 2004, 61. For a powerful response (and defense of Judaism), see Levinas 1990, 111–118. Levinas claims that Spinoza's account of Judaism as an "inevitable stage on the road to truth" encouraged Western Jewish intellectuals to view Judaism merely as a primitive stage in the human search for truth. See also Cohen 1924, 290–372.

[20] TTP 3, Spinoza 1925, III.54; 2004, 39. For more details on this theology of freedom, see Frankel 2002, 273–296.

[21] TTP 5, Spinoza 1925, III.75, 76; 2004, 60, 61.

characterized by constant obedience, a solution which is barely preferable to slavery (and only because it commands obedience to a *divine* master), Christianity is marked by its freedom from the law.[22] Christians need not obey any ceremonial law; its teachings are universal and manifest to the "natural light of reason" rather than the revelation of a particular political or ceremonial law.[23] In short, Christianity is characterized by freedom and self-determination which is expressed most clearly in the rational recognition of the truth.

The problem with rational freedom is that it is not available to the people that it purports to save. Universal faith involves reasoning based on empirical grounds, that is, "from what sense perception tells [us] occurs in nature," or "on the basis of self-evident intellectual axioms" and the careful deductions from those axioms. Because most people do not have the patience, care, or intelligence to deduce a long series of propositions from self-evident axioms, this natural or rational basis of faith is largely irrelevant to the political problem (that to live in communities, men need compulsion yet resent and resist it). As Spinoza argues in the *Political Treatise*,

> [T]he road which reason teaches us to follow is very steep, so that those who believe that ordinary people or those who are busily engaged in public business can be persuaded to live solely at reason's behest are dreaming of the golden age of the Poets or a myth.[24]

Spinoza suggests an alternative solution to the political problem. Scripture presents a teaching regarding "philosophic matters" presented in an easy-to-grasp historical narrative that requires no special training or intellectual ability to understand.[25] He concludes that although such

---

[22] "God is the God of all nations, i.e. since He is equally propitious to all, and since all were equally under the law and sin, [therefore] God sent to all nations His Christ, who would free all equally of bondage to the law" (TTP 3, Spinoza 1925, III.54; 2004, 39). In contrast to Moses, the greatest of the Hebrew prophets, Jesus was free of any defective knowledge of God: "If Moses spoke with God face to face, as a man speaks with his friend (*i.e.*, by means of their two bodies), Christ communicated with God mind to mind" (TTP 1, Spinoza 1925, III.21; 2004, 7).

[23] TTP 5, Spinoza 1925, III.76; 2004, 61.

[24] See TP 1, Spinoza 1925, III.275; 2000, 35–36, also see *Ethics* Vp42s on the difficulty of following reason, and *Ethics* Vp1–p10s on the ability of reason to moderate the passions. According to *Ethics* IVp4dem, a human being cannot be fully self-caused and therefore he "is necessarily always subject to passions."

[25] "[T]he greatest authority to interpret Scripture . . . must not be so difficult that it can be directed by the most acute Philosophers, but must be accommodated to the natural and common mental cast and capacity of men, as we have shown ours to be" (TTP 7, Spinoza 1925, III.117; 2004, 101). Mignini argues that reason can never have very much control over the passions and therefore religion is always necessary, even for rational men: "[T]he imagination is the instrument and impassable limit of fortune; if it is founded upon the relation between the human body and other bodies, as the representative structure of *affectiones*, one can understand why Spinoza affirmed that reason, considered as true knowledge, has no power of the imagination and can do nothing against the course of fortune and the emotions which it produces" (Mignini 1984,130).

narratives cannot provide knowledge of the truth, they can instill true opinions, for example, they can "still teach and enlighten men as much is sufficient for impressing obedience and devotion in their spirits."[26] Just before his critique of Maimonides, and in keeping with his account of Christianity as a faith characterized by freedom and rationality, Spinoza ostensibly adopts the Maimonidean view on the relation of reason and revelation. According to this view, Scripture presents the truths of reason in an imaginative language accessible to non-philosophers so that their lives are consistent with the teachings of reason. Of course, this does not fully cure them of superstition; nonetheless, they can still enjoy some measure of blessedness thanks to the compelling narratives of the Gospels.[27]

Thus, Spinoza's criticism of Maimonides in Chapter 5 is hardly intended as a rejection of the Maimonidean strategy of using the Bible to teach and edify the multitude. Rather, Spinoza's problem with Maimonides is limited to a particular defect of his theology, namely that it provides insufficient warrant for a universal faith. Even here, Maimonides is not fully to blame since he was forced to work within the confines of a highly particular theology to develop a religion with universal scope. A Spinoza quote from the *Mishneh Torah* confirms this view:

> *Everyone* who takes to heart the [Noahide laws] and diligently follows them, belongs to *the pious of nations* and is heir to the world to come . . . [if] he follows them because God has ordained them in his Law . . . But if he follows them through the guidance of reason, he is not a dweller among the pious nor among *the wise of the nations*.[28]

For Maimonides, the covenant with Noah represents Scripture's universal teaching, and such a covenant cannot be established on the basis of reason, but only on obedience to revelation. Spinoza's criticism here concerns merely a theological difference with Maimonides: if Scripture has a universal teaching, it should not be confined to a particular tradition but accessible

---

[26] TTP 5, Spinoza 1925, III.77–78; 2004, 63. Spinoza candidly admits that faith "cannot give us the knowledge and love of God . . . [but] is very useful with a view to civil life. For the more we have observed and the better we know the character and circumstances of men . . . the better will we be able to live more cautiously among them and accommodate our lives to their disposition as much as reason suggests" (TTP 4, Spinoza 1925, III.62; 2004, 46). David Lachterman suggests that the TTP retranslates a scientific concept of law back into the human domain so that the "pre-scientific understanding of law, legislation, legislators, obedience and disobedience can all be intelligently derived" (Lachterman 1991, 132).

[27] Steven Smith argues that Spinoza's positive presentation of Christianity "was dictated not by the methods of historical philology but by the need to gain genuine support for his universal religion of tolerance": Smith 1997, 105.

[28] TTP 5, Spinoza 1925, III.79–80; 2004, 64–65. I have added emphasis to the phrases which show the universal breadth of Maimonides' declaration.

to everyone.[29] Such access is possible only with a theology of freedom as is found in the Gospels, a teaching rooted in reason as the only sure path to blessedness. Despite this theological difference, Spinoza's critique of Maimonides reinforces their agreement on the irrationality of the multitude and their need for guidance. Spinoza also concurs with Maimonides that Scripture represents a practical solution to the problem of superstition, a solution made possible by the fact that reason teaches the very freedom celebrated in the Gospels. In Spinoza's interpretation, the Gospels liberate men from the Mosaic law and make possible a universal law.[30]

Given their overall agreement, it is surprising that when Spinoza returns to Maimonides in Chapter 7, he describes the Maimonidean approach to Scripture as "harmful, useless, and absurd."[31] His goal is nothing less than the annihilation (Spinoza uses the conjugated verb *explodimus*) of the Maimonidean method of interpretation. In contrast to his Maimonidean treatment of the Gospels in Chapter 5, Spinoza now urges restraint in explaining the meaning of Scripture and questions whether the text even has a single consistent teaching or the ultimate truth. He insists that the Bible be approached with the same caution as any ancient historical document, and in particular that we should not project foreign or imagined views onto Scripture.[32] One of the most egregious violations of this caution is

---

[29] Scripture is one of many, and perhaps not the most important, sources for theology. Hence, Spinoza asserts that "belief in historical narratives of any kind whatsoever has nothing to do with the Divine Law" (TTP 5, Spinoza 1925, III.79; 2004, 64).

[30] In order to appreciate the meaning of political freedom and how it leads to peace, we must distinguish it from both slavery and true freedom. True freedom – "he alone is free who lives with a full spirit solely on the basis of the guidance of reason" – is not politically relevant because such rationality is unavailable to most men. Slavery, of course, is the opposite of freedom but, according to Spinoza, it is not simply a matter of living in obedience to another's command (TTP 16, Spinoza 1925, III.194; 2004, 184). Rather the slave lives in obedience to commands that are not useful to himself. In contrast, the politically free individual or subject obeys commands – and in this sense is not free – but since those commands are for the benefit of the subject, he obeys them willingly. This willful obedience is the hallmark of political freedom. Obedience to law is freedom in a political sense because political authority depends in part on my perception of a harmony between my interests and the interests of the community. Freedom, particularly in a democracy, is the most stable and secure regime because it appears to accord most closely with my perception of my own conatus as freedom of will. As Spinoza remarks: a liberal democratic state "*seems* the most natural and to go along most with the freedom that nature grants to each" (emphasis added; TTP 16, Spinoza 1925, III.195; 2004, 185). The seeming freedom of liberal democracy is Spinoza's political theology. As with his biblical theology, Spinoza leaves us free to interpret it according to our capacity. Many individuals will undoubtedly see political freedom as the highest type of freedom, sanctioned by nature. Others will recognize that such freedom is an illusion, but is nonetheless the most effective superstition for producing political security and stability.

[31] TTP 7, Spinoza 1925, III.116; 2004, 100.

[32] Spinoza reports that Jewish theologians commonly hold the view that Scripture has infinitely many profound meanings, that everything in Scripture from the ancient marks above the letters to the contradictions within the narrative, is fraught with meaning (TTP 9, Spinoza 1925, III.140; 2004, 126). But if Scripture has infinite meaning, the result can be only infinite quarreling: "For if

Maimonides' claim that the prophets "were the most acute Philosophers" who grasped the truth of things.[33] After characterizing Christianity as teaching freedom consistent with rationality in Chapter 5, it would appear that Spinoza has violated his own rule and imposed a philosophical meaning onto scripture.

To grasp the meaning of Spinoza's critique of Maimonides in Chapter 7, we must clarify its purpose. Spinoza certainly does not reject Maimonides' views regarding the superiority of reason, or the rejection of religious and pagan superstitions. Rather, the issue concerns the authority of reason among the multitude. Spinoza insists that most men will not recognize the authority of reason or defer to the wisdom of philosophers. Maimonides' hermeneutic, in Spinoza's interpretation, attempts to establish covertly the authority of reason in politics by installing a "new type of priest," a philosopher who is adept at portraying rational truths in imaginative language.[34] To do this, Maimonides slyly suggests that regardless of the literal meaning of Scripture, there is a deeper, rational level to its teachings. The problem with this hermeneutical strategy is that it undermines, and ultimately dislodges, the literal sense of Scripture and thereby destroys "the certainty about the sense of Scripture which the vulgar can have by a straightforward reading . . . "[35] As a result, the meaning of Scripture is thrown open to superstitious speculation. Maimonides' superstitious followers concluded "that reason has to serve as the handmaid of Scripture, and submit to it completely."[36]

In contrast, Spinoza outlines an effective hermeneutical method which is accessible to the multitude.[37] This method accepts the literal meaning of the

interpreting Scripture in their mode were permitted everywhere, there would surely be no speech whose true sense we could not doubt" (TTP 10, Spinoza 1925, III.148; 2004, 135). Such a view serves those polemical theologians who are interested in promoting superstitious speculations about the meaning of Scripture. To be sure, Spinoza's method opens up the same possibilities, but not for superstitious speculations.

[33] TTP 5, Spinoza 1925, III.117; 2004, 101.

[34] In the Maimonidean solution, the wisdom for combining reason and revelation presumably moderates the political ambitions of the theologians and, at the same time, alleviates the resentment which attends all communities. Spinoza rejects this not only because passionate individuals stubbornly resist reason, but also because he doubts that reason can moderate either the political ambitions or superstitious tendencies of priests. See Frankel 1999, 897–924.

[35] TTP 7, Spinoza 1925, III.116; 2004, 100.

[36] TTP 15, Spinoza 1925, III.181; 2004, 169–170. Here, Spinoza refers apparently to the so-called Maimonidean controversy which began with the publication of the *Guide* in the twelfth century, which Menachem Kellner describes as "an event of major social and political significance, shaking the Jewish communities of Spain, Provence, and even France for well over one hundred years." See Kellner's account, which accords by and large with Spinoza's description, in Kellner 1991, 79.

[37] Spinoza devises a straightforward historical method for the interpretation of Scripture: "the universal rule in interpreting Scripture is to attribute nothing to Scripture as its teaching [*nihil Scripturae tanquam eius documentum tribuere*] which we have not understood as clearly as possible from its history" (TTP 7, Spinoza 1925, III.99; 2004, 85).

text even if it contradicts reason or seems absurd to philosophers. In addition, the method must explain the most important passages and the central teachings of Scripture, i.e. those that deal with salvation. As for the other, more obscure passages, "there is no reason why we should be so worried about the remaining things."[38] The Bible may contain irrational elements, but the critical teachings for our salvation are clear. Spinoza adds in a telling phrase that "in this perception" (*in hac perceptione*) the vulgar willingly acquiesce. He means by this that the vulgar believe they can grasp, without the help of interpreters, the critical teachings of Scripture on salvation.

But Spinoza's critique of Maimonides is not confined only to the problematic aspects of the Maimonidean hermeneutic. The failure to enlighten the multitude betrays a deeper, more serious problem with the political analysis that undergirds the project. Nor is this problem confined to Maimonides. Despite overwhelming evidence of the permanence of superstition in political life, philosophers cling to the belief that the goal of politics should be to make citizens rational or intellectually virtuous. They continue to imagine impossible political regimes, where reason rules and enlightens the multitude. This belief that reason could somehow gain political authority has rendered political philosophy ineffective and useless. Spinoza reports that philosophers

> have never conceived a theory of politics which could be turned to use, but such as might be taken for a chimera, or might have been formed in Utopia . . . As in all sciences, which have a useful application, so especially in that of politics, theory is supposed to be at variance with practice; and no men are esteemed less fit to direct public affairs than theorists or philosophers.[39]

In contrast to philosophers, statesmen have the practical task of directing the passions, and this requires seeing political life more truly, that is, without reference to reason. Such individuals – and here Spinoza seems to have in mind Machiavelli – "have written about politics far more effectively than philosophers."[40] Rather than judge politics and condemn "cunning

---

[38] TTP 7, Spinoza 1925, III.111; 2004, 96.   [39] TP 1, Spinoza 1925, III.273; 2000, 33.

[40] "[L]aw givers, with a view to exacting general obedience, have wisely set up another end, one very different from that which necessarily follows from the nature of the laws by promising to the upholders of the laws what the vulgar love most, and on the other hand, by threatening those who would violate them what the vulgar fear most" (TTP 4, Spinoza 1925, III.59; 2004, 44). Using hope and fear, that is, by appealing to men's strongest passions rather than their intellect, legislators have "wisely" found a way to restrain the multitude and prescribe to them a manner of living. See also TTP 14, Spinoza 1925, III.178; 2004, 165 and *Ethics* Vp41s: "If men did not have this hope and fear, but believed instead that minds die with the body, and that the wretched, exhausted with the burden of morality, cannot look forward to a life to come, they would return to their natural disposition, and would prefer to govern all their actions according to lust and to obey fortune rather than themselves."

and astute" statesmen according to the standard of rationality, philosophers must instead learn to appreciate how statesmen use the passions to create a stable unity or agreement among chronically superstitious citizens.[41] The proper task for philosophy is to learn and appreciate effective practice from non-rational statesmen.

Spinoza's restatement of the political problem

If Spinoza rejects Maimonideanism in Chapter 7, why does he use theology to support his own political agenda? Why does he portray Christianity as a religion of liberation? In fact, a closer look at Spinoza's theology shows that he does not present the theology of freedom as identical to the teachings of philosophy. As we shall see, his theology of freedom is no less superstitious than the belief in the Mosaic law. The belief in freedom is not a substitute for philosophy, nor does it contribute to the Enlightenment of the multitude. Instead, his theology conscientiously benefits the multitude by embracing superstitions that contribute to the stability and security of society.

The starting point of Spinoza's political thought is his famous doctrine of the *conatus*, that all things in nature seek to maintain an equilibrium of their parts and preserve their whole being.[42] The human manifestation of *conatus* is more complex because our perception of our being is partly conscious and involves beliefs about the objects of our desires and fears. Indeed, the status of these desires and fears is central to our perception of our *conatus*. Even though such perceptions are very likely erroneous – particularly the belief that I am free to choose a strategy for preserving – nothing in nature has greater authority or is more compelling to me than my own evaluation of my *conatus*. Reason has little power over these evaluations. Spinoza does not deny that philosophers can offer better strategies for self-preservation, but this is irrelevant to political life where "[e]ach deems that he alone knows everything, and wants everything to be modified on the basis of his own mental cast, and figures something is equitable or inequitable . . . insofar as he judges it to fall to his profit or harm."[43]

The primacy of the *conatus* and its tenuous relation to reason explains the unwillingness of the multitude to defer to philosophers or, for that matter, any authority. The suspicion of authority, even in the garb of reason and

[41] TP VI, III, IV, Spinoza 1925, III.291, 287, 293; 2000, 64, 51, 58.   [42] *Ethics* IIIp6–9, IVp22–26.

[43] TTP 17, Spinoza 1925, III.203; 2004, 193. Also see TTP 16, Spinoza 1925, III.190; 2004, 180: "The natural right of every man is thus determined, not by sound reason, but by desire and power." Spinoza's account of human action is developed in *Ethics* III, especially propositions 28–39. See also Skulsky 2009, 121–129.

philosophy, is reinforced by our experience and knowledge. Everyone – including the self-proclaimed philosopher – is concerned first and foremost with his own preservation, and is willing to employ any means, including deception, to secure it.[44] The primacy of my pursuit of my own self-preservation as I see fit is the basis for the enduring belief in equality. Were all men rational, the fact that there are better and worse strategies for self-preservation would naturally translate into greater authority for the wise. Unfortunately, reason is not equally distributed; to put it in Spinoza's memorable words, the sane have as much right as the insane.[45] Without natural sanction, the wise have no authority to decide what is best for others. This limitation forces us to lower the goal of politics, abandoning moral or intellectual perfection which is at best available only to a few, in favor of security and comfort, the benefit of which all men recognize.

The Maimonidean dream of making men rational serves only to distract us from the actual gulf between reason and passion which persists in political life.[46] This chasm becomes apparent when we perceive that the very terms men commonly invoke in political life are imaginings, the result of inadequate ideas. By exposing this fact, and showing our moral vocabulary to be illusory, reason corrodes the stability of actual regimes and contributes to their political and intellectual chaos. The TTP presents the most politically relevant examples of this chasm between inadequate and adequate ideas that separate philosophers from the many. The concept of "law" as an adequate idea, for instance, refers to those effects "which follow necessarily from the very nature or definition of a thing."[47] True laws are scientific descriptions of the universal and determined causal relations which explain all of nature. A philosopher perceives the "true object" of nature's laws and therewith the best manner of living. Such a rational being follows the law voluntarily since he recognizes that its aim is none other than happiness.

But this concept of happiness is irrelevant politically because most people "are completely ignorant of how things are really ordered and connected."[48] For the many, "it is better to consider things as open possibilities, and to consider law as created by men."[49] This notion is based on a framework of

---

[44] TP II, Spinoza 1925, III.280; 2000, 42. "The highest law of nature is that each thing endeavor, as much as is in it, to persevere in its state – and do so without regard to anything but itself" (TTP 16, Spinoza 1925, III.189; 2004, 179).

[45] The recognition of inequality of wisdom, that others have better strategies for self-preservation, is the starting point for education. The inability of most people to recognize this fact helps explain Spinoza's pessimism about educating the multitude.

[46] TP II, IV, Spinoza 1925, III.282, 284, 292–294; 2000, 45,47, 58–60.

[47] TTP 4, Spinoza 1925, III.57; 2004, 43.   [48] TTP 4, Spinoza 1925, III.58; 2004, 44.

[49] TTP 4, Spinoza 1925, III.58; 2004, 44.

inadequate ideas, including will and freedom. When human beings issue political laws, they presume the existence of an undetermined domain within which our choices are meaningful. This domain applies only to "the mind's perception of things"; or more specifically, to our inadequate ideas of our relation to other things. The realm of political authority involves concepts such as justice, law, right, and freedom which are illusory and impossible to harmonize with reason.[50]

The political problem, as Spinoza presents it, involves uniting non-rational citizens around a conceptual framework of justice, a concept which is itself neither natural or rational.[51] To achieve stability and peace among self-seeking individuals involves directing passions and interests so that people see the community as enhancing their interests or power. This is not a matter of educating the citizens about the true definition of justice or the greatest good or making the moral framework of political life consistent with rationality.[52] Such efforts will not contribute to the stability of the state; rather, the state must convince citizens that its power contributes to their own pursuit of self-preservation.[53] As Edwin Curley observes, "the problem of forming a society with any chance of enduring becomes the problem of designing a society whose members will continue to perceive it to be useful to them."[54] The political problem can be understood in terms of encouraging citizens to obey, by manipulating their perception of the legitimacy and usefulness of the state. A careful

---

[50] Douglas Den Uyl, responding to Smith's claim that democracy fosters rationality, makes a similar point: "Political action is never active in Spinoza's sense, and the effort to make it such carries with it confusions that can translate into social conflict. Politics for Spinoza has a simple limited function that in itself has nothing to do with perfection, activity, or blessedness . . . The best we could say is that 'democracy' does not contradict the perfected active life – not that it fosters it. To foster it would mean we would have some clear conception of how to bring activity about through political means" (Den Uyl 1983, 12–13).

[51] TP I, Spinoza 1925, III.282, 284; 2000, 45,47

[52] The traditional judgments about politics are framed in morality categories such as justice or the good. But such judgments are arbitrary and confuse our evaluation of politics. Moral claims merely "disguise exhortation as description" and "indicate nothing positive in things, regarded in themselves" (*Ethics* IV, Preface). Yet such illusions are critical to the perspective of superstitious citizens and therefore to the legitimacy of the state (see TP I, II Spinoza 1925, III.274, 279; 2000, 35, 41; and Ep 22). Philosophers must learn to respect the authority of these categories, even while recognizing that they are entirely conventional.

[53] As we have seen, Spinoza wishes to humble philosophers and force them to respect the wisdom of non-philosophic statesmen. To this end, he urges philosophers to contemplate political life objectively as a scientist contemplates natural phenomenon, without imposing moral judgments (TP I, Spinoza 1925, III.274; 2000, 35).

[54] Curley 1991–1992, 41. See also Stanley Rosen: "The state exists as the result of a common agreement by individuals to surrender their power to a sovereign authority for the sake of enhancing each man's power of self-preservation," in Rosen 1987, 472.

examination of Spinoza's theology shows that it has been designed to do just that.

Spinoza does not ignore the most common strategy employed by regimes to "persuade" its citizens to obey the law, namely the use of force. But force alone is not enough to ensure the perception of the legitimacy and usefulness of political power.[55] Citizens still retain some measure of power or *ius* even in the face of coercion. To achieve stability, therefore, a state must use other strategies including an appeal to superstition.

Spinoza's theology

Spinoza's presentation of the political problem helps us understand the critical role superstition plays in his theological account. It also explains why his theology contains an explicit attack on Scripture as a source of knowledge about God. Spinoza does not hesitate to criticize Scripture as corrupt throughout the TTP:

> Those who consider the Bible, such as it is, as an Epistle of God sent to human beings from heaven, will no doubt shout that I have committed a sin against the Holy Spirit – by stating that God's word is faulty, truncated, adulterated, not consistent with itself, that we have only fragments of it, and finally, that the transcript of God's compact that he compacted with the Jews has perished. But ... God's eternal word and compact, and true religion, are divinely inscribed in the hearts of human beings, that is, in the human mind ...[56]

The purpose of this critique is to limit the meaning of Scripture by exposing it as a corrupt text written for a largely ignorant audience. Spinoza's account of Maimonides makes clear why he pursues such a damaging critique with such energy. Maimonides had inadvertently expanded the possible meaning of Scripture with terrible consequences; superstitious readers were heartened and persecuted their enemies, often violently. Spinoza's portrait of

---

[55] TTP 17, Spinoza 1925, III.201; 2004, 191. Power is the result of a dynamic relation between the pursuit of one's *conatus* and the perception of authority. This distinction, according to Steven Barbone and Lee Rice, is presented in Spinoza's work in terms of the contrast between *potentia* and *potestas*: "when Spinoza uses the term *potentia*, he is almost always speaking of the ability or capacity to be able to do something. This ability is an innate ability or operation of the individual who has it; that individual exists and acts because of this power." *Potestas*, on the other hand, is the authority or privilege which permits us to do an action. Citizens always retain their *potentia* even when they transfer authority or *potestas* to the state (Barbone and Rice 2000, 16–17). In Chapter 17 of the TTP, Spinoza links an individual's *potentia* to his essence. Den Uyl shows that Spinoza "conceives political society to be a dynamic process of individual interactions" (Den Uyl 1983, 67). My account follows Den Uyl's explanation of collective power, especially the relation between political institutions and individual *conatus*.

[56] TTP 12, Spinoza 1925, III.158; 2004, 147.

Scripture as a corrupt text prevents us from establishing even Scripture's literal meaning with certainty. This, in turn, forces theologians and religious figures to turn their efforts away from superstitious interpretation toward unearthing the original meaning of the text which has been buried under layers of historical and linguistic data. Though these efforts are unlikely to produce a single, dogmatic interpretation of such an ancient text, Spinoza does not draw this conclusion.

He suggests instead that we can easily identify Scripture's authoritative moral teaching which promises salvation. Scripture's essential teaching concerns moral truths, which can be readily confirmed by our hearts or minds. The ambiguity between hearts and minds is revealing. Although at times the TTP appears to suggest that Scripture's teachings can be discovered or verified by reason, and further, that some prophets and apostles were also philosophers, Spinoza does not build his case for their teachings on their rationality. To the contrary, he provides ample evidence for doubting the truth of revelation.[57] His universal tenets of faith, for example, include the belief in a deity who promises eternal rewards in exchange for obedience to moral law, notions which are clearly inconsistent with his metaphysics.[58] The teachings of Scripture are "effective truths," that is, they are superstitions that have a salutary effect on their adherents. The truth of such beliefs is irrelevant as long as they lead people to act in a kind and charitable fashion.[59] The moral truths in Scripture are in our hearts, that is, they have nothing to do with metaphysics or knowledge:

> [W]e conclude that the intellectual knowledge of God which considers his nature just as it is in itself . . . does not pertain to faith and to revealed religion

---

[57] Spinoza's claim that the apostles were philosophers, who understood and taught philosophical truths in a language that the multitude could grasp, is consistent with Maimonides, who repeatedly asserts the hermeneutical principle that the "Torah was written in the language of the sons of man" (see, for example, *Guide* I.26, 29, 33, 47). By this, he means that in order to understand the meaning of Scripture and the divine law, we must grasp how the law accommodates itself to frailties and practices of the ancient Israelites. To take one example, the Torah's obsession with laws of sacrifice reflects the efforts of Moses to wean the Israelites off of ancient, idolatrous practices by redirecting their practices. See Klein-Braslavy 2006, 137–164.

[58] See Smith 2003; Curley 1990.

[59] Spinoza urges philosophers to accept the intellectual limitations of the multitude in a manner consistent with Christian teachings. To this end, he reminds them of Paul's teaching that "true knowledge is not a command, but a divine gift, and that God asks of man no knowledge [of Himself] other than knowledge of His divine justice and loving-kindness" (TTP 13, Spinoza 1925, III.169; 2004, 156). Spinoza urges men who have been blessed with such a gift not to insist on knowledge as the sole criterion of piety because the "common people, the uneducated multitude" can aspire only to imitate the truly pious by practicing *caritas* (TTP 13, Spinoza 1925, III.171; 2004, 159). This helps explain why the particularities of various superstitions or religion are largely a matter of indifference to Spinoza's philosophers.

in any mode; and, consequently, human beings can err about it astronomically without impropriety.[60]

The notion that one can separate moral from intellectual virtue, or that one can adopt correct moral principles based on a false set of premises, is hardly tenable for philosophers.[61] But Spinoza does not insist that anyone should be forced to accept the intellectual claims. He asks only that philosophers, those who recognize the effective truth of Scripture, adapt their views to the language of Scripture.

Spinoza supplements his theological teachings with political superstitions. The theological teaching of the TTP (Chapters 1–15) prepares the ground for his solution to the political problem (Chapters 16–20), where he builds the case for liberal democracy as the regime which best preserves natural rights of equality and freedom. The belief in such rights stands in sharp opposition to Spinoza's metaphysics. The meaning of freedom, for example, is highly suspect if every individual is fully determined by an infinite series of prior causes. Similarly, the belief in equality is also questionable in light of Spinoza's account of the fixed, superstitious disposition of the multitude. Still, such doubts do not mitigate the efficaciousness and widespread appeal of such beliefs. Indeed, given the weakness of reason in political life, the belief in these political superstitions represents the best practical solution to the political problem.[62]

Democracy offers neither moral nor intellectual perfection to the multitude, but this should not blind us to its other virtues. For one thing, it is less harsh than the superstitious, and often violent, manipulation commonly found in theocracies. Instead, it encourages an attitude of toleration of diverse beliefs. Separating reason and revelation into exclusive domains – "there is no connection or relationship between faith, or Theology, and Philosophy" – means that religious beliefs and practices are no longer judged by the standards of reason.[63] Rather than entrust philosophers with the religious or political authority to enlighten the multitude, Spinoza crafts a theology of religious freedom while circumscribing its actual scope or domain of authority.[64] From a Maimonidean point of view,

---

[60] TTP 13, Spinoza 1925, III.171; 2004, 159.
[61] Philosophers know that such morality is nothing more than the pursuit of self-interest as informed by superstition: TTP 14, Spinoza 1925, III.179; 2004, 166.
[62] See also Frankel 2011, 55–76.   [63] TTP 14 and Preface, Spinoza 1925, III.179, 10; 2004, 166, xxi.
[64] From the TP II, Spinoza 1925, III.280; 2000, 42: "In my lexicon one is altogether 'free' only to the extent that one is led by reason. To that extent one's act are determined by causes that can be adequately understood only by reference to one's own nature, even as if causes they determine one's acts necessarily. Freedom . . . does not rule out necessity, freedom presupposes necessity."

perhaps, Spinoza's toleration represents an attitude of indifference to the intellectual welfare of the multitude. But Spinoza has already shown that the intellectual perfection of the multitude is a self-defeating project; indeed, caring for the multitude is possible only if philosophy abandons the goal of making them rational. His liberal democracy offers an unprecedented level of security and comfort for mankind.

Conclusion: Spinoza's enlightenment

We began our discussion with the disagreement among scholars on the relation between Spinoza and Maimonides: some scholars emphasize Spinoza's kinship with Maimonides, while others focus on the comprehensiveness of his critique. We can now see that these positions reflect the particular elements of Spinoza's treatment of Maimonides in Chapters 5 and 7 of the TTP.

The first attack in Chapter 5 is meant to appeal primarily to Spinoza's Christian audience by presenting the Gospels as more rational than the Hebrew Bible in the sense that they promote freedom. Despite this difference, Spinoza's overall project of using religion to direct superstitious individuals to act in accordance with reason appears consistent with his account of Maimonides. The difference between the two appears largely rhetorical and theological, that is it reflects the different audiences of the respective works. In fact, Spinoza does not insist on the rationality of Scripture, but only that its essential teaching is freedom from the law. By substituting freedom – a superstition – for rationality, Spinoza radically departs from the Maimonidean project. This difference becomes clear in his second attack on Maimonides, as Chapter 7 exposes a more radical critique. What appears to be a mere disagreement over hermeneutical issues reveals the dramatic failure of the Maimonidean project to enlighten the multitude by making politics and religion more consistent with reason.

In analyzing this failure, Spinoza alludes to the unbridgeable chasm between philosophy and religion or politics. Men are directed by their passions to pursue self-preservation without consulting reason. The absence of reason in nature is apparent in politics as well. The conceptual world of politics rests on a host of inadequate ideas, such as law and freedom. The political ambitions of philosophers like Maimonides consistently fall short because they ignore the limits of reason in political life. Spinoza rejects such utopian projects and suggests instead a set of religious superstitions that contribute to the stability of the regime. The most stable regime is liberal democracy, which is rooted in the most natural and enduring superstitions, freedom and equality. The virtue of this regime is toleration which, from the point of view of philosophy, represents a studied indifference to the inadequacy of political superstitions.

The seeming contradiction between Spinoza's critiques on Maimonides dissolves therefore when we recognize that Spinoza's political thought eschews the goal of making the multitude rational in favor of the lower, more practical goal of stability and security. This separation of reason from politics allows Spinoza's students to embrace superstitions which have a salutary effect on the multitude. As for theologians and philosophers, Spinoza teaches them to tolerate various theologies as long as they culminate in the practice of *caritas*. This political teaching represents nothing less than the complete rejection of the Maimonidean project of enlightenment.

'Ishq, ḥesheq, *and* amor Dei intellectualis

Warren Zev Harvey

There are many parallels between Maimonides' *Guide of the Perplexed*, III.51, and Spinoza's *Ethics*, Part Five, propositions 21–42.[1] My remarks in this chapter are about some of them, and in particular about the connection between the Arabic *'ishq*, the Hebrew *ḥesheq*, and the Latin *amor Dei intellectualis*.

Guide, III.51, begins the climactic conclusion of the work. It treats of the intellectual knowledge of God, its attendant pleasure and love, and eternal life. These are also the topics of the climactic concluding propositions of the *Ethics*. In his prefatory comments to *Guide*, III.51, Maimonides states that the chapter is "a kind of conclusion," adding nothing not discussed in previous chapters, save guidance regarding the intellectual knowledge of God and the eternal life of the intellect.[2] In his prefatory comments to *Ethics* Vp21–p42, Spinoza similarly states that he has already said everything he wishes to say about "this life," and the concluding propositions will deal with "the duration of the mind without relation to the body."[3]

Although the *Guide* is on the whole an Aristotelian book, it is characterized by the wide stylistic diversity of its chapters. Yet III.51 stands out even amid such diversity. It is non-Aristotelian, poetic, and spiced with allusions to mystical literature.[4] It marks a change of tone in the *Guide*, even as Vp21–p42 mark a change of tone in the *Ethics*.

In their respective discussions of our knowledge of God in *Guide*, III.51, and *Ethics* Vp21–p42, Maimonides and Spinoza attribute or seem to

---

An earlier version of this paper was delivered at a conference of the Jerusalem Spinoza Institute on *Ethics* V: Love, Knowledge, and Beatitude, June 1999.

[1] See W. Harvey 1981, 167.

[2] Maimonides 1963, 618. Quotations from Pines's translation will sometimes be modified. References to Ibn Tibbon's Hebrew translation, used by Spinoza, are to Maimonides 1872. References to the Arabic text are to Maimonides 1931. On the theory of love in *Guide*, III.51, see Vajda 1957, 133–140.

[3] *Ethics* Vp20s, Spinoza 1925, II.294. Translations from the *Ethics* are based on Spinoza 1985, but sometimes modified.

[4] Hekhalot, Merkabah, and Sufi tropes may be detected. See S. Harvey 1991, 47–45. Cf. Blumenthal 1977, 51–68, and 1987, 86–106.

attribute pleasure and love to the intellect "without relation to the body." This is a problem. According to Maimonides' Aristotelian psychology, pleasure and love cannot, on the face of it, be attributed to the intellect; for the intellect is separate from the body, and pleasure and love are in the animal soul, which is inseparable from the body.[5] Similarly, according to Spinoza's psychology, pleasure and love cannot, on the face of it, be attributed to the intellect; for the intellect is distinct from the body, and pleasure and love are affects, that is, "affections of the body" or imagined ideas of those affections.[6] It would seem that for Maimonides and Spinoza "intellectual pleasure" and "intellectual love" are oxymora. If then there are attributions of pleasure or love to the intellect in *Guide*, III.51, or *Ethics* Vp21–p42, what are we to make of them?

The position we should expect Maimonides to hold regarding the knowledge and love of God is the one he sets down in *Guide*, I.39, when defining the commandment to love God "with all thy *heart*" (Deuteronomy 6:5). He takes "heart" to refer by metonymy to "all the forces of the body." The commandment is fulfilled by directing all one's bodily forces toward the knowledge of God: the knowledge is intellectual, but the love is a bodily passion.[7] Spinoza gives a comparable description of the love of God in *Ethics*, Vp16, describing it as involving "all the affections of the body."[8] However, in *Guide*, III.51, and *Ethics*, Vp21–p42, Maimonides and Spinoza seem to attribute pleasure or love to the intellect "without relation to the body."

Reactions and evaluations

Guide, III.51, and *Ethics*, Vp21–p42, have given rise to extreme positive and negative responses among readers.

Rabbi Shem Tov ben Joseph ibn Shem Tov, a major fifteenth-century commentator on the *Guide*, praises III.51, and says it presents "a wonderful

---

[5] On the separateness of the intellect, see e.g. *Guide*, I.1, Maimonides 1963, 23; I.68, 163–166; I.74, 221. In his *Eight Chapters*, 1, Maimonides assigns love to the appetitive faculty (Maimonides 1912, 42–43).

[6] The human intellect, according to Spinoza, is distinct from the body in the sense that the attribute of *cognitio* is distinct from that of *extensio* (*Ethics*, Ip10s, *realiter distincta concipiantur*; IIp1–p2, p11, IIIp2s, Spinoza 1925, II.52, 86–87, 94–95, 141). Love (*amor*), joy (*laetitia*), and pleasure (*titillatio*) may be "passive" or "active" affects (*Ethics*, IIIp11, p21, p58–p59; Definitions of the Affects, definitions 2 and 6, Spinoza 1925, II.148–149, 156, 187–188, 191–192), but are always either *corporis affectionis* or imagined ideas (*Ethics*, IIIdef3, Spinoza 1925, II.139; cf. IIp17–p18, p40; IIIp53, Spinoza 1925, II.104–107, 120–122, 181–182). Imagined ideas are dependent on the body (*Ethics*, IIp17–18; IIIp27, Spinoza 1925, II.104–107, 160–161) for the imagination is "corporeal" (TIE, 82; Spinoza 1925 II, 31). Maimonides similarly describes the imagination as a faculty of the soul "that cannot disengage itself from matter" (*Guide*, I, 73, 10th premise, Maimonides 1963, 209).

[7] *Guide*, I.39, Maimonides 1963, 8.   [8] *Ethics*, Vp16, Spinoza 1925, II.290.

regime" for the individual who is both religious and philosophical. However, he also reports the views on the chapter held by certain non-philosophic rabbis, outraged by its radical intellectualism.

> "Many rabbinic scholars," he writes, "have said that the Master did not write this chapter, and if he did write it, it deserves to be buried or, better, burned, for how could he say that those who know the natural things are on a higher level than those who occupy themselves with religion?"[9]

Other writers have, on the contrary, held that III.51 is too religious and its philosophic argumentation not sufficiently rigorous. The great Maimonidean scholar Salomon Munk, editor of the Arabic text of the *Guide* and author of its French translation, inserted the following note in the course of his translation of III.51: "The reflections contained in this paragraph are more religious and edifying than rigorously philosophical, and the author could not have seriously thought that they can serve to solve the problem."[10]

Similar bipolar views have been voiced about *Ethics*, Vp21–p42. Whereas Novalis thought that the author of the final propositions of the *Ethics* was *ein gotttrunkener Mensch*,[11] others seem to think he was simply drunk when he wrote them. Albert Einstein surely spoke from his own experience when he declared: "If those searching for knowledge had not been inspired by Spinoza's *amor Dei intellectualis*, they would hardly have been capable of that untiring devotion which alone enables man to attain his greatest achievements."[12] According to Morris Raphael Cohen, "the doctrine of the intellectual love of God" is "the central doctrine in Spinoza's philosophy," and "an ideal which may still serve as a beacon to illumine current tendencies in life and thought."[13] However, Jonathan Bennett pronounced *Ethics*, Vp21–p42, to be "an unmitigated and seemingly unmotivated disaster," and "rubbish which causes others to write rubbish."[14] And Edwin Curley confided: "I . . . do not feel that I understand this part of the *Ethics* at all . . . I also believe that no one else understands it adequately either."[15]

An Aristotelian problem

This problem of the attribution of pleasure or love to the intellect is found not only in Maimonides and Spinoza. It goes back to Aristotle. To say the least, Aristotle was not consistent in denying pleasure or love to the intellect,

---

[9] Maimonides 1872, III, 64b, 68a.   [10] Maimonides 1856–1866, III, 446.
[11] Friedrich von Hardenberg 1960–2006, III, *Fragmente und Studien 1799–1800*, no. 562, 651.
[12] Einstein 1954, 52.   [13] Cohen 1946, 307–308.   [14] Bennett 1984, 357, 374.   [15] Curley 1988, 84.

even though he had explicitly taught its separateness from the other parts of the soul and from the body (e.g. *De Anima*, III.4, 429a–430a). He sometimes knew how to declare that the pleasure in thinking is distinct from thinking (e.g. *Nicomachean Ethics*, X.5, 1175b 34–35), but at other times he flatly attributed *hedone* to *dianoia* (e.g. *Nicomachean Ethics*, III.10, 1117b 27– 31). His most famous assertion of the disembodied pleasure of *nous* is found in *Metaphysics*, XII.7, 1072b16 and 24, where he goes so far as to attribute *hedone* to the Prime Mover. In the same chapter, he describes the Prime Mover as the object of the *eros* of the world (1072b3). In *Nicomachean Ethics*, X.8, 1179a24–31, he suggests that "the gods take pleasure" in the human intellect *in actu*, and the happy human being who pursues intellectual activity is "beloved of the gods." If Maimonides, in *Guide*, III.51, and Spinoza, in *Ethics*, Vp21–p42, attribute pleasure or love to the intellect, they perhaps contradict themselves, but they have a good Aristotelian precedent for doing so.[16]

In his discussion of the love of the human intellect for God in *Guide*, III.51, Maimonides uses the Arabic *'ishq* and its Hebrew cognate *ḥesheq*, terms which designate intense, intimate, passionate love. The use of *'ishq* to designate our love for God was favored by some Sufi mystics, but avoided by most philosophers, who considered it too erotic for such a usage.[17]

Al-Farabi (*c.* 870–950), the founder of medieval Aristotelianism, did not use *'ishq* to designate our love for God, but did use it to designate the First Cause's intellectual self-love. In his *Political Regime* and in his *Virtuous City*, he affirmed that the First Cause is not only knower and known, but also *'āshiq* (passionate lover) and *ma'shūq* (passionately loved), and moreover has immense pleasure (*ladhdhah*) in His self-knowledge.[18] The term *ma'shūq*, a passive participle derived from the root of *'ishq*, reflects here Aristotle's reference to the Prime Mover as *eromenon* at *Metaphysics*, XII.7, 1072b3. The description of the First Cause by the term *'āshiq*, an active participle derived from the root of *'ishq*, has no precedent in Aristotle.

Avicenna (980–1037), an Aristotelian who had a penchant for mystical imagery, used the term *'ishq* without inhibitions. Like Al-Farabi, but more

---

[16] Already Aspasius criticized Aristotle for attributing pleasure to mind, and explained that "rejoicing and pleasures . . . are not in the intellect, but in the emotive part of the soul" (Aspasius 2006, 89, on *Nicomachean Ethics* III.10, 1117b 27–31). A similar criticism was elaborated by Crescas in his *Light of the Lord*, I.3.5, and II.6.1: see W. Harvey 1988. Cf. Anscombe 1963, 77: the concept of pleasure "reduced Aristotle to babble, since . . . he both wanted pleasure to be identical with and to be different from the activity that it is a pleasure in."

[17] See S. Harvey 1997.

[18] Al-Farabi 1964, 46–47; translated in Al-Farabi 2007, 90–91. See also Al-Farabi 1985, 86–89, 96–97, 345, 352, 361.

liberally, he used it to teach that the First Cause is passionate lover and passionately loved. Moreover, in his celebrated "Epistle on '*Ishq*" and in other works, he writes of the passionate love that accompanies our intellectual knowledge of God. For Avicenna, this love is part of the love of all creation for the First Cause.[19]

Anti-Aristotelian philosophers, like Al-Ghazali (1058–1111) and Rabbi Judah Halevi (*c*. 1075–1141), who were influenced by Sufism but also by Avicenna, described the true worshipper as a "passionate lover" (*'āshiq*).[20]

The usage of '*ishq* in *Guide*, III.51 is clearly influenced by Al-Farabi and especially Avicenna. Maimonides, who like his contemporary Averroës had reservations about Avicenna's philosophical rigor, was nonetheless drawn to his metaphysics. He may have felt that in metaphysics, which is in any case not amenable to logical proof, it is helpful to turn to a philosopher like Avicenna who knows the language of vision.[21]

Love vs. Intellectual Love

Maimonides uses the terms '*ishq* and *ḥesheq* in various grammatical forms, nine times in *Guide*, III.51,[22] but not once in the rest of the book. All nine uses refer to our love of God, and none to God as lover. He contrasts '*ishq* and *ḥesheq* (passionate love) with *maḥabbah* and *ahabah* (love). Passionate love is "an excess of love, so that no thought remains that is directed toward a thing other than the beloved."[23] The true worship of God is "to apply intellectual thought in passionately loving Him always."[24] This intellectual thought and this passionate love involve pleasure. The intellect "rejoices in what it apprehends."[25] The intellectual thought, the passionate love, and the joy become stronger and stronger until the intellect is separated from the body at death in intense pleasure, and remains eternally in this state of pleasure "which does not belong to the genus of bodily pleasures."[26] These statements do not prove that Maimonides attributed passionate love to the

---

[19] Avicenna 1960, VIII.7, 369–370; IX.2, 391–393. See Fackenheim 1945; cf. Goichon 1938, 222–225, and S. Harvey 2013.

[20] The description appears often in Al-Ghazali, e.g. *Iḥyā' 'Ulūm al-Dīn* (Revival of the Religious Sciences), IV.36; Al-Ghazali 2011. See Abrahamov 2003. It appears once in Judah Halevi's *Kuzari*, IV.15, Halevi 1905, 222. See Lobel 2000, 152–153, 243–244.

[21] See W. Harvey 2008. Cf. Pines's translator's introduction to *Guide*, Maimonides 1963, xciii–ciii.

[22] *Guide*, III.51, Maimonides 1963, 621, 627–628. Cf. Maimonides 1931, 457.13 (*fi 'ishqihi*), 462.13 (*ḥashaq*), 462.15 (*wa-'ashiqanī*), 462.16 (*ḥosheq*), 462.17 (*al-'ishq*), 462.20 (*li-'ishqihi*), 462.24 (*w'al-'ishq*), 463.4 (*al-'ishq*), 463.5 ('*ishqihi*).

[23] *Guide*, III.51, Maimonides 1963, 627.   [24] Maimonides 1963, 621.   [25] *Ibid.*, 627.

[26] *Ibid.*, 627–628. In distinguishing intellectual from bodily pleasure (628), Maimonides refers us to his books on Jewish law. He has in mind two passages, both of which quote the Talmudic dictum: "in the

intellect. They do prove that he attributed "pleasure" to it, but this pleasure is said to be not merely of a different species from bodily pleasures, but even of a different genus, i.e. it is not pleasure in any recognized sense of the term. It is plausible to understand Maimonides as holding that the distinction between love (*maḥabbah, ahabah*) and passionate love (*'ishq, ḥesheq*) corresponds to that between the two genera of pleasure. Under this interpretation, Maimonides attributes "passionate love" to the intellect, but passionate love, whatever it is, is not a bodily emotion. Maimonides makes no attempt to explain what he means by a pleasure that is not a bodily emotion.

Spinoza's distinction between *amor* and *amor Dei intellectualis* may be said to correspond to Maimonides' distinction between "love" and "passionate love," and his distinction between *laetitia* and *beatitudo* may be said to correspond to Maimonides' distinction between the two genera of "pleasure." According to Spinoza's exposition, intellectual love is the only eternal love because it is the only love not dependent on the body.[27] Beatitude is the eternal perfection of the intellect.[28] *Amor Dei intellectualis* and *beatitudo* constitute eternal salvation.[29] And "the mind delights in this divine love or beatitude."[30] Spinoza is less guarded than Maimonides. Whereas Maimonides had not explicitly attributed *'ishq* or *ḥesheq* to the disembodied intellect, Spinoza explicitly attributes *amor Dei intellectualis* to it.

Unlike Maimonides, Spinoza valiantly, if imprudently, tries to give a reasoned explanation for the attribution of joy and love to the intellect. He tries to justify the leap from "joy" and "love" to "beatitude" and *amor Dei intellectualis*. The critical argument occurs at *Ethics*, Vp32–p34, and runs as follows. Since the highest intellectual knowledge of God,

---

world to come ... the righteous ... *enjoy* the radiance of the Shekhinah" (Babylonian Talmud, *Berakhot* 17a). The first passage is in his *Commentary on the Mishnah*, introduction to *Sanhedrin* 10; the second in his *Mishneh Torah*, Hilkhot Teshubah 8:2. In the first passage, it is explained that "the soul [i.e. the intellect] will have pleasure in what it cognizes of the Creator, just as the *ḥayyot* [the angelic order identified with the Prime Mover] and the other orders of angels have pleasure in what they cognize of His existence," and there is no bodily pleasure to which this pleasure can be likened (Twersky 1972, 411–412, translation modified). In the second passage, it is explained that the "enjoyment" of the souls figuratively means that the righteous "know ... of the true reality of the Holy One, blessed be He, what they did not know while in the crass and lowly body" (Maimonides 1962, 90a, translation modified). In both passages, the attribution of pleasure to the intellect is considered either incomprehensible or metaphoric. The allusion in the first passage to the pleasure of the Prime Mover connects the Talmudic dictum about the afterlife with Aristotle's statements about intellectual pleasure in *Metaphysics*, XII.7, 1072b16 and 24. See Berzin 2004, 93–102.

[27] *Ethics* Vp34, Spinoza 1925, II.301.   [28] *Ethics* Vp33s, Spinoza 1925, II.301, 303.

[29] *Ethics* Vp36s, Spinoza 1925, II.303 (cf. the bold use of *laetitia* at line 9).

[30] *Ethics* Vp42, Spinoza 1925, II.308 (*Mens ... gaudet*).

scientia intuitiva, is eternal, then so is our pleasure in it, which is *mentis acquiescentia* or *beatitudo*, and so is our concomitant *amor Dei intellectualis*.[31] However, it is not explained why an affection of the body (joy or love) should be anything but an affection of the body just because it arises from eternal intellectual knowledge.[32] The replacement of the odd philosophic term *mentis acquiescentia* by the old religious term *beatitudo* may be effective rhetorically, but has no explanatory value. In the end, Spinoza's argument for the eternality and incorporeality of *amor Dei intellectualis* begs the question.

The invulnerable intellect

One of the parallels between *Guide*, III.51, and *Ethics*, Vp21–p42, concerns the notion that the intellectual love of God conquers death because the intellect is invulnerable.

Interpreting Psalms 91, Maimonides teaches that the passionate lover of God fears not death. In the psalm, God says:

> Thou shalt not be afraid of the terror by night ... A thousand may fall at thy side, and ten thousand at thy right hand; it shall not come nigh thee ... *Since he hath set his passionate love upon Me*, therefore I will deliver him. (Psalms 91:7–14)

According to Maimonides' exegesis, as explained by his commentators, the sword can destroy the body, but not the disembodied intellect. Maimonides quotes also other verses: e.g. "Fear thou not, for I am with thee" (Isaiah 41:10), "The Lord is for me, I will not fear" (Psalms 118:6), and "Acquaint now thyself with Him, and be at peace" (Job 22:21). The one who knows and passionately loves God has no fear of death, because the intellect cannot be physically harmed; and this eternal freedom from the bodily passions is true "peace."[33]

---

[31] *Mentis acquiescentia* ("contentment of mind," "peace of mind") or *acquiescentia in se ipso* ("self-contentment," "being at peace with oneself") is defined at *Ethics* III, Definitions of the Affects, definition 25, as the joy (*laetitia*) that results from knowledge of our power (Spinoza 1925, II.196); in definition 26, it is said to be the opposite of humility and repentance (Spinoza 1925, II.196–197). At Vp33s, *beatitudo* is substituted for *mentis acquiescentia* (see Vp32; Spinoza 1925, II.300) and understood as the supreme pleasure (Spinoza 1925, II.301).

[32] Cf. Nadler 2006, p. 258: "[W]hy is the love of God not just another passion? ... [H]asn't Spinoza just substituted one (albeit more controllable and reliable) passion for the others?"

[33] *Guide*, III.51, Maimonides 1963, 626–627. Cf. commentaries on the *Guide*, *ad loc.* by Moses of Narbonne (Narboni 1852, 65), Ephodi (Maimonides 1872, p. 67b, *zayin*), and Shem Tov ben Joseph ibn Shem Tov (Maimonides 1872, 67a–68a).

In *Ethics*, Vp38–p39, Spinoza echoes Maimonides, and argues that *amor Dei intellectualis* removes the fear of death, since the intellect is invulnerable.[34] The more the mind has intellectual knowledge, the more it remains "unharmed."[35] Consequently, those who have eternal intellectual knowledge "hardly fear death."[36] The connection made by Spinoza between *mentis acquiescentia* and *amor Dei intellectualis*[37] may have been suggested by Maimonides' use of Job 22:21.

In *Ethics*, Vp38, Spinoza makes the claim that intellectual knowledge, that is, knowledge of the second and third kinds, frees us from the affects, which are "evil." The idea that all or some affects are "evil" is repeated in the demonstration of the proposition. The idea is Maimonidean, although it may be traced to earlier philosophers.[38]

God's intellectual love

Maimonides speaks in *Guide*, III.51, of the human being's passionate love for God, but not of God's passionate love for human beings or for the world. However, Rabbi Levi ben Gershom, known as Gersonides (1288–1344), the foremost Jewish Aristotelian after Maimonides, and described by Spinoza as "a most erudite man," wrote not only of our passionate love for God, but also of God's passionate love for the world. In this sense, his metaphysics of love was more Avicennian than was Maimonides'. Inspired by Maimonides' discussion of the intellectual love in *Guide*, III.51, he explicitly attributed passionate love (*ḥesheq*) to the intellect *in actu*, whether the human, the celestial, or the divine.[39] He moreover held that the belief that God's joy is the only perfect joy is a major dogma of the Law, and thereby turned Aristotle's thesis in *Metaphysics*, XII.7, 1072b, into a foundation of Judaism.[40] In a sentence that evidently had a strong impact on Spinoza, he states that God "passionately loves the intelligible system of the world, which is God in some mode"

---

[34] Cf. *Ethics*, Vp38–39, Spinoza 1925, II.304–305.   [35] *Ethics*, Vp38, Spinoza 1925, II.304.
[36] *Ethics*, Vp39s, Spinoza 1925, II.305.   [37] *Ethics*, Vp38s, Spinoza 1925, II.304.
[38] *Ethics*, Vp38 (cf. Vp10dem, Vp39dem, Vp42dem). See *Guide*, I.54, Maimonides 1963, p. 126. Cf. III.51, Maimonides 1963, pp. 625–626. Cf. Aquinas, *Summa Theologiae* Ia2ae, q. 24, a. 2: "the Stoics said all passions are evil."
[39] See W. Harvey 1998, 102–105, and Touati 1973, 119–120, 484–485. Cf. Gersonides, *Wars of the Lord*, I.13, Vc.11–12, VIb.8, Levi ben Gershom 1984, 224–225; 2000, 170–174, 465–467 (where *ḥesheq* is translated "desire"). Spinoza refers to Gersonides in TTP 9, n.16, Spinoza 1925, III.256–257. See also W. Harvey 2012.
[40] Levi ben Gershom 1888, on I Chronicles, end, *to'elet* 6, 62; cf. on 16:27, 51. Cf. W. Harvey 1998, 102, n.14.

(*she-hu' ḥosheq be-zeh ha-siddur ha-muskal asher la-'olam, asher hu' ha-Shem yit'aleh be-'ofen mah*).[41]

Gersonides was not the first Jewish philosopher who went beyond *Guide*, III.51, and attributed passionate love to God, but he was the most significant. After Gersonides, many Jewish philosophers did so, and some of them, like Rabbi Hasdai Crescas (*c.* 1340–1410/11), who rejected the concept of intellectual love, and Leon Ebreo (*c.* 1465–after 1523), who accepted it, had a distinct influence on Spinoza's theory of *amor Dei intellectualis*.[42]

In *Ethics*, Vp17, Spinoza proves that God has no joy, and the corollary of this is that He loves no one. This is all evident for God has no inadequate (i.e. imagined or non-rational) ideas and is immutable.[43] However, in Vp35, he contradicts both the proof and its corollary. He writes that "the nature of God rejoices";[44] and having attributed joy to God, he attributes intellectual love to Him.[45] God rejoices in His infinite perfection, and intellectually loves Himself. In attributing joy and intellectual love to God, Spinoza parts company with Maimonides, and follows Avicenna and Gersonides.

In *Ethics*, Vp36c, Spinoza goes further: God loves not only Himself, but also human beings (despite Vp19!). He explains God's love of human beings by referring to IIp3: "In God, there is necessarily an idea both of His essence and of everything that necessarily follows from His essence." Knowing Himself, God knows all things; loving Himself, He loves all things.[46] In arguing that God's self-knowledge entails His knowledge of all things, Spinoza follows Themistius' interpretation of Aristotle's view in *Metaphysics*, XII.7 and 9. According to the prevalent interpretation of Aristotle's view, God knows only Himself, and thus does not know all things; according to Themistius' interpretation, God knows only Himself, but since all things are in Him, He knows all things. It is debatable whether Maimonides had accepted Themistius' interpretation. However, Gersonides

---

[41] Levi ben Gershom 1993–, on Genesis 2:2, 79. Cf. W. Harvey 1998, 104, n.17.
[42] See W. Harvey 1998, 105–117. Cf. the use of *ḥesheq* by Abulafia and Shalom, cited in the postscript. On Leon's debt to Avicenna, Maimonides, and other medievals, see Pines 1983.
[43] *Ethics* Vp17, Spinoza 1925, II.291.
[44] *Ethics*, Vp35, Spinoza 1925, II.302. Cf. III, Definitions of the Affects, definition 16 (*gaudium*), Spinoza 1925, II.195. Cf. also Vp36s, Spinoza 1925, II.303, where a reservation is expressed about the use of *laetitia* regarding God.
[45] *Ethics* Vp35, Spinoza 1925, II.302. God's intellectual love of Himself is demonstrated on the basis of our intellectual love of God.
[46] *Ethics*, Vp36, Spinoza 1925, II.302. The reference at line 24 to Vp35 includes the citation there of IIp3.

embraced it, and further argued that God loves His creation.[47] Again, Spinoza follows Gersonides.

Glory

Awareness of the parallels between *Guide*, III.51, and *Ethics*, Vp21–p42, can help us solve riddles concerning Spinoza's discussion. For example, in *Ethics*, Vp36s, after having expounded on *amor Dei intellectualis* and *beatitudo*, Spinoza remarks that these concepts are called in Scripture "glory" (Hebrew: *kabod*).[48] He is doubtless repeating a motif found often in medieval Jewish philosophy, according to which the divine glory is identified with intellect. But to which particular verse is he referring? To solve this riddle, all we have to do is search *Guide*, III.51, for a citation of a relevant biblical text containing the word "glory." Lo and behold, there is such a text. After having expounded on "passionate love" (*'ishq* or *ḥesheq*) and on the pleasure of the disembodied intellect, Maimonides quotes Isaiah 58:8, which reads literally: "Thy righteousness shall go before thee, and the *glory* of the Lord shall be thy rearguard [*ya'asfekha*]." As Maimonides understands it, the text means: if you are righteous, i.e. if you love God passionately, then upon your death the divine glory shall gather you up [*ya'asfekha*], i.e. your intellect will be united with the eternal active intellect.[49] The similarities between the literary contexts of Spinoza's remarks about "glory" and Maimonides' citation of Isaiah 58:8 prove that Spinoza's remarks allude to Maimonides' citation. There is also an external confirmation of this. In his TTP, Chapter 5, Spinoza argues that Isaiah 58:8 presents the clearest statement of the prophetic teaching on ethics and *beatitudo*, and interprets the verse after the manner of Maimonides: if you are righteous in this life, then after your death *gloria Dei te aggregabit*.[50]

Conclusion

In conclusion, Spinoza's discussion of *amor Dei intellectualis* in *Ethics*, Vp21–p42, is indebted to Maimonides' discussion of the passionate love of God in *Guide*, III.51. The term *amor Dei intellectualis* recalls the Arabic *'ishq* and the Hebrew *ḥesheq*, as used in *Guide*, III.51. The history of these

---

[47] See Pines 1987b, 177–204; and Pines 1991, 179–183. Cf. Themistius 1999, 33, 37–39, 92–93, 115, 142–143, 149.

[48] *Ethics*, Vp36s, Spinoza 1925, II.303.   [49] *Guide*, III.51, Maimonides 1963, p. 628.

[50] TTP 5, Spinoza 1925, III.71, and note *. See W. Harvey 2000.

three terms for the intellectual love of God may be traced from Al-Farabi, through Avicenna, Maimonides, and Gersonides, to Spinoza. However, the idea of intellectual passion goes back to Aristotle. In Aristotle the idea is problematic, and remains so in Maimonides and Spinoza. If it seems more problematic in Spinoza, it is only because he exerted the greatest effort to make philosophic sense of it. *Sed omnia praeclara tam difficilia explanandorum quam rara sunt.*

Postscript

The connection observed above between Spinoza's *amor Dei intellectualis* and *'ishq* and *ḥesheq* is conceptual, not linguistic. However, Moshe Idel has drawn attention to a compelling linguistic precursor of Spinoza's term. In a kabbalistic book by Rabbi Abraham Abulafia (1241–after 1291), *Or ha-Sekhel* ("The Light of the Intellect"), Part 9, there occurs the Hebrew phrase *ahabah elohit sikhlit*, literally "intellectual divine love," which could be translated into Latin as *amor Dei intellectualis*. Abulafia writes:

> Since between two lovers there are two parts of love, which become one when the love is actualized, so the Name [i.e. the Tetragrammaton] is composed of two parts, which are the conjunction of intellectual divine love [*ahabah elohit sikhlit*] with intellectual human love [*ahabah enoshit sikhlit*], and is one [love] . . . This is the power of the human being that he is able to connect the Lower Realm with the Upper, and the Upper descends and kisses that which ascends toward it, as a groom actually kisses his bride, out of the abundance of true passionate love [*ḥesheq*], designated for their mutual pleasure . . .[51]

As Idel has noted, the relevant passage in Abulafia's book is adapted (without citation) by the Maimonidean philosopher, Rabbi Abraham Shalom (d. 1492), in his *Neveh Shalom* ("Dwelling of Peace"), VI, 1, who also borrows the term *ahabah elohit sikhlit*. Now, while it is unlikely that Spinoza read Abulafia's arcane mystical book, which was available only in rare manuscripts, it is likely he read *Neveh Shalom*, a popular philosophic work, available in print (Venice, 1575). Here is the passage from *Neveh Shalom*, which interprets the verse describing Jacob's ladder, "And he dreamed and behold a ladder set up on the earth, and the top of it reached

---

[51] Abulafia 2001, 109. See Idel 1979, 5–6; English translation in Idel 1988, 66–67, 70. See also Idel 2000, 154, 167, 172; published without Hebrew texts in Idel 1988, 7–8, 20, 24. In Hebrew numerology, the Tetragrammaton = 26 and *ahabah* (love) = 13. The Tetragrammaton (26) is thus composed of two loves (13 + 13), divine and human.

to heaven, and behold the angels of God ascending and descending on it" (Genesis 28:12):

> The Separate Intellects are called "angels of God." However, there are also "angels of God" on earth, and they are the perfect scholars . . . [who] sanctify themselves through the contemplation of the *intelligibilia* and through the worship in the heart . . .
>
> This is the power of the human being that he is able to connect the Lower Realm with the Upper such that the Lower ascends and conjoins with the Upper, and the Upper descends and kisses that which ascends toward it. This is the intent here in the phrase "ascending and descending." For the [human] intellects are the [angels] *ascending* from the depths of lowliness by means of the Ladder of Wisdom, and the Separate Intellects are the ones *descending* toward them out of the abundance of the true passionate love [*ha-ḥesheq*], designated for their mutual pleasure . . . In this way, the intellectual divine love [*ha-ahabah ha-elohit ha-sikhlit*] conjoins with intellectual human love [*ahabah enoshit sikhlit*].[52]

In the passage from *Or ha-Sekhel*, two allusions may be discerned to *Guide*, III.51, namely, the description of the intellectual love between God and human beings as *ḥesheq*, and the reference to the intellectual divine "kiss."[53] These two allusions are found also in the passage from *Neveh Shalom*, which contains an additional very explicit allusion; namely, the reference to the perfect scholars contemplating the *intelligibilia* and engaging in the "worship in the heart."[54]

It seems, therefore, that not only was Spinoza's discussion of *amor Dei intellectualis* indebted to medieval discussions of 'ishq and ḥesheq, and in particular to the exposition in *Guide*, III.51, but even his phrase *amor Dei intellectualis* was indebted to them.

---

[52] Shalom 1575, 87ab. The phrase is printed erroneously as *ha-ahabah ha-elohit ve-sikhlit* ("the divine and intellectual love"), not *ha-ahabah ha-elohit ha-sikhlit* ("the intellectual divine love"), but a competent reader would automatically correct the error.
[53] Maimonides 1963, 627–628.   [54] *Ibid.*, 620–621.

Monotheism at bay: the Gods of Maimonides and Spinoza

Kenneth Seeskin

There is much that Maimonides and Spinoza have in common. Both devoted their entire lives to trying to relieve humanity of its tendency to conceive of God in anthropomorphic terms. Both decry the use of the imagination to lead one to truth. Both argue that human beings are only a small part of a vast universe and have no reason to think that it has been designed to accommodate their needs. Both deny that God rewards virtue or punishes vice in a direct or obvious way. Both stress that the goal of human life is to weaken our attachment to temporal things and achieve a higher level of understanding culminating in the intellectual love of an impersonal God.[1]

In the introduction to Book I of the *Guide of the Perplexed*, Maimonides says that his primary purpose is to explain the meaning of certain terms occurring in the works of the prophets. For the rest of that book he devotes over thirty-five chapters to examining words that seem to imply that God has bodily or personal qualities. When the Bible says that humans are made in the image of God (Genesis 1.26), Maimonides replies (*Guide* I.1) that all this means is that humans have intellectual apprehension. When the Bible says that God saw something, all that is meant is that God understood something (*Guide* I.4). When the Bible ascribes place to God, all that is meant is that God occupies a unique rank in the order of existence (*Guide* I.8). When the Bible says that God spoke to a prophet, what is meant is that the prophet understood something that pertains to God (*Guide* I.65). All of this is of a piece with the view that God is immutable and does not experience emotion (*Guide* I.35). It follows that when we say God is jealous or merciful, we are not talking about God himself but the consequences of divine activity as manifested in the created order (*Guide* I.54). Thus "God is merciful" does

---

[1] For recent essays that discuss Maimonides' influence on Spinoza's conception of God, see Fraenkel 2006, 169–215, W. Harvey 1981, 151–71, and Melamed (forthcoming). Needless to say, the *opus classicus* on this topic is Wolfson 1934. For more on Fraenkel, see n.6 below.

not mean that God is moved by prayers of entreaty but rather that God has provided each species with the resources needed to gather food and defend itself from danger.

Although Spinoza disagrees with Maimonides about the prophetic understanding of God, arguing that the prophets *did* ascribe bodily or personal qualities to God, when it comes to his own view, he too takes up the task of depersonalization.[2] *Ethics* Ip17s says explicitly that intellect and will do not pertain to the nature of God so there is no respect in which God exercises free choice. As stated in the appendix to *Ethics* I, one of Spinoza's primary purposes is to show that God acts by the same necessity with which he exists. Thus any suggestion that God acts with an end in view or has made everything for the sake of human beings is nonsense. At *Ethics* Vp17c, he affirms that strictly speaking, God does not love or hate anyone, from which it follows (*Ethics* Vp19) that someone who loves God should not expect God to love him in return.

The thrust of both philosophies is to depersonalize our understanding of God and argue that our primary way of relating to God is intellectual. For Maimonides, divine providence is consequent on the perfection of the intellect (*Guide* III.18): the more perfection one achieves, the closer to God one gets. For Spinoza, insofar as the human mind perceives things truly, it is part of the infinite intellect of God (*Ethics* IIp43s). Yet for all their efforts at depersonalizing God, Maimonides and Spinoza wind up in different places when it comes to how to respond to God. In a famous passage in the *Mishneh Torah*, Maimonides writes:[3]

> When a man reflects on these things, studies all these created beings, from the angels and spheres down to human beings and so on, and realizes the divine wisdom manifested in them all, his love for God will increase, his soul will thirst, his very flesh will yearn to love God. He will be filled with fear and trembling, as he becomes conscious of his lowly condition, poverty, and insignificance, and compares himself with any of the great and holy bodies; still more when he compares himself with any one of the pure forms that are incorporeal and have never had association with any corporeal substance. He will then realize that he is a vessel full of shame, dishonor, and reproach, empty and deficient.

From Maimonides' standpoint the chief theological virtue is humility, to bow one's head in the face of something too vast to understand.

---

[2] See, for example, Ep 19, G IV.93: "They [the prophets] constantly depicted God in human form, sometimes angry, sometimes merciful, now looking to what is to come, now jealous and suspicious, and even deceived by the devil." Also see TTP, Chapter 7.

[3] *Mishneh Torah* 1, Principles of the Torah, 4. 12. Cf. *Guide of the Perplexed* III.52.

Even a cursory reading of the *Ethics* shows that Spinoza had something very different in mind. For him humility is "Sadness [*tristitia*] born of the fact that a man considers his own lack of power, or weakness."[4] In reading this, we must keep in mind that according to Spinoza, the nature or essence of each thing is a striving (*conatus*) to persevere in its own being. Thus consciousness of weakness or lack of power runs contrary to our very nature, which is why it is experienced as sadness.

On the other hand, an increase in power is experienced as joy (*laetitia*). The best way to experience increased power is to take an active role with respect to one's emotions, and the way to do that is to understand what causes us to have them. The more we understand ourselves and our emotions, the more we will come to love God, who is the primary cause of everything (*Ethics* Vp15). The more we love God, the more we enter into a state of blessedness (*Ethics* Vp36s). The result is that humility is not a virtue and does not arise from a correct use of reason (*Ethics* IVp53).[5] By contrast, its opposite, self-esteem, can arise from a correct use of reason, in which case it is the highest thing we can hope for. This chapter explores the difference between the two thinkers on this topic.

I

Although there is still debate over whether Maimonides believed in a God who created the world according to will and purpose or one who is the source of a necessary and eternal emanation, there is no doubt that he put severe limits on the knowledge we can have of God.[6] At a prominent place in the *Guide*, he claims it is well known that God is not susceptible to definition.[7] The reasoning is that there is no wider category under which

---

[4] *Ethics* IIIp58def26.
[5] Some qualifications are in order. In the *Short Treatise* (KV 2.8), humility, which is defined as knowing one's own imperfection without regard for others' disdain for one, is regarded as a virtue, while feigned humility or self-deprecation is regarded as a vice. So the question seems to be whether one's humility is based on a correct or incorrect assessment of the mind's ability to know God. As we will see, the basic difference between the two thinkers is that Maimonides believes that the human mind cannot know God directly, Spinoza that it can. According to *Ethics* IIIp58def29, humility is very rare because most of what people refer to as *humble* behavior is an outgrowth of ambition and envy. Note, as Curley (1988, 111) does, that even in the *Ethics* (IVp54s), Spinoza praises humility for its social value. On this point, I am indebted to Cooper (forthcoming), Chapter 3.
[6] For a book-length study of this debate and a defense of the view that Maimonides was committed to will and purpose in God, see Seeskin 2005.
[7] *Guide* I.52.

God can be subsumed and therefore no possibility of a cause prior to God as *living thing* is prior to *mammal*. If no definition can be given of God, then: "His essence cannot be grasped as it really is."[8]

What, then, do we say about knowledge, life, and power in God? Maimonides rejected any suggestion of similarity between God and humans so that terms like 'knowledge' or 'power' are strictly equivocal "having nothing in common in any respect or in any mode."[9] As a rigorous proponent of the *via negativa*, he argued that all positive claims about God's knowledge, life, or power should be understood as negations. Thus "God is wise" means "God does not lack wisdom or possess it in a way comparable to us." His reason for preferring negation to affirmation is that the former does not appear to give us essential knowledge and therefore does not deceive us into thinking we can have it.[10]

It is worth noting that in Maimonides' opinion even negations are suspect because by putting God under a description, they too can lead one to think that we know what God is. In his words, negations are useful to the degree that they "conduct the mind" to the utmost of what must be believed about God. They are the best linguistic tool we have. But at the highest level, all linguistic tools fail. As he tells us: "The bounds of expression in all languages are very narrow indeed . . . "[11] The final answer, then, is to follow Psalm 65 and recognize that the highest praise we can

---

[8] *Guide* I.54. For further discussion of this point and the historical precedents behind it, see Altmann 1969.

[9] *Guide* I.58, Maimonides 1963, 137. Although Maimonides says this several times (e.g. *Guide* I.35, I.56), there is a long-standing debate over how committed he was to this principle. In the negative theology chapters (*Guide* I.52–59), he seems to be completely committed to it. But at *Guide* I.68, he appears to back pedal by suggesting that the formal structure of cognition in God is the same as it is in us. The principle in question is the Aristotelian view which holds that when the mind is active, the intellect, the intellectually cognizing subject, and the intellectually cognized object are one and the same. It is generally agreed that Spinoza refers to *Guide* I.68 in his discussion of parallelism at *Ethics* IIp7s. If God contemplates the order and connection of ideas, then he must be identical to it. By the same token, if God contemplates the order and connection of things, he must be identical with that as well. Putting the two together, we get the conclusion that the order and connection of ideas is the same as the order and connection of things. Thus Fraenkel 2006, 169–215, cites *Guide* I.68 as a crucial text for establishing a link between Maimonides and Spinoza. In response to Fraenkel, note two things. Because *Guide* I.68 appears to contradict the negative theology chapters, it is by no means clear that it represents Maimonides' final view of the matter. It could be nothing more than his way of saying that the Aristotelian view of cognition is as far as philosophic speculation can take us, but that in the end, it too asserts more than we can possibly know. Second, as Fraenkel admits, identifying God with the order and connection of things would mean that extension is an attribute of God. While Spinoza would applaud this result, Maimonides' Neoplatonism would cause him to shudder. According to *Guide* III.8, matter is the source of sin, corruption, and death.

[10] *Guide* I.58.   [11] *Guide* I.57, Maimonides 1963, 132.

offer to God is a studied silence.[12] In this context, silence is another name for intellectual humility. More fully:[13]

> Glory then to Him who is such that when the intellects contemplate His essence, their apprehension turns into incapacity; and when they contemplate the proceeding of His actions from His will, their knowledge turns into ignorance; and when the tongues aspire to magnify Him by means of attributive qualifications, all eloquence turns into weariness and incapacity!

To be sure, the ignorance Maimonides is talking about is a learned ignorance that may take years to achieve. But learned ignorance is still ignorance, which means that for Maimonides, as for Socrates, there are cases where ignorance is a virtue.

The only exception that Maimonides recognizes to his rule of silence is the Tetragrammaton: Y.H.V.H.[14] In his view, it is the proper name of God because it is the only one used exclusively of God, the others (e.g. the Merciful, the Just, or the Gracious) being used of both God and humans. Thus the Tetragrammaton is the only name that gives an unequivocal indication of God's essence rather than an indication of His consequences or effects.[15] In Jewish tradition, the Tetragrammaton was to be pronounced only by the priests in the Temple and the High Priest on the Day of Atonement. Since the destruction of the Temple, and the abolition of the priesthood, not only is it forbidden to pronounce it, no one can be sure how it should be pronounced. The standard practice is to substitute *Adonai*, a title derived from *Adon* (Lord), or *HaShem* (The Name).

---

[12] *Guide* I.59. For the skeptical interpretation of Maimonides, see Stern 2005. For the traditional interpretation, see Davidson 1992–1993. My view is that while Maimonides thought the truths of metaphysics were the penultimate step in coming to understand God, in the end, they too reveal their inadequacy and must give way to silence.

[13] *Guide* I.58, Maimonides 1963, 137.

[14] *Guide* I.61. The Tetragrammaton is first used in its official capacity at Exodus 4:15 and then again at Exodus 6.3, where God says: "I appeared to Abraham, Isaac, and Jacob as God Almighty [*El Shaddai*], but by my name Y.H.V.H., I was not known to them." I say its first "official capacity" because even though God says he was not known to the Patriarchs by this name, the narrative portion of Genesis uses the Tetragrammaton in numerous places (e.g. 13:4,15:2, 22:14, 26:22, 28:13). In Chapter 13 of the TTP, Spinoza explains this by saying that the author did not employ names that were in use at the time to which he was referring but rather names that were familiar to people at the time he was writing. For further comment on Maimonides' analysis of the Tetragrammaton and its influence on Spinoza, see Melamed 2012.

[15] Cf. Spinoza, TTP, Chapter 13: "Again, it should be observed that in Scripture no word but 'Jehova' [the Tetragrammaton] is to be found to indicate the absolute essence of God, as unrelated to created things. That is why the Hebrews contend that this is, strictly speaking, God's only name, the other names being forms of address; and it is a fact that the other names of God, whether substantive or adjectival, are attributes belonging to God insofar as he is considered as related to created things, or manifested through them."

At first blush, Maimonides suggests that the Tetragrammaton is indicative of necessary existence but does not completely commit himself. His suggestion is based on the fact that however it was pronounced, the Tetragrammation is derived from the Hebrew verb *hayah* (to be). The connection between them is made explicit at Exodus 3:14 with the words *Eheyeh asher eheyeh*, which employs the first person singular form of the verb and is usually translated as "I am that I am" or "I am and shall be" or even "I shall be what I shall be." God then tells Moses: "You shall say to the Israelites 'I AM [*Ehyeh*] has sent me to you.'" The next verse then employs the Tetragrammaton or third person form of the verb with the words: "You shall tell the children of Israel that Y.H.V.H., the God of your fathers . . . has sent me to you." In short, the Tetragrammaton is a shortened form or name derived from "I am that I am."

Maimonides interprets the passage to mean that in the case of God, the subject is identical with the predicate, so that God does not exist *through* (i.e. by means of) existence in the sense that existence is external to the subject and has to be added to it.[16] The reason for this is not hard to discern. If existence were something added to the essence of God, there would have to be an agent other than God responsible for the addition, which is clearly absurd. Therefore in God and God alone, essence involves existence, which is another way of saying that God's existence is necessary. In Maimonides' words: "There is a necessarily existent thing that has never been, or ever will be, nonexistent."

Maimonides concludes his discussion of God's existence by returning to the subject of the Tetragrammaton, only this time he is more decisive:[17]

> This name is not indicative of an attribute but of simple existence and nothing else. Now absolute existence implies that He shall always be, I mean He who is necessarily existent.

With the benefit of hindsight, we are inclined to ask how, given his analysis of the Tetragrammaton, Maimonides still could hold that God's essence is unknowable. Why, in other words, is necessary existence not a perfectly adequate account of what God is? And why did Maimonides not use this insight to propose a version of the ontological argument?

The answer is that he thought necessary existence so unlike ours that we have no hope of understanding it. Once again: "The term 'existent' is predicated of Him . . . and of everything that is other than He, in a purely equivocal sense."[18] Although Aquinas's position on the equivocal nature of

---

[16] *Guide* I.63. [17] *Guide* I.63, Maimonides 1963, 156. [18] *Guide* I.56, Maimonides 1963, 131.

divine names is not as extreme as Maimonides', he too maintains that while
"God exists" may be self-evident in itself, it is not self-evident to us.[19] More
fully, the essence of God, while knowable in itself, cannot be known by
anyone in this life or by natural means.[20] In fact, both Maimonides and
Aquinas cite Exodus 33 ("No one can see my face and live") to underscore
their point.[21] So while it is true to say that God is existence itself, this still
leaves us ignorant of what God's essence is.

II

For Maimonides, not only is God shrouded in mystery, so are important
parts of the world for which God is responsible. Even if we suppose that
God acts from will and purpose, at *Guide* III.13 Maimonides insists that we
are not in a position to know what that purpose is and should not deceive
ourselves by thinking that everything was created to serve human ends.[22]
More broadly, Maimonides devotes seven chapters of the *Guide* to an
argument derived from the *Kalam* known as the "argument from particularity."[23] Briefly stated, the argument asks: "Why this rather than that?" If
the rationalist account of the universe is correct, then there ought to be a
sufficient reason for everything that happens. If so, why does Venus move
this way and Mercury that way? Why is the orbit of the sun tilted 23.5
degrees to the plane of the earth rather than, say, 24.5 degrees? Why does
this quadrant of the night sky have a large number of stars while that
quadrant has comparatively few?

The demand for a reason could be met in either of two ways: by giving
the efficient cause of the phenomenon in question or by showing what
purpose it serves. So let us ask what purpose is served by having Venus and
Mercury move in opposite directions or the angle of the sun's orbit at 23.5
degrees? In the absence of a convincing explanation, proponents of
the argument concluded that the only way we could understand the

---

[19] *Summa Theologica* 1.2.1.
[20] *Summa Theologica* 1.12.4, 1.12.11, 1.13.11. For a twentieth-century Thomist, see Owens 1963, 353:
"From the standpoint of what is originally conceived through simple apprehension, the human
intellect cannot form any notion at all of the divine essence. In this respect one can state categorically
that we do not know what God is."
[21] *Guide* I.54 and *Summa Theologica* 1.12.11.
[22] This exempts Maimonides from much of the criticism Spinoza directs against traditional religion in
the appendix to *Ethics* I.
[23] See *Guide* I.73 and II.19–24. Wolfson 1976, 434–452 traces this argument to the Asharite theologian
Al-Juwayni. Its best-known version and that which had a direct impact on Maimonides is Al-Ghazali
1997, 12–27.

phenomenon is that God chose to make it one way rather than another. In its extreme form, the argument went on to assert an atomist metaphysics according to which each atom is qualitatively indistinguishable from every other.[24] If so, why does this atom occupy this region of space and that atom occupy a different one? Because no scientific explanation could ever be forthcoming, the answer was to say that God's will is responsible for the placement of every atom and is therefore the cause of every natural phenomenon.

Maimonides' response to the argument is to say that when it comes to the earthly realm, Aristotle has provided us with satisfactory explanations for why things happen as they do, but when it comes to the heavenly realm, human knowledge is so limited that we cannot hope to obtain truth and must settle for mathematical models that merely save the phenomena.[25] From the standpoint of empirical accuracy, the best model of the day was Ptolemy's. But Maimonides objected to his theory because it overturned Aristotle's concept of natural motion by introducing epicycles and eccentric orbits to account for planetary motion. While Aristotle's theory according to which all heavenly spheres rotate around the center of the earth made more intuitive sense, its predictions were not always accurate. Faced with this dilemma, Maimonides himself admits to perplexity.

Although Maimonides admits that the phenomena that are perplexing to him might one day be clear to someone else, we should not make too much of this. It took a major paradigm shift in science – something neither Maimonides nor any of his contemporaries could have imagined – for this possibility to be borne out. His skepticism is even more pronounced in Book III of the *Guide*, when he argues at length that matter – even heavenly matter – is a strong veil that prevents us from apprehending things that are separate from matter as they truly are.[26] In the case of God, apprehension of the true reality is completely impossible.

Again Aquinas concurs, maintaining that the mode of knowledge follows the mode of the nature of the knower. Because our soul, as long as we live in this life, has its being in corporeal matter, it knows naturally only what has a form in matter or what can be known by such a form.[27] To return to Maimonides, existence is anything but an open book, which is why he never misses an opportunity to emphasize the importance of humility in dealing

---

[24] *Guide* I.73.
[25] *Guide* II.24. For more on Maimonides' doubts about medieval astronomy, see Seeskin 2005, Chapter 5.
[26] *Guide* III.9. [27] *Summa Theologica* 1. 12. 11.

with our ability to make sense of it. We can see this in another way by looking at Maimonides' characterization of Moses.

In his discussion of character traits in the *Mishneh Torah*, Maimonides points out that while it is normally advisable for a person's behavior to follow the middle way between extremes, there are some exceptions – the most obvious being humility.[28] In fact, it is not enough merely to be humble, a person must hold himself low and have no pretensions. In support of this, he cites Numbers 12:3, which says that Moses was not just humble but *very* humble. He goes on to cite the Mishnaic tractate *Pirke Avot* (4.4), which bids us to hold ourselves "very, very low." Roughly the same point is made in the *Guide* when Maimonides points out that Moses hid his face and was afraid to look on God at Exodus 3:6, while the nobles of Israel were overhasty at Exodus 24:11 and achieved only an imperfect apprehension as a result.[29]

Maimonides' praise for humility can also be found in his treatments of Job and Rabbi Akiba. On Maimonides' reading, Job is described as righteous at the beginning of the story but not wise or understanding.[30] By the end of the story, however, he comes to realize that the things he used to value, e.g. health, wealth, and children, are not the ultimate values and cannot compare to knowledge of God. Thus far Spinoza would agree. But we should not lose sight of the fact that Job's recognition is accompanied by a large measure of self-deprecation. Thus Job 42:3: "I have uttered what I did not understand, things too wonderful for me" and 42:6: "I despise myself and repent in dust and ashes." For Spinoza, both would count as paradigm cases of sadness, which would disqualify Job as a hero.

Rabbi Akiba is mentioned in connection with *Hagigah* 14b, which recounts the legend of the four rabbis who entered the garden of paradise (*pardes*).[31] In keeping with Jewish tradition, Maimonides interprets *pardes* as exposure to esoteric subjects. The legend tells us that one Rabbi died, one went mad, one became an apostate, and only Akiba entered and went out in peace. Maimonides invokes the legend to stress the virtue of epistemological humility:[32]

> For if you stay your progress because of a dubious point; if you do not deceive yourself into believing that there is a demonstration with regard to matters that have not been demonstrated; if you do not hasten to reject and categorically to pronounce false any assertions whose contradictories have

---

[28] *Mishneh Torah* 1. Character Traits, 2.3. For more on Maimonides' view of humility, see Weiss 1991, 38–46, 102–105, 107–115.
[29] *Guide* I.5.   [30] *Guide* III.22.   [31] *Guide* I.32.   [32] *Guide* I.32; Maimonides 1963, 68.

not been demonstrated; if, finally you do not aspire to apprehend that which you are unable to apprehend – you will have achieved human perfection and attained the rank of Rabbi Akiba . . .

Simply put: if you recognize your limits and stay within them, you will achieve the same status as one of Israel's greatest sages.

III

The metaphysical picture changes dramatically when we get to Spinoza. By the seventeenth century, many of the astronomical phenomena that befuddled Maimonides and his contemporaries were finally explained in a satisfactory way. The ontological argument that Maimonides seemed to be hinting at became explicit. More important, Spinoza did not think that biblical language contained hidden truths that only a few people were capable of deciphering.[33] On the contrary, the prophets addressed themselves to general audiences and taught only simple doctrines.[34] Nor does he believe that, once identified, the truths he is discussing can never be made fully explicit. Again the contrary is true: when it comes to God, these truths are available to everyone and can be expressed with geometric precision.

In a letter to Boxel, Spinoza admits that he does not have complete knowledge of God. Of the infinite attributes God manifests, he can understand only two.[35] But this admission is followed by a strong qualification: from the fact that he does not know all or even most of God attributes, it does not follow that he does not know some. Because an attribute constitutes the essence of substance, by knowing thought and extension, he claims he has as clear an idea of God as he does of a triangle. In fact, at *Ethics* IIp47, he says without hesitation that the human mind has an adequate knowledge of the eternal and infinite essence of God. To this we may add that even if one were to imagine an unknown attribute of God, according to the doctrine of parallelism presented at *Ethics* IIp7, the order and connection of things conceived under that attribute would be no different from the order and connection of things conceived under thought or extension.[36] So looking at the world under the aegis of a previously unknown attribute would not generate any surprises.

The extent of Spinoza's disagreement with the medievals can be seen as early as the *Short Treatise*, where he objects that the indefinability of God

---

[33] The difference between Maimonides' and Spinoza's views on biblical language, and how these differences affect their view of God, are explored by Chalier 2006, 76–85.
[34] TTP, Chapter 13.   [35] Ep 56.   [36] *Ethics* IIp7.

presupposes the Aristotelian view according to which all definitions must proceed by genus and specific difference.[37] As readers of the *Ethics* well know, he begins his magnum opus with definitions of 'self-caused', 'substance,' and 'God,' none of which proceeds according to genus and specific difference. By the same token, 'thought' and 'extension' cannot be placed within a wider genus because they are not conceived through anything else. But Spinoza never doubts that we know what they are.[38]

To return to the *Short Treatise*, not only is the medieval view of definition wrong, in Spinoza's opinion it leads to a thorough going skepticism because it leaves the most fundamental category of the system undefined.[39] I will have more to say on this point below. For the present, it is noteworthy that while the medievals may well have understood definition in the way Spinoza indicates, we saw that their view of God was motivated by other considerations as well. In the first place, there is the scriptural evidence provided by Exodus 33. In the second place, there is the view that in this life, the soul can only know a form that is combined with matter.

Needless to say, Spinoza would not have been persuaded by either consideration. If Moses thought that humans cannot see the face of God and live, Spinoza would say the reason is not that he thought God was unknowable but because he believed that something terrible would happen to you if you tried to look at God. In regard to the second argument, while it is true that the constant flux to which material things are subject prevents us from acquiring adequate knowledge of them, this has no tendency to show that we cannot have adequate knowledge of things that are eternal and immutable like triangularity and the essence of God.

Consider 'self-causation,' which Spinoza defines as that whose essence involves existence or whose nature can be conceived only as existing. This is compatible with *Ethics* Ip20, which says: "God's existence and his essence are one and the same." If God's essence involves existence, then nothing external to God can prevent God from existing. This is another way of saying, as Spinoza does at *Ethics* Idef3, that God is conceived through himself so that the conception of God does not require the conception of anything else.

It follows that the only way to deny God's existence would be to show that the idea of self-causation is incoherent. In his second proof for the

---

[37] KV 1.7, Spinoza 1925, I.44–45.

[38] This reading rejects the interpretation of Wolfson 1934, 76, 142, who argues that since Spinoza's God cannot be subsumed under a genus, Spinoza must have agreed with the medievals that God's essence is unknowable. It seems to me that this is contradicted by Ep 56 mentioned above as well as *Ethics* IIp47.

[39] Cf. Bruaire 1974, 21, who argues that negative theology is tantamount to atheism.

existence of God, Aquinas rejects the suggestion that something can be the efficient cause of itself on the grounds that if this were so, it would be prior to itself. According to the medieval understanding, the efficient or agent cause is something that confers existence on another thing.[40] If we take self-causation to mean that God somehow *brings* himself into existence, then Aquinas would be right: the idea of self-causation is incoherent. Obviously this is not what Spinoza means. His point is that unlike every other essence, which requires the work of an external agent in order to be realized, God's essence alone is sufficient to account for God's existence. Incoherence would arise only if it could be shown that existence must come to something from an external source. But, Spinoza would object, there is no reason why we have to grant this. If not, self-causation is both coherent and comprehensible.

If more understanding of God's essence is sought, Spinoza has a ready answer. Eschewing the faculties of intellect and will, which often lead to mystery, he turns to thought and extension, two terms known to everyone and which, according to Melamed, serve to depersonalize God even further.[41] Suppose someone were to ask: "What is it that exists necessarily?" Unlike the scholastics, Spinoza's answer is: we can conceive of it either as an infinite system of ideas or as an infinite plenum of material things. We have seen that given the claim that God has an infinite number of attributes, some ways of answering this question are unknown to us. Spinoza insists, however, that this fact does not diminish the clarity or the legitimacy of the two answers we do have.

To carry this point a step further, whichever way we choose to understand God, we will see that it "expresses eternal and infinite essence."[42] On the meaning of eternity, Spinoza is equally explicit: "By eternity I mean existence itself, as it is conceived to follow necessarily from the definition alone of an eternal thing."[43] This is another way of saying that either way of understanding God will give us something whose existence does not derive from an external source but is inseparable from its own nature. To understand why, we should keep in mind that the infinity Spinoza is talking about is absolute so that "whatever expresses essence and involves no negation pertains to its essence."[44]

If we conceive of God as an infinite system of ideas linked in causal order, we will recognize that it is impossible for anything outside the

---

[40] *Summa Theologica* 1.44.1: "It pertains to everything to have an efficient cause in so far as it has being."
[41] See Melamed 2012.   [42] *Ethics* Idef6.   [43] *Ethics* Idef8.   [44] *Ethics* Idef6.

system to be responsible for its existence. The reason is that anything outside the system will be either an idea or something else. By *Ethics* Ip3, if it is not itself an idea, it cannot be the cause of a whole system of ideas. If, on the other hand, it is an idea, it must already be contained in the system and be part of the causal order that links every idea with every other. The same is true for an infinite plenum of material things or an infinite something-or-other conceived under an attribute beyond our comprehension. So however we conceive of God, existence is internal to His nature.

In addition to understanding God through the attributes of thought and extension, there is Spinoza's famous identification of God with nature (*Deus sive Natura*). One reason why the identification is problematic is that having distinguished between nature understood as *Natura naturans* and nature understood as *Natura naturata*, Spinoza does not tell us whether God should be understood as only the first, i.e. nature in its active capacity considered as a self-caused and self-sustaining thing, or as the totality of nature.[45] Because the former consists of "the attributes of substance that express eternal and infinite essence," there is no question that it pertains to God. While the latter consists of the modes that follow from the necessity of God's nature, it is nonetheless true that they exist in and can neither be nor be conceived without God.

No matter what interpretation one picks, there is no getting around the fact that Spinoza's identification of God with nature constitutes one more step in the process of depersonalization. People recognized as early as the Book of Job that natural phenomena such as floods, droughts, and earthquakes affect everyone equally, making no distinction between the virtuous and the vicious.[46] They strike without mercy, cannot be appeased, and are oblivious to love, hate, or any other form of emotion. This accords with Spinoza's view that God acts by necessity and does not love or hate anyone. But in addition to depersonalizing God, Spinoza is also attempting to remove any sense of mystery from God. If God and nature are identical, then to use a medieval term, the ways and works of God are perfectly intelligible. Put otherwise, if nature is infinite so that everything exists in and is conceived through it, then it is impossible to form a coherent idea of anything correctly described as *super*natural. For all intents and purposes,

---

[45] *Ethics* Ip29s. For a defense of the view that God is identical only with *Natura naturans*, see Curley 1969, 42–43 and 1988, 42–43. For a recent critique of Curley, and of the view that the relation between substance and modes is a causal one, see Melamed 2009, 17–82, especially 31–34.

[46] See Job 9:22.

Spinoza has lifted the veil of ignorance that surrounds God and found nothing that we are incapable of understanding.

The debate over how to interpret Spinoza's naturalism has long revolved around two poles: (1) that by denying the traditional God of Scripture, he is an atheist, and (2) that by identifying God with nature and claiming that everything exists in and is conceived through God, he was God intoxicated. It does not require great insight to see that the normal terms in which the debate is phrased are too vague to shed any real light on Spinoza's views. He was hardly the first person to maintain that the traditional conception of God has to be reformulated to stand up to critical scrutiny. And his understanding of self-causation has a solid textual basis in Exodus 3.14. Though he could have eliminated the word 'God' from his writing altogether and spoken entirely in terms of nature or substance, he chose not to, knowing full well what the connotations of the word are.

When Velthuysen accused him of introducing atheism by stealth, Spinoza responded that he had "perversely" misinterpreted his meaning.[47] So it would be better to say that Spinoza thought he was purifying our conception of divinity rather than destroying it. To repeat: God is existence itself conceived either as an infinite system of ideas or an infinite plenum of material things. To some, this will seem like a divinity *manqué*. Spinoza would only point out that the material that is lacking – will, purpose, likes, dislikes, and in general everything included under the rubric of personality – is the stuff of mythology. To the degree that humanity sets itself the task of pleasing such a God through entreaties or the performance of rituals, it is subjecting itself to a form of self-imposed tyranny.

In view of this, I suggest that Steven Nadler is right to say that the real question is not so much how we think of God but the proper attitude to take *toward* God.[48] Maimonides too argued for an impersonal God who could not be swayed by entreaties, but he wanted us to stand in awe of such a God and bow our heads in reverence. For him, Aristotle has given us such an accurate picture of the sublunar realm that anyone who doubts it is a fool. The picture changes dramatically when we get to the heavenly realm and becomes highly speculative. By the time we get to God, we are left with something that stubbornly resists our attempt to understand it. The proper attitude, then, is not to press on with further inquiry, but to recognize our limits and stop.

Nadler is also right to say that nothing could be further from the spirit of Spinoza. Having rejected the ritual component of the law, Spinoza still

<hr />

[47] Ep 42 and 43, Spinoza 1925, IV.218, 219.　　[48] Nadler 2006, 119–21.

could have argued that we have no choice but to stand in awe of God or nature as something too great for us to understand. If he had, then the God-intoxicated epithet might be accurate. The truth is, however, that he argued for the opposite: the goal of human life is to become so familiar with the causal structure of nature that one sees intuitively how everything that happens follows from God. As he says in the appendix to *Ethics* I, the dispelling of ignorance entails the disappearance of wonder. By dispelling ignorance, the mind moves from a passive to an active state, which, as we have seen, is experienced as joy and culminates in love of God.

Love for Spinoza is "Joy, accompanied by the idea of an external cause" (*Ethics* IIIp59def6). The highest achievement is to view everything that happens to us as governed by necessity and as related to the idea of God. As we saw, love of God leads to a state of blessedness, which Spinoza associates with what Scripture terms glory (*kavod*, *Ethics* Vp36c). Putting all this together, we arrive at the conclusion that blessedness is not a matter of being singled out by God but of coming to accept a proper conception of God and the mind's ability to know God. From Spinoza's perspective, Maimonides and the medievals are too pessimistic. There is no room for fear and trembling in his thought and no awareness of ourselves as a vessel full of shame and dishonor. On the contrary, love of God is a form of empowerment. Without it, our lives are subject to the whims of fortune as one emotion follows another without any rhyme or reason.

IV

We are now in a position to understand why the two thinkers took such different paths. While they both set out to oppose anthropomorphic conceptions of God, they have different strategies for how to go about it. For Maimonides, the need to renounce anthropomorphism is directly related to the rejection of predication by analogy. The rationale for his view is clear: if you cannot know what God is, then any comparison between God and us is immediately suspect. The depth of his conviction can be seen in his repeated warning that even to suggest that God has multiple attributes is to go down the wrong path.[49] Not only should one refrain from making comparisons with God, one should refrain from saying anything at all about God lest one put God under a description and destroy His uniqueness.

Spinoza's disdain for anthropomorphism is aptly summed up in his letter to Boxel: if triangles could speak, they would assure us that God is

---

[49] *Guide* I.51 and I.53.

eminently triangular, and if circles could speak, they would assure us that God is circular. His way of avoiding anthropomorphism is to naturalize God. Once the identification with nature is established, and with it the recognition that there is no force operating above and beyond nature, the only way we can think about God is in terms of cause and effect. As Spinoza tells us, nature is everywhere and always the same.[50] I take this to mean that nature makes no decisions and that there is no such thing as being in its good graces. To repeat: this means that in the strict sense, God does not love or hate anyone.

It is clear, however, that by taking such extreme positions, both thinkers ran risks. If God is unknowable, one has to embrace a large dose of skepticism to relate to God in an appropriate way. At *Guide* I.59, Maimonides anticipates the objection that if what he says is true, there will be nothing to distinguish the fool from the wisest of people. This is the passage where he says that it may take years of study for a person to see that categories applicable to a science are not applicable to God. While the answer is true in principle, the objection anticipates dissatisfaction with the *via negativa* and the idea that ultimately all we can do is contemplate God in silence. A critic could easily press the objection a step further by asking: what exactly are we contemplating? Maimonides' answer, a familiar one in the Middle Ages, would be to say that while we can know *that* God is, we will never be in a position to know *what* God is. As we saw, we can know the consequences or effects that follow from God but not the nature of what has caused them. In medieval parlance, this means that any demonstration we offer of God's existence must be a demonstration *quia* rather than a demonstration *propter quid*.[51]

From Spinoza's perspective, this entire approach is suspect. We can understand the nature of his objection in simplistic form by going back to his correspondence with Boxel. When Boxel claims that ghosts express the image of God better than corporeal creatures, Spinoza replies that he cannot believe in something if he cannot form a clear idea of what it is.[52] It follows that if God's essence is unknown to us, belief in the existence of God would be sheer folly. Looked at another way, if the knowledge of an effect depends on and involves knowledge of the cause, then to the degree that we cannot know what God is, it is impossible for anything to be conceived *through* God. So whatever mystery we attribute to God will permeate everything that God is responsible for, meaning that there will be a veil of ignorance surrounding the entire universe. This opens the door to superstition and

[50] *Ethics* III Preface.   [51] See *Summa Theologica*, 1.2.1.   [52] Ep. 54, Spinoza 1925, IV.253.

wild speculation about why things happen as they do – precisely what the rejection of anthropomorphism is supposed to avoid!

On the other hand, there are also risks associated with naturalism. Spinoza's position requires one to hold that whether you think of it under the attribute of thought or under the attribute of extension, nature is a seamless web of causal relationships culminating in the eternal and infinite essence of God. Maimonides argued that if nature is everywhere and always the same, there are particular features of nature that science cannot explain. While our understanding of nature has undergone profound changes since Maimonides' day, we may ask whether we are not in much the same boat as he was.

With the mathematization of natural science came the discovery of physical constants like the force of gravity or the mass and charge of the electron. Take any physical constant and one can raise the same question: why this rather than that? Why does the mass of a particle or strength of a force take on what seems like an arbitrary value? The question is apt given that even the slightest variation in these values would lead to a universe vastly different from ours. If the force of gravity were more than it currently is, the universe would collapse in what has come to be known as the big crunch; if it were less, the inflation would be so great that it would be impossible for stars and galaxies to form. So why is it that the force of gravity appears to have been finely tuned to be compatible with the formation of stars and thus the existence of life?[53] "Fine tuned" is just another name for particularity so that, like the medievals, we are faced with the question of how far to press the need for a scientific explanation.

According to the classic view, explanation begins with a localized description of the universe at a particular time and a general law under which that description can be subsumed. In this case, however, we are not asking how one event leads to another but why the general law has the specific character it does. The problem is that physical constants are so basic to our understanding of nature that it is difficult to find anything more general to which we can appeal for an explanation. For a rationalist like Spinoza, there is always the possibility of saying that just because no explanation is currently available, it does not follow that there is none.

---

[53] On this issue, see Hawking 2010, 160–161: "Most of the fundamental constants in our theories appear fine-tuned in the sense that if they were altered by only modest amounts, the universe would be qualitatively different, and in many cases unsuitable for the development of life . . . The emergence of the complex structures capable of supporting intelligent observers seems to be very fragile . . . Were it not for a series of startling coincidences in the precise details of physical law, it seems, humans and similar life-forms would never have come into being."

While this reply may shift the burden of proof temporarily, it still leaves Spinoza in a precarious position, for despite the pervasive character of his naturalism, it is hard to see how he could get from the eternal and infinite essence of God to something with the specificity of a physical constant. In a famous letter, he claims that motion and rest are produced directly by God viewed under the attribute of extension and that from motion and rest we get "the face of the whole universe" (*facies totius universi*), which, although varying in infinite ways, yet remains the same.[54] But this, even this together with the physical interlude of *Ethics* II and the common notions, are still too general to account for the exact force of attraction that we measure with our instruments. In his letter on the infinite, he argues that we can conceive of quantity in two ways: either abstractly, under the guise of infinite and indivisible substance, or superficially as divisible, finite, composed of parts, and multiplex.[55] From the latter come time and measure as conceived by the imagination: time as a limit to duration, measure as a limit to quantity. If so, how could the measurements taken by the modern natural scientist be anything but superficial, which is to say ideas of the imagination?

Maimonides used the specificity of planetary motion to argue for will and purpose in God. Spinoza went to great lengths to show that this conception of God is incoherent. This is not the place to argue for or against the coherence of voluntarism. Nor is it fair to criticize Spinoza for failing to anticipate developments in science that did not occur until centuries after his death. In an autobiographical statement published in 1949, Einstein, an admirer of Spinoza, still expressed a faith in the intelligibility of nature, which he took to mean that there are no arbitrary constants but only strongly determined laws from which one could derive completely determined constants.[56] But many scientists no longer share this view. According to Stephen Hawking: "Not only does God definitely play dice, but He sometimes confuses us by throwing them where they can't be seen."[57]

Playing dice is, of course, a metaphor. In most cases, we give odds for things when we lack sufficient knowledge, thereby confirming Spinoza's view of contingency. If, for example, we had sufficient knowledge of the size, mass, and shape of the dice along with the force with which they were thrown and the distance they had to fall, we could give a satisfactory account of why a particular outcome was realized. But the kind of probability physicists talk about today is different because there is no possibility of

---

[54] Ep. 64, Spinoza 1925, IV.278.   [55] Ep. 12, Spinoza 1925, IV.56–57.   [56] Einstein 1949, 63.
[57] www.hawking.org.uk/does-god-play-dice.html.

explaining why the path of an electron took one direction rather than another. In this case, probability is ultimate. To use a different metaphor, suppose someone were to ask why Susan won the lottery while John did not. If the winner is determined by a random process, there is no deep level explanation of the outcome: all we can says is that Susan's chances of winning were the same as John's and that her number happened to be the one that was picked.

If God does play dice, and if, as Hawking and others have suggested, our universe is but one of a vast number of universes arising from random conditions and containing different physical constants, there would be no deep level explanation – either scientific or theological – for why our universe has the particular features it does. The fine-tuning that we observe is due to the fact that this is the universe we are in. Asking "Why this rather than that?" would be like asking why Susan won the lottery.

My point is that by identifying God with nature, Spinoza ran the risk that if our understanding of nature should change, our understanding of God would have to change as well. Though many still hold out hope for a single theory that would explain all natural phenomena, no one knows for sure whether such a theory is possible. I mention this because to the degree that our understanding of nature no longer resembles a seamless web, awe and humility in the face of nature begin to look like legitimate responses. Despite his belief in strongly determined laws, Einstein would have struck a responsive chord with Maimonides when he said:[58]

> The most beautiful and most profound experience is the sensation of the mystical. It is the sower of all true science. He to whom this emotion is a stranger, who can no longer wonder and stand rapt in awe, is as good as dead. To know that what is impenetrable to us really exists, manifesting itself as the highest wisdom and the most radiant beauty which our dull faculties can comprehend only in their primitive forms – this knowledge, this feeling is at the center of true religiousness.

To be sure, Einstein would not have said that there are clearly demarcated boundaries beyond which further inquiry must stop, but he does say that no matter how much we inquire, we are likely to find something in nature that calls forth a religious response.

If the medievals used the fine-tuning of planetary motion to argue for an anthropomorphic conception of God, in today's world, many use the fine-tuning of physical constants to argue for the same thing. It is

---

[58] See Mitchell 1991.

significant, however, that neither Maimonides nor Spinoza would agree with this. However mysterious nature is, Maimonides would argue that God is even more mysterious. By contrast, Spinoza would insist that no matter how complicated our picture of nature, we can never be satisfied with the suggestion that things happen without a reason why. Whatever the differences, their steadfast opposition to a God conceived along the lines of a glorified human being puts both squarely within Jewish tradition.

CHAPTER 7

Moral agency without free will: Spinoza's naturalizing of moral psychology in a Maimonidean key

Heidi M. Ravven

The doctrine of free will, in its most basic and minimal version, is the claim that we are the originators of our actions (at least substantially) and hence that we are responsible for them. While some philosophers hold that free will presupposes choice of action between alternatives, others now maintain that only substantial origination in oneself alone is necessary for an action to be considered freely willed. Some philosophers believe that this notion of free will, sometimes called "guidance control," is compatible with causal determinism. I argue in this chapter, against some recent claims that Spinoza is a free will compatibilist,[1] that Spinoza's position does not meet even this reduced and compatibilist criterion for free will.

Spinoza's account of the interactive nature of perception

Spinoza insists that perception is always of our constitutive relations, and never, *pace* Descartes, a mere peering inward into an inner self to which we have direct access. Spinoza makes the claim very explicitly that we have no direct introspective self-perception. Instead, all perception, of both internal states and of external world, originates in the awareness of how the body is affected. Spinoza writes in *Ethics* IIp19:

> The human Mind does not know the body itself, nor does it know that it exists except through ideas of affections by which the Body is affected.

Nor is there ever any direct access to external objects or events, for "the ideas that we have of external bodies indicate the condition of our own body more than the nature of external bodies."[2] Peering into our own individual

---

[1] See, for example, Lenz, "Whose Freedom? Spinoza's Compatibilism," as well as Kisner 2013 and Kashap 1987.
[2] *Ethics* IIp16c2.

minds or those of others can never reveal clear ideas or motives, for Spinoza maintains that

> the idea that constitutes the nature of the human Mind is not, when considered in itself alone, clear and distinct; we can also demonstrate the same of the idea of the human Mind, and the ideas of the ideas of the human Body's affections [viz. they are confused], insofar as they are referred to the Mind alone.[3]

"The ideas of the ideas of the human Body's affections" are emotions, according to Spinoza's definition (IIIdef3). Hence emotions, which include what we would call today motivations, when considered as within an individual alone, cannot be clearly discerned. Spinoza tells us why: it is because "the human Body requires a great many bodies by which it is, as it were, continually regenerated" so that,

> this idea [of each of our minds] will be in God insofar as he is considered to be affected by the ideas of a great many singular things. Therefore, God has the idea of the human Body, *or* knows the human Body, insofar as he is affected by a great many *other* ideas, and not insofar as he constitutes the nature of the human Mind. [My emphasis]

Even from the infinite or eternal perspective, and not only from the human one, insofar as God constitutes the nature of *this particular* human mind, it cannot be understood. Minds are never discrete: neither their ideas nor their motivating emotions are ever discrete; they never have their source in any singular mind/body. My claim is that the mind does *not* have its source in a single mind–body entity. All the evidence I am citing shows that Spinoza is arguing against the free will claim that a single discrete person is an uncaused cause of action, an unmoved mover. If a person is embedded in causal networks that together produce effects (which is Spinoza's claim) then no person is an unmoved mover, which is the same as to say that no person has free will. This claim would seem already to constitute strong evidence that Spinoza does not hold the view that we have a free will, originating in oneself alone or substantially, which is the source of our actions. Even God does not have this kind of free will, although Spinoza does maintain that God alone is "free," for Spinoza in *Ethics* Ip32c1 writes, "God does not produce any effect by freedom of the will." Free will is not the kind of freedom, we realize, that Spinoza is attributing to God. At bottom, perceptions, the basis of all knowledge, are fundamentally confused if and when they are thought to reveal our bodies or minds, for "the ideas of

[3] *Ethics* IIp28, 28s.

the affections of the human Body, insofar as they are related only to the human Mind, are not clear and distinct but confused," Spinoza informs us in IIp28. Instead, God knows the human mind only in its interactions and hence we can come to know our own minds only by taking note of, that is, perceiving our interactions and interrelations, and how those affect us both physically and mentally. Yet at the same time, to know those interactions *is precisely what it is* to know the human mind not only for us but for God:

> But the ideas of the affections of the Body are in God insofar as he constitutes the nature of human Mind; *or* the human Mind perceives the same affections (by P12), and consequently (by P16) the human Body itself, as actually existing (by P17). Therefore to that extent only, the human Mind perceives the human Body itself, q.e.d.[4]

God knows the human mind only in its interactions, and hence we can know our own minds only by our perceptions that capture our interactions and interrelations and how those affect us both physically and mentally. The clarity comes with the grasp of the interaction. There is not an individual, constituted of mind and body, prior to the engagement who *then* interacts. Hence, just these ongoing *interactions* and *interrelations* that our minds perceive (and our bodies enact) *are* what constitute the nature of the human mind in God. Unpacking the metaphor, we become who we are through our interactions and interrelations. We know ourselves in them and as them. We are co-constituted. We also come to act *as* them, for "[a] thing which has been determined to produce an effect," Spinoza writes, "has necessarily been determined in this way by God; and *one which has not been determined by God cannot determine itself to produce an effect*" (my emphasis).[5] We produce effects as embedded in causal networks, for individual things exist as modes in God within the infinite causal concatenation of finite causes within the universe, for

> [t]he idea of a singular thing which actually exists has God for a cause not insofar as he is infinite, but insofar as he is considered to be affected by another idea of a singular thing which actually exists; and of this [idea] God is also the cause, insofar as he is affected by another third, and so *to infinity*.[6]

From our human perspective, "the idea of any mode in which the human Body is affected by external bodies must involve the nature of the human Body and at the same time the nature of the external body."

---

[4] *Ethics* IIp19 and dem.   [5] *Ethics* Ip26.   [6] *Ethics* IIp9.

For all the modes in which a body is affected follow from the nature of the affected body, and at the same time from the nature of the affecting body . . . And so the idea of each mode in which the human Body is affected by an external body involves the nature of the human Body and of the external body. . . . From this it follows . . . that the human Mind perceives the nature of a great many bodies together with the nature of its own body.[7]

We perceive and come to know ourselves only as embedded in contexts and as interactively constituted by them.

For Spinoza images capture and express our relations and interactions

The relational character of our perception is captured as well in Spinoza's conception of "images." He says that "we shall call images" "the *affections of the human Body* whose ideas present external bodies as present to us."[8] Hence, images are changes in and states of our own body that enact and embed the effects of our interrelations with the world within (and as) the self. Hence it is hardly surprising that "the ideas we have of external bodies indicate the constitution of our own body more than the nature of external bodies."[9] Nevertheless, "the Mind does not know itself, except in so far as it perceives ideas of affections of the Body,"[10] and hence the mind does not know itself directly through introspection, an internal gaze into itself, but rather only through experience, which is to say, through being affected and thinking about how it is affected – either thinking imaginatively or, instead, rationally and intuitively. Interactions can be perceived because they affect one's own body, and that is the only route to experience (perception) and knowledge. One can come to know oneself only through these encounters, these interactions, Spinoza insists, and never directly (for "the human mind has no knowledge of the body except" [*pace* Descartes]).

Further:

[W]hen we say that the human Mind perceives this or that, we are saying nothing but that God, not insofar as he is infinite, but insofar as he is explained through the nature of the human Mind, *or* insofar as he constitutes the essence of the human Mind, has this or that idea; and when we say that God has this or that idea, not only insofar as he constitutes the essence of the human Mind, but insofar as he also has the idea of another thing together

---

[7] *Ethics* IIp16 and dem. [8] *Ethics* IIp17s (my emphasis). [9] *Ethics* IIp16c2. [10] *Ethics* IIp23.

with the human Mind, then we say that the human mind perceives the thing only partially or inadequately.[11]

Moreover, this perceiving and knowing in the human person, and not only in God, *is* what ideas are (*Ethics* IIdef3). For a mind is not a thing that *has* ideas but is the *process* of forming ideas, that is, *thinking*. Thinking, a dynamic process and not a container of ideas, is also what a mind *is*:

> Because the essence of our Mind consists only in knowledge, of which God is the beginning and foundation (by Ip15 and IIp47s), it is clear to us how our Mind, with respect both to essence and existence, follows from the divine nature, and continually depends on God.[12]

Hence our minds encounter both self and world not only *in* but *as* interactions, as particular interactions affect us (our body–mind) and constitute our idea of the body, which is to say, the self, for the urge of the *conatus* spans mental and physical. Body and mind bring together self and world, imbuing the relation with the urge to persist. The idea of the mind, its structure as well as its content, is rooted in and comes about in our engagements, our embeddedness in our environments. The activity of the mind, which the mind is – and which ideas are, too – relates, brings together, self and world because it captures the body's interactions, the body's actions, and not the body in isolation prior to its actions and interactions.

The relational character of individual bodies

Even the individual body itself in its internal constitution has a relational character, Spinoza contends, for he defines an individual body not as a substance (as Descartes did) but in terms of its stable internal relations of parts:

> bodies are not distinguished in respect to substance; what constitutes the form of the Individual consists [NS: only] in the union of bodies . . . But this [NS: union] by hypothesis is retained even if a continual change of bodies occurs. Therefore, the individual will retain its nature.[13]

An individual he defines as "an unvarying relation of movement among themselves" of "a number of bodies of the same or of different size," so that they "are united with one another" by contiguity or so "that they communicate their motions to each other in a certain fixed manner."[14]

---

[11] *Ethics* IIp11c.   [12] *Ethics* Vp36s.   [13] *Ethics* IIp13, lemma 4dem.   [14] *Ethics* IIp13ax2 def.

If the parts composing an Individual thing become greater or less, but in such a proportion that they all keep the same ratio of motion and rest to each other as before, then the Individual will likewise retain its nature as before.[15]

And this obtains for an object in motion as well as at rest.[16] Such composite individuals "can be affected in many ways, and still preserve [their] nature." Moreover such composite individuals are not discrete but can be nested in each other, in larger and larger ones to infinity so that "we shall easily conceive that the whole of nature as one Individual, whose parts, i.e., all bodies, vary in infinite ways, without any change of the whole individual."[17]

The interactive accuracy of perceptions

Moreover, "the human Mind is a part of the infinite intellect of God."[18] Hence, Spinoza draws the conclusion that "[t]he human Body," again *pace* Descartes, "exists, as we are aware of it,"[19] for what we are aware of are the relations, the responses of, our bodies to and within the environment. These, taken in and of themselves, are accurate, for they capture and express our responses to the relations obtaining *between* self and environment. So perception, and not only true knowledge as ratio and as intuition, is accurate (although not "adequate") since it is relational and captures relations considered in themselves (as fragments), relations which constitute the mind and the body. True knowledge, as *ratio* and intuition, is also relational, in fact, infinitely relational and contextual, and hence truer and more adequate in part because of their broader contextualization. While perception captures accurately the experience we have of each encounter between self and world when thought of in isolation, our *understanding* and *explanation* of our affections in these encounters can be either fragmented and ordered according to the various associative cognitive operations of the imagination (the common order of nature and happenstance), or come to be known within the true causal order of nature (that is by the power of the mind to actively think and reflect and reconstitute its understanding via reason and intuition). In either case, it is the contextual relational nature of mind/body and world, their co-construction, which is being captured and expressed by the mind (and enacted by the body).

Moreover, we must recall that for Spinoza the mind's thinking is not outside the world looking in but is the expression of the world "worlding" in

---

[15] *Ethics* IIp13c, ax3, lemma 5.   [16] *Ethics* IIp13c, ax3, lemmas 6 and 7.   [17] *Ethics* IIp13, lemma 7s.
[18] *Ethics* IIp11c.   [19] *Ethics* IIp13c.

us, so to speak, just as much as body is. Hence thinking *enacts* a constitutive structure of self and world and is as much an *expression* of reality, of God or nature, as is extension. The mind cannot have thoughts that are merely *about* the world and not constitutive of its own self-constitutive enacting relations, for thinking is a doing and being in and with and within infinitely extending contexts. Hence as the mind reconstructs the mind–body's causal origins and ongoing relations, the ideas of those origins and relations become explicitly what the mind–body is since a mind does not *have* ideas but *is* its ideas as acts of thought. Hence there is no boundary where the mind stops but rather it enlarges in scope to encompass its actual embodied relations. It is one of Spinoza's basic principles (*Ethics* IIp7) that "[t]he order and connection of ideas is the same as the order and connection of things." Hence, the mind in thinking, like the body in (inter)acting, is always co-constituting itself anew in relation to the environment. Thinking is a type of action and interaction.

The common notions: the basic relational building blocks of all knowledge

What Spinoza refers to as the "common order of nature" is the world co-constructed in perception by the imaginative associative operations of the mind. This imaginative linkage of perceptions (in which each idea is itself a co-construction accurately expressing a relation of body–mind to immediate environment) captures an immediate location through application of the mind's provincial associations – understanding and explanation via similarity, emotional contagion, prejudice, the idiosyncrasies of culture and language, and the like. In the cases of rational and intuitive understanding and explanation, percepts (each consisting of an accurate yet isolated grasp of self and world de-coupled from its imaginative associations – although not from images *per se*) are linked, instead, in terms of true universals.

A transition from associative imaginative thinking to rational thinking is possible because of the common notions which span all things. Common notions are defined as "those things that are common to all things and are equally in the part as in the whole, [and hence] can be conceived only adequately."[20] They are categories that do not suffer from the distortion of imaginative association since they gather together universal features that are ubiquitous and therefore cannot be misconstrued – their local grasp of the self in the immediate environment captures a universal pattern. The common

---

[20] *Ethics* IIp38.

notions cut the world at its joints (in contrast to most imaginative universals, which create categories via arbitrary and often idiosyncratic temporal and other associations and similarities). Imaginative categories generally capture only the common order of nature, which is expressive of the arbitrariness of our experience, culture, language, and the like. Common notions, however, since they cannot be perceived but accurately because of their ubiquity (and hence cannot be distorted by time and place, partiality and prejudice), form the bridge between imagination and reason. Rational understanding, the second kind of knowledge, is built upon common notions and is general in character. The common notions, according to *Ethics* IIp44c2dem, "are the foundations of Reason." There are not only universal common notions but also subordinate common notions of a more limited scope and range of knowability.

A common notion is an imaginative universal that, because of its ubiquity, grasps a rational truth and cannot distort it. (The ideas of motion and rest are Spinoza's paradigmatic examples of common notions.) Spinoza illustrates what he means by 'common notions' with a mathematical rule. Rather than a single concept or an abstraction, a common notion is a principle that operates in every case of a given phenomenon and explains it. Thus common notions are concrete rather than abstract imaginative universals. In *Ethics* IIp38 and p39, Spinoza offers a more detailed account of common notions:

> P38: Those things which are common to all, and which are equally in the part and in the whole, can only be conceived adequately . . .
> Cor.: From this it follows that there are certain ideas, *or* notions, common to all men. For (by L 2) all bodies agree in certain things, which (by P38) must be perceived adequately, *or* clearly and distinctly, by all.
> P39: If something is common to, and peculiar to, the human Body and certain external bodies by which the human Body is usually affected, and is equally in the part and in the whole of each of them, its idea will also be adequate in the Mind.
> Cor.: From this it follows that *the mind is the more capable of perceiving many things adequately as its Body has many things in common with other bodies.*[21]

---

[21] My emphasis. I note here in passing Spinoza's profound commitment to the material basis of cognition. This flies in the face of those who view Spinoza as the quintessential rationalist for whom reason is divorced from body and world. Nothing could be further from the truth. James (1997, 205) remarks: "Turning to the claim that reasoning is divorced from everything bodily, we have seen that this is as far as possible from Spinoza's view." See also Collier 1991.

Hence the common notions are not only the bridge between imaginative thinking and reason (and from the latter to intuition) but also between self and environment, for they neutralize the distortion of one's own body and mind upon perception. "What is common to all things . . . and is equally in the part and in the whole, does not constitute the essence of any singular thing."[22] Ratio is based on common notions, and Spinoza says of it in Part Five that it is abstract or universal knowledge in contrast with intuitive knowledge, which is knowledge of singular things. Intuitive knowledge is the knowledge of singulars as they are shown to be within (*Ethics* Vp36s) and dependent upon God for their essence and existence. It is intuitive knowledge that becomes the basis for the true understanding of the self in nature because it traces knowledge of singular essences to their divine attribute (*Ethics* IIp40s2), or, vice versa (*Ethics* Vp36s), from the attribute to the singular essence. Common notions neutralize the character of the *conatus* of the mind that makes percepts more about ourselves than about the world. Thus they give us a *true relation* enabling us to build rationally (and then intuitively) upon categories that put ourselves into universal nature implicitly and, ultimately, explicitly via intuitive knowledge, which is knowledge of particulars in God (or alternatively, the knowledge of God modally down to each singular thing, especially the singular things we care most about, ourselves, in self-knowledge in God).

Because they cannot but be true, common notions form the basis of rational knowledge, the possibility of rendering the localism of imaginative association into universal causal explanation in God or nature. Here in the common notions a *relation* is expressed that constitutes not only body and environment, self and other, but is true universally of nature in every part and whole. Hence they cannot but be true when perceived even in isolated fragmented ways. They are ubiquitously and universally embodied and embedded so that in these cognitive building blocks of interactions of self and world (for example, an expression of self and world interaction in a proportion of motion and rest), each common notion expresses a (concrete universal) relation that is the same whether imaginatively expressive of local context or rationally expressive of the universal natural causal context. In these common notions, the relations and interactions that constitute experience are true because no provincial bias or idiosyncratic point of view befogs them. They are windows into the self in nature as well as self in immediate context as well as into the world. This is Spinoza's answer to the

---

[22] *Ethics* IIp37.

cogito. The common notions serve to locate each of us in our embeddedness in the world. Not only are the ubiquitous common features the source of our immediate experience, but they serve as the basis of the possibility of adequate ideas, that is of knowledge. They guarantee that knowledge is to be found neither within our minds alone nor in an external nature from which all subjectivity has been extracted but instead in the shared features and meeting of mind and world.

To introduce one's own mind–body into these categories by explaining oneself in terms of them is to place oneself, the singular individual, within the infinitely contextual and causally explanatory systems of nature. In contemporary terms, it is to come to understand oneself within bodies of scientific explanation, for rational knowledge not only employs categories true to nature but also traces the causes of the self to infinity within nature or God. It is causally explanatory as well as rationally categorized or principled. These are Spinoza's finite series of infinite causes (i.e. *natura naturans*, the attributes, which are in certain respects analogous to what we would call today the most general scientific principles and laws) and the infinite series of finite causes (i.e. *natura naturata*, the modes, the causal series and webs that gives rise to singular events and objects).[23] Intuitive knowledge, in contrast to *ratio*, revises self-understanding in terms of larger and larger bodies of knowledge of the world as well as identifying the particular causal paths that result in this singular object, person or event, thereby re-situating (in each of our cases) the *conatus* of the mind(–body) within its true constitutive contexts to infinity, that is within God.

> The idea of a singular thing which actually exists has God for a cause not insofar as he is infinite, but insofar as he is considered to be affected by another idea of a singular thing which actually exists; and of this [idea] God is also the cause, insofar as he is affected by another third [NS: idea], and so on, to infinity.[24]

For "the essence of man is constituted by certain modifications of God's attributes."[25] Yet

> the being of substance does not pertain to the essence of man (by Ip10). Therefore it is something (by Ip15) which is in God, and which can neither be or be conceived without God, *or* (by Ip25c) an affection, *or* mode, which expresses God's nature in a certain and determinate way.[26]

---

[23] *Ethics* Ip29s.   [24] *Ethics* IIp9.   [25] *Ethics* IIp10c.   [26] *Ethics* IIp10c dem.

The power of thinking

Spinoza makes it very clear in *Ethics* Vp4s that "*the Mind has no other power than that of thinking and forming adequate ideas*" (my emphasis). Hence action is not a discrete process separable from thinking. Yet there are distinctions in the quality of one's thinking, and hence of one's agency. Spinoza distinguishes between the passive and active character of thinking. In *Ethics* IIp29s he says that:

> the Mind has, not an adequate, but only a confused [NS: and mutilated] knowledge, of itself, its own Body, and of external bodies, so long as it perceives things from the common order of nature, i.e., so long as it is *determined externally*, from fortuitous encounters with things, to regard this or that, and not so long as it is *determined internally*, from the fact that it regards a number of things at once, to understand their agreements, differences, and oppositions. For so often as it is *disposed internally*, in this or in another way, then it regards things clearly and distinctly. (My emphasis)

The power of the mind, Spinoza tells us, is only in its thinking and the power of thinking resides only in its capacity for internal determination. For "so often as it is *disposed internally*, in this or in another way, then it regards things clearly and distinctly."[27] What does that mean? The internality of thinking refers to both ratio and intuition but means something different in each case. In ratio it refers to the mind when it "regards a number of things at once, to understand their agreements, differences, and oppositions," which is the rational reconstruction of the common notions, the common properties of things, and what follows logically from such a secure basis. In intuitive knowledge, Spinoza tells us in *Ethics* Vp24, it refers to a tracing of causes from God to singulars or from singulars to God as cause. While, "[i]nadequate and confused ideas follow by the same necessity as adequate or clear and distinct ideas" (*Ethics* IIp36), and action follows from either case and is a necessary outgrowth of the type of mental operation involved (whether clear or confused), since there is no power of acting independent of understanding, it is the origin and character of our ideas that make the difference. The intellectual difference is a fundamental difference in mental operation, a difference between internal versus external, active versus passive mental operations. In imaginative cognitive operations we are passive because the links that fill our causal explanatory grasp of self and world are picked up passively by the mind from the ways in which the common order of nature (the local context) connects things with each other and

---

[27] *Ethics* IIp29s.

ourselves with our immediate world. The mind's passivity, its weakness occurs when it is determined principally by its embeddedness in immediate circumstances and narrow contexts, which write themselves unreflectively upon the mind, filling it with imaginative associations of time and place. The mind is dominated by these association – which it superficially is and enacts, until educated by its own active rational and intuitive reflective thinking processes. These are the only two ways that we conceive things as actual, Spinoza says, thereby forming a conceptual (and motivational) world for ourselves, "either insofar as we conceive them to exist in relation to a certain time and place, or insofar as we conceive them to be contained in God and to follow from the necessity of the divine nature" (*Ethics* Vp29s).

Such an active reconstruction of one's own experience via discovering its rational causal constitution to infinity – that is, in God (*Ethics* Ip15), for "God is the immanent, not the transitive, cause of all things" (*Ethics* Ip18) – is an emotionally rich process with emotionally therapeutic consequences that inform action. According to *Ethics* Vp14 and its demonstration:

> The Mind can bring it about that all the Body's affections, or images of things, are related to the idea of God.
>
> Dem.: There is no affection of the Body of which the Mind cannot form a clear and distinct conception (by P4). And so it can bring it about (by IP15) that they are related to the idea of God, q.e.d.

What results is that, "[h]e who understands himself and his affects clearly and distinctly rejoices (by IIIp53), and this Joy is accompanied by the idea of God (by P14)" (*Ethics* Vp15dem). The consequence is the intellectual love of God, a full-scale transformation in emotion and motivation if ever there was one. "The greatest striving [*conatus*] of the Mind, and its greatest virtue is understanding things by the third kind of knowledge." And, "[t]he more the Mind is capable of understanding things by the third kind of knowledge the more it desires to understand them by the this kind of knowledge" (*Ethics* Vp25, Vp26). Moreover, according to *Ethics* IVapp5, "things are good only insofar as they aid man to enjoy the life of the Mind." Emotion and desire, a person's central motivation, their *conatus*, their essence, their very self as we would say today, has become transformed. That is Spinoza's ethics or theory of moral agency.

Instead of accounting for moral agency in terms of a free will that somehow originates its own actions in and due to a self beyond contextual explanation and description, Spinoza's moral agency embraces the notion that each of us lies at a series of causal nexuses, with the expansive boundaries between these series constantly shifting. The original constitutive images in which *each image brings together self and world* in passive reflection of the common order of nature, the localism of time and place, and which harbor and drive all our originally passive emotions, are reconnected through acts of self-understanding in God with a consequent wholesale transformation in motivation toward discovering love and joy in nature. Understanding thus reframes personal experience, making us realize ever more completely our embeddedness in the world. It is a far cry from, and perhaps Spinoza's answer to, Descartes's subjective turn that aims to control the mental content of the mind so that it acts *upon* the world, upon nature, upon body in an imagined increased independence *from* it. Spinoza's understanding of the power of mind enables each of us to free ourselves (to varying degrees) from the ongoing pain of pasts passively shaped by narrow provincial worlds, from the tyrannies and agonies of memory, their constitutive shaping of and power over our *conatus*, our intimate emotional self and settings, through recasting ourselves via an intellect that captures the true contours and scope of self within nature and universe. For "we feel and know by experience that we are eternal. For the Mind feels those things that it conceives in understanding no less than those it has in the memory."[28] Hence the two visions of human agency, the Spinozist versus the Cartesian – whose echoes I believe can still be heard in contemporary compatibilism's notion of the moral agency as a will that in some significant respect originates its own actions and then acts *upon* (rather than within) body and environment – are diametrically opposed. Why should we wish upon Spinoza a latter-day version of the Cartesian normative stance?

Ethics within the Arabic Aristotelian philosophic orbit: the education of desire[29]

Medieval Arabic philosophy benefited from having inherited the Greek philosophical naturalism and intellectualism of the Alexandrian School of Neoplatonism of late antiquity. By the sixth century the philosophic focus in that school had shifted decisively toward Aristotle, and specifically toward a markedly embodied and naturalist understanding of Aristotle. Rather than serving the primary purpose of supplying an introduction to the Neoplatonic curriculum, and particularly to the dialogues of Plato, as Aristotle's philosophy had done in the Athenian School of Neoplatonism

---

[28] *Ethics* Vp23s.
[29] See Adamson and Taylor 2005; Black 2005; D'Ancona 2005; Ravven 2013, 182–239; Reisman 2005 (Reisman's extensive quotation [55] is from Al-Farabi's *Appearance of Philosophy*). On Alexandria versus Rome, see Niehoff 2011. On the philosophic religion of Al-Farabi, see Fraenkel 2009.

in its heyday, in the Alexandrian School, it was Aristotle himself who was deemed the epitome of philosophic achievement and the model of philosophic endeavor. The Alexandrian reading of Aristotle emphasized the intelligibility of nature to the human mind, and the divine gift of reason as binding together God, cosmos, and human soul. The spiritual path toward God, in this view, was available to all human beings via reason, which is to say, through the study of philosophy and science. The intellectual spirituality of the Alexandrian school became the foundation of Arabic philosophy when the area around Alexandria fell into Muslim hands and rule at the end of antiquity, in the seventh century, early in the rise and expansion of Islam. The Alexandrian School, perhaps representing the most naturalist and rationalist version of the classical Greek philosophical tradition, thus came within the Muslim orbit.[30]

In the Arabic philosophical tradition, Aristotle's moral intellectualism was accentuated and developed further by the *falasifa* who, at the same time, downplayed his notion of practical moral virtue.[31] In interpreting Aristotle, the *falasifa* emphasized the sections of the *Nicomachean Ethics* about the divine nature of the pure intellectual life, reading the sections on practical reason in the light of the sections on the spiritual attainment (and the concomitant transformation in desire) emerging from the ecstatic joy of the discovery of the underlying principles of nature and universe. They downplayed Aristotle's account of the training of character via the practical intellect and the choice of the mean between two extremes in favor of the passages in which Aristotle introduced a vision of God as engaged in theoretical contemplation of the scientific order of the universe, a natural order of which God's activity of theoretical thinking was itself the eternal necessary and ongoing source (a Neoplatonic reading). A quote from Averroës captures the thrust of this approach:

> This power [of practical intellect] is a power common to all people who are not lacking in humanity, and people only differ in it by degrees. As for the second power [the theoretical intellect], it is clear from its nature that it is very divine and found only in some people, who are the ones primarily intended by Divine Providence over this species.[32]

Aristotle held that training in habits would promote the kind of character which, in turn, would make possible ethical discernment or moral perception of the virtuous mean between extremes, resulting in a life of moderation.

---

[30] D'Ancona 2005, 10–31.
[31] Regarding the general moral intellectualism of the *falasifa*, see Adamson 2010.
[32] Averroës, *Talkhis kitab al-nafs*, quoted in Black 2005, 323.

The lesser practical virtue of moderation, following Galen, was associated with the body and generally thought of on the medical analogy as the health of the (lower parts of the) soul, those that governed the body. Yet this Aristotelian notion of practical training in habits of virtuous character was largely denigrated within the Arabic philosophical milieu as somewhat trivial and insufficiently intellectual to be transformative of the whole personality. Hence it was downplayed by the Arabic philosophers in favor of the passionate and immoderate embrace of intellectual virtue, the rigorous pursuit of universal theoretical truths. The pursuit of intellectual virtue, in contrast, was thought of in terms of ultimate spiritual transformation and ecstatic rapture. Attainment of a degree of intellectual virtue thus was thought to offer a taste of the joy of eternity.

There were ascetic and moderate versions of the moral intellectualism that ascribed virtue strictly to intellectual endeavors for their own sake. Both versions focused on coming to know "intelligible objects," that is, the bodies of knowledge of the theoretical sciences and philosophy. The moral ascetic believed that intellectual aims alone were worth pursuing, while the moral moderate believed that practical and social goods could have instrumental benefit or were indifferent. The two positions could also be reconciled in a "two-level ethic" that ascribed to the elite alone the goal of the pursuit of intellectual virtue and the intellectual life, whereas the rest of humanity was relegated to having as its proper moral aim the mundane life of moderation and practical virtues. Only the philosophically and scientifically educated had the opportunity to pursue the superior moral life of intellectual virtue, which developed the (theoretical rational) soul, rather than having to settle for the pursuit of the lesser virtue of moderation, a virtue focusing on developing the (mental abilities associated with the) body and the social body.

Maimonides' psychology of moral agency: naturalism meets intellectualism[33]

I argue here that Maimonides is squarely in the intellectualist and naturalist tradition of Greek classical moral theory as it was intensified in the Arabic philosophical appropriation of it. Al-Farabi's naturalist approach to human nature admirably expresses that of Maimonides, and, in my view, of Spinoza as well:

---

[33] This section is a response to Parens 2012, Chapter 6.

Man is a part of the world, and if we wish to understand his aim and activity and use and place, then we must first know the purpose of the whole world, so that it will become clear to us what man's aim is, as well as the fact that man is necessarily a part of the world, in that his aim is necessary for realizing the ultimate purpose of the whole world.[34]

Sarah Stroumsa, in her portrait of Maimonides in his Islamic Mediterranean world, describes even his ongoing desire to increase his professional medical knowledge, and not just his philosophical and scientific endeavors, in terms of his intellectual commitments. Stroumsa writes that "Maimonides' reflections on medicine highlight his continuous monitoring of human intellectual activities. On the one hand, he avidly strives for the acquisition of knowledge and understanding, pushing himself to exhaustion in the desire to learn more." It is his intellectual integrity and seriousness, not any disdain for the rational enterprise itself, she argues, that led Maimonides to take extraordinary care in evaluating intellectual arguments and sources, so that he "on the other hand" also "restrains the craving for unattainable knowledge and warns against false pretense that comes with it."[35] We clearly hear an echo of Maimonides' "intellectual thought in constantly loving Him should be aimed at" in Spinoza's intellectual love of God.[36] Maimonides writes in *Guide* III.51, for example,

> if . . . you have apprehended God and His acts in accordance with what is required by the intellect, you should afterwards engage in totally devoting yourself to Him, endeavor to come close to Him, and strengthen the bond between you and Him – that is, the intellect.[37]

Shlomo Pines famously proposed that Maimonides' innovation was to radicalize the intellectualist tendency of Arabic Aristotelianism by proposing an opposition between the true and the good.[38] In the *Guide*, Maimonides notes that:

> fine and bad . . . belong to things generally accepted as known, not to those cognized by the intellect. For one does not say: it is fine that heaven is spherical, and it is bad that the earth is flat; rather one says true and false with regard to these assertions . . . Now man in virtue of his intellect knows truth

---

[34] Al-Farabi, *Philosophy of Plato and Aristotle*, 'The Philosophy of Aristotle', quoted in Reisman 2005, 69.
[35] Stroumsa 2009, 137. Stroumsa thus weighs in on the intellectualist side of the scholarly debate about the meaning of Maimonides' comments on the limits of knowledge, a debate initiated by Shlomo Pines in his famous paper, "The Limitations of Human Knowledge According to Al-Farabi, ibn Bajja, and Maimonides" (Pines 1979), still ongoing, and recruiting a new generation of scholars taking sides. See particularly Altmann 1987 for a definitive rebuttle to Pines.
[36] *Guide of the Perplexed* III.51, Maimonides 1963, 621.   [37] *Ibid.*, 620.   [38] Pines 1990.

from falsehood . . . [W]ith regard to what is of necessity, there is no good and evil at all.[39]

Maimonides' version of moral intellectualism, Pines argued, may be the purest in the history of philosophy. Maimonides' doctrine includes a moral theory and not just an account of the overriding value of theoretical intellectual endeavor over conventional moral endeavor, in that the intellectual life has within it its own sources of moral agency and the shaping of motivation. A careful review of several passages in the *Guide* will, I think, convince the reader that for Maimonides theoretical study for its own sake – the true – was the *only* avenue to the deep moral transformation of motivation, while the training and habituation in moral action according to the mean could serve merely as a helpful preparation for engaging in philosophy, thereby also contributing to social stability and political utility. Spinoza's intellectualist account of moral agency dovetails with this reading of Maimonides. The overall thrust of Maimonides' transformation of the heart through theoretical endeavor, the philosophic and scientific knowledge of God, and its anticipation of Spinoza's intellectual love of God, is nicely set forth by Kraemer in his biographical study:

> Knowing the nature of the universe is a way to attain love of God, which is realized only through apprehension of the whole of being and the contemplation of God's wisdom manifested in it. This contemplation consists of correct opinions concerning the whole of being, which corresponds to the various theoretical sciences by which these opinions are validated. This philosophical interpretation of the love of God is closer to Spinoza's intellectual love of God (*amor Dei intellectualis*) than to any description of the love of the divine in the Talmud and Midrash. Maimonides clarified at the start that his main concern was science and the study of nature, the foundation of his restoring Judaism as a religion of reason and enlightenment.[40]

The argument of this chapter is that Spinoza recruited Maimonides' psychology of philosophical religion as the basis for his account of moral psychology, the perfected moral agency of a Spinozist philosopher.

Maimonides' natural determinism

In the Aristotelian philosophical tradition, mind, as form, was believed to be more amenable to scientific natural explanation than matter was. In contrast to the recalcitrance and only approximate character of the way that physical principles were embodied in singular objects, the human mind, in

---

[39] *Guide of the Perplexed* I.2, Maimonides 1963, 24–25 (my emphasis)   [40] Kraemer 2008, 326.

the act of knowing, could capture, and hence conform with, the divine causal principles it extracted and abstracted from natural physical processes (in this reading of especially Aristotle's *De Anima* Book III). Maimonides makes clear in the *Guide* that he believed that the natural necessity that holds sway in the universe was also true of the human person and precisely of human action. He puts it explicitly and succinctly: God is

> He who arouses a particular volition in the irrational animal and who has *necessitated this particular free choice in the rational animal* and has made the natural things pursue their course – chance being but an excess of what is natural [emphasis added].[41]

Hence the human will was as embedded in the divine necessary natural causality in the same way that objects are subject to the laws of physics, on the one hand, and animals follow their desires, on the other. Hence, for neither Maimonides nor Spinoza could the human will be regarded as outside nature, choosing beyond its constitutive causes, beyond its desires.

Maimonides is here following Aristotle (who argued that "mind is never found producing movement without appetite, for wish is a form of appetite") in maintaining that all action originates in desire and never in reason or thinking alone.[42] It was the intellect that could transform desire, all motivation, into the love of God, thereby making the love of God's world, the divine presence in and the divine origin of nature the spring of all one's being and actions – positions recruited and built upon by Spinoza. Maimonides perhaps even out-Aristotles Aristotle in his version of the motivationally transformative power of the intellectual life; and that moral vision is an important inspiration for Spinoza's rethinking of moral agency.

Maimonides' downplaying of practical morality

In the *Guide*, reason designates the philosophic life and never practical moral deliberation. Maimonides is on firm Aristotelian ground in distinguishing sharply between the theoretical and practical intellects insofar as Aristotle repeatedly tells the reader that "practical wisdom is not scientific knowledge." Aristotle distinguishes between the theoretical and the practical in content as well as in mental operations. Theoretical thinking is the highest human virtue and also divine; it is an activity engaged in for its own sake, and it results in divine-like human fulfillment and joy, according to Aristotle's *Nicomachean Ethics*, Book X.

---

[41] *Guide of the Perplexed* II.48, Maimonides 1963, 410.   [42] Aristotle, *De Anima*, III.10, 433a 24–25.

In that book, too, Aristotle explicitly maintains that the divine thinking of the ideas that become the natural principles inherent in embodied singulars in the world is strictly an engagement in theoretical knowing; it does not partake at all of practical intellect or moral practice. And human contemplation follows that pattern as well:

> But that perfect happiness is a contemplative activity will appear from the following consideration as well. We assume the gods to be above all other beings blessed and happy; but what sort of actions must we assign to them? Acts of justice? Will not the gods seem absurd if they make contracts and return deposits, and so on? Acts of a brave man, then . . . ? Or liberal acts? . . . Is not such praise tasteless, since they have no bad appetites? If we were to run through them all, the circumstances of action would be found trivial and unworthy of the gods. Still, everyone supposes that they *live* and therefore they are active . . . the activity of God, which surpasses all others in blessedness, must be contemplative and of human activities, therefore, that which is most akin to this must be most of the nature of happiness . . . Happiness extends, then, just so far as contemplation does, and those to whom contemplation more fully belongs are more truly happy . . . Happiness, therefore, must be some form of contemplation.[43]

It is philosophers, Aristotle concludes in this chapter, who are most like the gods in their strictly contemplative activity, and who are thus also the happiest. Maimonides honors statesmen, the prophets, who are philosophers but still return to the cave of ordinary social and political life and the demands and responsibilities of leadership. Nevertheless, when envisioning Adam before his rebellion in what he regards as the story or allegory of the Garden of Eden, Maimonides depicts him as engaging in pure contemplation. Adam "had no faculty that was engaged in any way in the consideration of generally accepted things," Maimonides informs the reader. Yet at the same time, Maimonides says of him, "[t]hrough the intellect one distinguishes between truth and falsehood, and that was found in [Adam] in its perfection and integrity."[44] In an ideal world, in an Eden, practical intellect and conventional values would not be necessary because desires would not be unruly or need training or coercive management. In Eden there would be no good or evil but only true or false – just as Aristotle maintains.

Maimonides, however, in the *Guide*, does not attribute the moral and political life to the practical intellect but instead, following al-Farabi, to the

---

[43] *Nicomachean Ethics* X.8, 1178b8–1178b32.
[44] *Guide of the Perplexed* I.2, Maimonides 1963, 25 and 24.

imagination.[45] It is still cognitive but no longer rational; conventional social ethics and justice are matters merely of the imagination. They have no spiritual transformative force in themselves (although the imagination also renders some basic truths of philosophy into accessible narrative form for the masses and thereby provides a window into truth); nevertheless, they lack the power to transform the emotions in all but superficial and external ways, leaving moral motivation largely untouched and unchanged. Intellectual love can transform the heart, Maimonides writes near the conclusion of the *Guide*: "As for the opinions that the Torah teaches us – namely, the apprehension of His being and His unity, may He be exalted – these opinions teach us *love*." These opinions "include the apprehension of His being as He, may He be exalted, is in truth." Obedience to the actions prescribed by the Law, in contrast, Maimonides concludes, is the result of fear rather than love.[46] Adam, as Maimonides interprets what he regards as the allegorical biblical story, had no need of anything but the theoretical intellect and could be completely engaged in the fulfillment of his divinely ordained human end of coming to understand the natural world with its concomitant rapturous love of God, up to his moment of turn to the lure of bodily desires, which for Maimonides includes and encompasses all cognitive and affective mental capacities beneath (or other than) theoretical reason or intellect.

So the moral of Maimonides' tale is that theoretical wisdom and its pursuit have no need for augmentation as the source of moral motivation. Human nature *in toto* is fulfilled in the intellectual life. It is the transformation of the heart through the rigorous engagement of the mind in theoretical intellectual pursuits, pursuits that aim toward the knowledge of God in the only way that that knowledge is possible to the extent that it *is* possible, which is the nature of consummate moral agency for Maimonides. Summarizing his position in the *Guide*, Maimonides writes:

> [True] worship ought only to be engaged in after intellectual conception has been achieved. If . . . you have apprehended God and His acts [i.e. physics] in accordance with what is required by the intellect, you should afterwards engage in totally devoting yourself to Him, endeavor to come closer to Him, and strengthen the bond between you and Him – that is, the intellect . . . The Torah has made it clear that this last worship to which we have drawn attention . . . can only be engaged in after apprehension is achieved; it says: To love the Lord your God, and to serve Him with all your heart and with all

---

[45] For an extended treatment of Maimonides' relegation of the political and the social to the imagination in the *Guide*, see Ravven 2001a; 2001b; and 2001c.

[46] *Guide of the Perplexed* III.52, Maimonides 1963, 630.

your soul. Now we have made it clear several times that love is proportionate to apprehension [i.e. theoretical understanding].[47]

This passage is Spinoza's source for his famous doctrine of the intellectual love of God, a Maimonidean-inspired account of the life of the mind that Spinoza explicitly designated "ethics," and what we today would call moral agency. Moreover, Spinoza also follows Maimonides in distinguishing between the moral life of the philosopher, which for Spinoza is the theory of motivational transformation and moral agency of the *Ethics*, versus the imaginative practical yet coercive moral life of the masses, which is the subject of the TTP.

The unification of the mind with nature:
Aristotle, Maimonides, Spinoza

While the more fully systematically elaborated and rationally explicated moral theory that Spinoza develops in the *Ethics* can help the reader of the *Guide* understand Maimonides' underlying theoretical thrust, an Aristotelian doctrine originating in the *De Anima*, which Maimonides refers to several times, can help the reader better understand (or become aware of) Spinoza's identification or unification of the mind (and the body) with nature. Kraemer points out that Maimonides repeatedly emphasizes (in *Guide* I.68) "a dictum of the philosophers that 'God is the intellect, the intellectually cognizing subject, and the intellectually cognized object'."[48] That philosophical position is an elaboration of Aristotle's claim in the *De Anima* that the activity of theoretical thinking brings together the reason inherent in natural processes and the reason inherent in thought. Kraemer goes on to propose that in maintaining this position, Maimonides is anticipating Spinoza:

> The statement that God is the intellect, the intellectually cognizing subject, and the intellectually cognized object has far-reaching implications, for if God knows the system of forms, or natural laws, existing in the universe, we must consider him as identical with these forms and laws, which constitute the scientific world system. If so, Maimonides' God is like Spinoza's divine attribute of intellect.[49]

In respect to moral agency, if the mind in active theoretical knowledge of the laws of nature becomes one with its objects, and if the mind is not a container of ideas but the active process of thinking, the identity of the

---

[47] *Guide of the Perplexed* III.51, Maimonides 1963, 620–621   [48] Kraemer 2008, 330.   [49] *Ibid.*, 331.

knower becomes one in scope and content with all natural causal explanations beginning with oneself. For Spinoza, it is not only mind that so expands, but the body's scope is extended to the systems in which it is nested and from which it derives. Each human body is continuous and within the infinite body of nature. Motivation is transformed to express the desire for survival of the nested natural systems within systems to infinity.

Aristotle argued that in the activity of theoretical thinking, which is to say, the study of nature for its own sake, the mind and its object (the principles of nature) become identical: "In every case the mind which is actively thinking is the objects which it thinks."[50] Maimonides follows Aristotle in maintaining that the activity of the intellect in theoretical thinking and its object are one and the same. Hence, the mind's boundaries extend infinitely beyond the skin, potentially to all scientific principles. This is possible because the mind is not a thing that thinks and contains ideas but the activity of thinking itself, for "in the case of every intellect," Maimonides writes, "its act is identical in essence; for intellect in *actu* [that is, the intellect engaged in active thinking] is not one thing and its act another thing" – a position that Spinoza also holds (*Ethics* IIdef3). Maimonides is somewhat cagey, we see here in *Guide* I.68, about whether he believes that when the human person achieves intellectual perfection to the extent possible in coming to understand principles of nature (physics), the human mind in that knowing approximates some infinitesimal corner of the divine mind. For he also maintains that we cannot know God's essence but only his attributes of action, which is to say the manifestation of the divine in and as natural processes. Nevertheless, our mind in engaging in the rigorous understanding of nature comes as close to the divine, manifesting divine natural principles in its thinking, as possible. Uniting with those principles of nature, it extends beyond the bounds of the body to natural laws wherever they are located, finding in the event rapture and contentment, fulfillment of the personality and transformed agency – an Edenic world in which the heart through intellectual love does freely what only coercion and institutional regulation enforce in the masses post-Eden.

Moral psychology and immortality

Alfred Ivry has maintained that "Maimonides subscribed to the dominant epistemological paradigm of the period as laid out by Al-Farabi, Avicenna before him, and by Alexander of Aphrodisias in the third century."[51]

---

[50] Aristotle, *De Anima*, III.7, 431b 17–18.   [51] Ivry 2009, 54.

This paradigm involved the rational laws of nature being located in the heavens in a cosmic entity, the agent or active intellect. The agent intellect, held to be "a repository of universal ideas," endows all natural objects with their natural forms. "It is that supernal intelligence," Ivry writes, "that informs all sublunar objects and renders them intelligible, enabling us to comprehend them." He further notes that Maimonides in the *Guide* and also in *Sefer ha-Madda* in the *Mishneh Torah* "identify[ies] the soul with the rational faculty, treating that faculty alone as constituting the form of man." All other mental as well as corporeal faculties, thus, derive elsewhere than from the agent intellect, which endows the human person with intellect. Hence the human intellect alone has the capacity to become eternal, insofar as it derives from a non-corporeal and eternal source outside the body. In the dynamic act of cognition there is a "complete merging of subject and object," a merger in this case with the natural rational principles or laws residing in the divine hypostasis, the agent intellect. "The act of cognition is regarded as a joining of subject and object, and thus the acquired active intellect [in us] may be said to be with the Agent Intellect, and to be it." Hence only the intellect in the active theoretical grasp of physical science, and not those other mental capacities emerging from embodiment and that constitute individuation, are immortal and merged with the eternal agent or active intellect. Moreover, Ivry continues, "the pleasure to be had from this identification with eternal and therefore divine being is such as to absorb a person's entire life."[52] The intellect, in contrast with practical reason, whose functions in the *Guide* are absorbed into the imagination, does not engage in choice. Ivry reminds us that the theoretical intellect is not "that part of the rational faculty that is said to deliberate, cogitate, discern, and make choices." As he puts it,

> there is no choice for the theoretical intellect. It must embrace the truth once it meets it. It naturally desires the good, which is eternal being. At the level of the acquired intellect, there is no person choosing to know, there is no ghost in the machine ... As long as one wishes to know the truth, he or she is a recognizable individual. Once a person *attains* the truth, all or most of it, that individuality is lost.[53]

Ivry concludes that "Maimonides' theory of cognition subordinates will to intellect, and ultimately leaves volition behind altogether." The ultimate stage "for Maimonides and loyal Maimonideans like Narboni," he points out, is "the submerging of the self in the whole of being, in life as well as in

[52] *Ibid.*, 55–6.   [53] *Ibid.*, 57.

death."[54] My burden in this chapter has been to show that Spinoza is to be counted as one of the "loyal Maimonideans."

Understanding Spinoza's moral agency via Maimonides

Spinoza's is a Maimonidean-inspired vision of theoretical intellect producing the consummate moral agency, a freedom of enlarged perspective, which for Spinoza entails an independence of mind (and heart) from narrow local and coercive origins, yet without the conceit of the self-origination of free will. For Spinoza, as for Maimonides, the hoped-for ideal is to act always from joy and transformed desire, a desire that spans the rediscovery of oneself in nature or God.

In this chapter my intent has been to argue that Spinoza's ethics, his moral psychology of agency, must be understood as an embrace, modification, and elaboration of that of Maimonides. The Maimonidean perfecting of human intellect and motivation as the unification of mind with *the divine reason in nature* through engaging in rigorous philosophical scientific thinking becomes in Spinoza's *Ethics* the expansion and unification not only of human mind but of body as well, toward the infinite and universal scope of our natural constitutive causes, mental and physical. We are nested within, and come to act explicitly as, the infinite scope and co-constitution, embeddedness and embodiedness, of self-in-nature. Spinoza replays the Maimonidean story with crucial modifications: the introduction of the identity of mind and body; the immanence of the divine principles in nature rather than hypostasized in a separate intellect; the relational character of all cognition and hence the merger of self and natural environment at every scale and at every level and not just in the final intellectual grasp. Nevertheless, I hope I have drawn attention to the Maimonidean inspiration informing Spinoza's morally transformative vision of finding oneself beyond the confines of the body and within the embrace of the divinity and infinity of nature.

[54] *Ibid.*, 58.

Virtue, reason, and moral luck: Maimonides, Gersonides, Spinoza

Steven Nadler

Few works in the canon of Western philosophy stand at a richer intersection of intellectual traditions than Spinoza's *Ethics*. An informed study of the treatise's definitions, axioms, propositions, and arguments reveals the variety of influences that lie behind its metaphysical, epistemological, psychological, moral, and political doctrines. These include Descartes, Hobbes, Aristotle, ancient Stoicism (especially Seneca), and contemporary Dutch philosophical, religious, and political writings. What seems to have gone underappreciated, however, is the extent to which the *Ethics* also reveals Spinoza's engagement with medieval Jewish philosophy. While it is fairly common and relatively easy to situate the TTP in a Jewish philosophical context – especially since Spinoza explicitly discusses in that work such thinkers as Abraham ibn Ezra and Maimonides – the Jewish angle, so to speak, of the *Ethics* is quite a bit more opaque.

The Judaic philosophical dimensions of the *Ethics* are particularly evident when Spinoza turns to moral and (for lack of a better term) eschatological matters in Parts Four and Five. I have elsewhere examined how the apparently puzzling doctrine of the eternity of the mind, in Part Five, begins to make a little more sense when read in the context of medieval Jewish discussions of immortality, especially Maimonides (Moshe ben Maimon) and Gersonides (Levi ben Gershom).[1] In this chapter, I show how another feature of Spinoza's moral philosophy – what is essentially his discussion of moral luck – is best situated in the context of the views of Maimonides and Gersonides.

The topic of moral luck concerns the extent to which a person's well-being and flourishing – what the ancient Greeks called *eudaimonia* – is subject to chance, to circumstances beyond his/her control. Can the happiness of a good person be undermined by bad luck? A good deal of moral philosophy since antiquity is concerned with whether or not there is such

[1] See Nadler 2001.

a thing as moral luck – Socrates, for example, denied that the happiness of the virtuous person can be undermined by bad luck in his/her external circumstances – and, if there is, how best to minimize its role in one's life.[2]

Moral luck was certainly a major theme in medieval Jewish philosophy, particularly among rationalists like Maimonides and Gersonides, much as it was for Aristotle, their guide in many philosophical matters. As we shall see, these two of the most important philosophers in Jewish history insisted on the intimate, even necessary connection between intellectual perfection (which, as a function of human reason, is under a person's control), true virtue, and the proper happiness of a human being. Moreover, they argued, the virtue and happiness achieved through perfecting the intellect by rational understanding provides a person with protection against the vicissitudes of nature. Essentially, the more you understand through reason, the better off you are and the more your well-being can withstand the onslaught of unfortunate and unforeseen events in your life. The rational and virtuous person enjoys a kind of immunity from moral luck, while the happiness of the vicious person is at the mercy of chance.

The relationship between knowledge, virtue, happiness, and moral luck is also central to Spinoza's ethical thought. In fact, I argue that Spinoza's conclusions on these matters can be seen as representing the logical culmination of that particular naturalistic and intellectualist tradition in medieval Jewish rationalism.[3]

I

In the philosophical writings of Maimonides and Gersonides, their views on the relationship between virtue – understood as the perfection of the intellect through the pursuit of rational understanding – happiness, and immunity from moral luck (or at least the reduction of the role of luck in a person's life) are found in their accounts of divine providence. For both thinkers, providence is to be understood in fairly naturalistic terms, whereby the actively virtuous person, precisely through his higher cognitive achievements, enjoys a kind of protection from the vicissitudes of fortune in his flourishing. This protection, which represents an advantage that a person may have in the world, does not come by any special actions of God, and certainly not by any miracles; rather, it is simply the natural consequence of the pursuit of intellectual knowledge.

[2] For recent discussions of moral luck, see Nagel 1979 and Williams 1981.
[3] This essay brings together and elaborates upon material I have published elsewhere; see Nadler 2005a, Nadler 2005b, and Nadler 2008.

After rejecting a number of theories of divine providence in his *Guide of the Perplexed* (including the Epicurean view, which is essentially a non-starter because of its denial of a providential God, the Asharite view, and the Aristotelian view), Maimonides proceeds to offer his own account, one that he insists is in accordance with the Law. He explains that in this sublunar realm the only *individuals* to which God's providence extends are human beings. For all other creatures, providence covers only the species and their preservation; and everything in the lifetime of a non-human individual that does not derive from the species to which that individual belongs – for example, speed in a cheetah or hunting instincts in a wolf – is left to chance (*keri*), as the Aristotelian view claims. Moreover, *all* of the events and activities of a human life, without exception, are a matter of divine justice and therefore fall under providence.

> I for one believe that in this lowly world . . . divine providence watches only over the individuals belonging to the human species and that in this species alone all the circumstances of the individuals and the good and evil that befall them are consequent upon the deserts, just as it says: "For all his ways are judgment."[4]

Thus, if a ship at sea is sunk by a storm or a hard wind blows a house down, this is due to "pure chance" – or, more properly, to the regular but (from the perspective of human expectations) unforeseen and uncontrollable causal order of nature[5] – no less than the fact that a particular leaf has fallen off a tree at a particular moment. But the fact that certain people had voluntarily gone on board the ship that sank or had been sitting in the house that was blown down is due not to chance but to "divine will in accordance with the deserts of those people as determined in His judgments."[6]

Now one possible, even natural way of conceiving the divine *modus operandi* in providence for Maimonides needs to be ruled out from the start. There are passages in which Maimonides speaks as if God, seeing the virtues and vices of particular human beings, actively and intentionally chooses to reward and punish them as individuals – perhaps in just the way that the multitude think of providence, with God sending a thunderbolt against one person while snatching another person from the jaws of

---

[4] *Guide of the Perplexed* (henceforth, *Guide*), Part III, Chapter 17, Maimonides 1963, p. 471.
[5] The events are not a matter of "chance" in the sense of being uncaused and random. The sinking of the ship or the blowing down of the house is no less determined by nature's causal order than any other event. Chance enters into the picture only from the perspective of human plans. What is a matter of "chance" or "accident" is the fact that these events are uncontrollable, unforeseen, unfortunate and inconvenient with respect to human endeavors, as well as unrelated to human deserts.
[6] *Guide* III.17, Maimonides 1963, 472.

death (e.g. saving Daniel in the lions' den by an ad hoc intervention). To be sure, Maimonides insists that the people are on board the ship because of the "divine will in accordance with the deserts of those people as determined in His judgments," just as he elsewhere notes how the fate met by many people is "due not to neglect and the withdrawal of providence, but was a punishment for those men because they deserved what befell them."[7] But it is clear that too literal and anthropomorphic a reading of these passages, with God intervening to save or punish a person as if through a miracle, is ultimately inconsistent with what Maimonides considers the proper conception of God. Such language may thus be only an element of Maimonides' exoteric writing, geared for the unsophisticated and unprepared reader, with the truth hidden (among the contradictions that Maimonides acknowledges he has intentionally inserted into the work) for the more philosophical reader.

Indeed, for Maimonides, God's role in providence is, so to speak, much more passive and naturalistic than a superficial reading of such passages would have us believe. God has put into place a system that is there for individual human beings to take advantage of or not, as they choose. And it is the virtuous – understood as those who pursue intellectual virtue, and not merely moral virtue – who choose to do so, while all others are left without its protection.

Maimonides distinguishes between general providence (in Samuel ibn Tibbon's authorized, late twelfth-century Hebrew translation, *hashgaḥah minit*, or providence of the kind), which is constituted by the species' characteristics oriented to its preservation and is (barring unusual circumstances) provided equally to all members of the species, and individual providence (*hashgaḥah 'ishit*), which is particularized to individuals and distributed only according to merits. Both varieties of providence are understood in highly naturalistic and Aristotelian terms. The latter kind of providence, however, comes into play only in the realm of human agency.

Individual providence, Maimonides says, is a function of the emanation and overflow of knowledge from God through the separate intellects governing the spheres of the cosmos (including, penultimately, the agent intellect, the separate intellect whose domain is the sublunar realm) to the human intellect. To the extent that a person receives this overflow, he is under the protection of providence:

---

[7] *Ibid.*, 473.

Divine providence is consequent upon the divine overflow . . . providence is
consequent upon the intellect and attached to it. For providence can only
come from an intelligent being, from One who is an intellect perfect with a
supreme perfection, than which there is no higher. Accordingly, everyone
with whom something of this overflow is united, will be reached by providence to the extent to which he is reached by the intellect.[8]

Individual providence is not an all or nothing affair, but proportionate to
the degree to which a person is virtuous – not simply morally virtuous and
endowed with a good character, which is only a necessary condition for the
summum bonum, but intellectually or rationally virtuous.[9] That is, individual providence is proportionate to the degree to which a person has turned
toward God, directed his attention to the knowledge flowing from God and
thereby perfected his intellect:

When any individual has obtained, because of the disposition of his matter
and his training, a greater proportion of this overflow than others, providence will of necessity watch more carefully over him than over others – if,
that is to say, providence is, as I have mentioned, consequent upon the
intellect. Accordingly, divine providence does not watch in an equal manner
over all the individuals of the human species, but providence is graded as
their human perfection is graded.[10]

In this sense, providence is a reward for (intellectual) virtue and the
perfection of our highest faculties. And despite Maimonides' claim that
the suffering of many is "due not to neglect and the withdrawal of providence, but was a punishment for those men because they deserved what
befell them," it seems clear that it is precisely through approach and withdrawal – that is, the human being's willful approaching to and withdrawing
from the overflow – that providence operates. As long as a person is actively
enjoying the epistemic connection to the divine overflow, that person is *ipso
facto* protected; providence is watching over – or, better, engaged in – such a
person and he is guarded from the vagaries of chance. On the other hand,
when one is not attending to God (either because one has never made the
effort or because, having achieved the connection, one has temporarily
become distracted, perhaps by the pleasures of the senses), one is abandoned
to chance and left to one's own devices in the face of the slings and arrows of
outrageous fortune. The person who is not experiencing the overflow is not
enjoying its benefits. He is at the mercy of nature's elements and his well-
being is subject to whatever may or may not come his way. Providence is no
longer watching over him – not because God is actively punishing him, but

[8] *Ibid.*, 471–472, 474.   [9] See *Guide* I.34.   [10] *Guide* III.18, Maimonides 1963, 475.

because through his own actions he has taken himself outside of the care that providence (the overflow of knowledge) offers and is now exposed to what chance brings:

> With regard to providence watching over excellent men and neglecting the ignorant, it is said: "He will keep the feet of his holy ones, but the wicked shall be put to silence in darkness; for not by strength shall man prevail." It says thereby that the fact that some individuals are preserved from calamities, whereas those befall others, is due not to their bodily forces and their natural dispositions ... but to their perfection and deficiency, I mean their nearness to or remoteness from God. For this reason, those who are near to Him are exceedingly well protected ... whereas those who are far from Him are given over to whatever may happen to befall them. For there is nothing to protect them against whatever may occur; for they are like one walking in darkness, whose destruction is assured.[11]

Those who do not strive for intellectual perfection have no more providential protection than non-human animals. They enjoy only general providence and whatever tools for survival the species confers upon them (as well as upon everyone else). For such people, there is a great deal of moral luck in their lives, insofar as their happiness and well-being, their flourishing, is subject to chance, to circumstances beyond their control.

But what exactly does Maimonides have in mind here? There is some ambiguity as to just what *is* the nature of the protection that, according to Maimonides, divine providence provides and *how* it provides it. The key passage I want to focus on – a passage that has long troubled commentators – is in Part Three, Chapter 51. At one point in this chapter, Maimonides suggests that what the knowledge brought to the human intellect by the divine overflow gives to the righteous person is a way actually to escape the evils around him. Maimonides seems to say here of the intellectually perfected person that he is literally protected from suffering any harm in the world:

> The providence of God, may He be exalted, is constantly watching over those who have obtained this overflow, which is permitted to everyone who makes efforts with a view to obtaining it. If a man's thought is free from distraction, if he apprehends Him, may He be exalted, in the right way and rejoices in what he apprehends, that individual can never be afflicted with evil of any kind ... For the thing that necessarily brings about providence and deliverance from the sea of chance consists in that intellectual overflow ... A human individual's being abandoned to chance so that he

---

[11] *Ibid.*, 475–476.

is permitted to be devoured like the beasts is his being separated from God.
If, however, his God is within him, no evil at all will befall him ... If you
should happen to pass on your way a widely extended field of battle and even
if one thousand were killed to your left and ten thousand to your right, no
evil at all would befall you.[12]

This is a very extraordinary claim for Maimonides, or any philosopher, to
make. It seems to suggest that the virtuous person can truly escape from the
vicissitudes of fortune that affect all beings in this world – to become, in
effect, immune from the forces of nature that govern all events and affect the
well-being of all creatures and that make life a chancy thing. Can
Maimonides really mean this?

This question has been asked by many of Maimonides' readers. It was the
subject of a letter from Samuel ibn Tibbon to Maimonides in 1199, and it has
bedeviled his most recent commentators. Speculation has ranged from those
who suggest that Maimonides must see such extreme divine protection as
involving constant miracles from God to ward off evils from the virtuous, to
those who argue that the stated immunity from external harm comes through
the perfection of the intellect because in achieving such perfection we become
more like disembodied celestial beings, pure intelligences, and are thus
untouched by the physical harms brought by terrestrial events.[13]

Most scholars rightly reject such suggestions as inconsistent with
Maimonides' overall approach to these topics, and especially the naturalistic
tenor of his account of providence. They have therefore concluded by

---

[12] *Guide* III.51, Maimonides 1963, 625–627.
[13] Samuel ibn Tibbon considers the first reading, grounded in miracles, only to conclude that it is
inconsistent with Maimonides' view on the order of nature; in the end, he decides that it is unclear
how Maimonides should be read here. Moshe Narboni argues for the second reading of the chapter.
See Diesendruck 1936 for a summary of these views and the text of Samuel ibn Tibbon's letter in
which he discusses *Guide* III.51. Among more recent commentators, Raffel (1987) believes that
Maimonides, in order to be making a plausible claim, should be interpreted in III.51 as redefining
the locus of personal identity from the mind/body (or form/matter) composite to the intellect alone.
The "I" that is untouched by the evils of this world is not the embodied human being (who obviously
cannot escape all physical harms), but the intellect itself; a virtuous person, when he perfects his
intellect, thereby transcends the physical world and consequently is not touched by its evils. "If the
physical body, then, is not the 'I' which escapes these evils, who or what is? Maimonides' shift on the
nature of human identity, consummated in the Job account, prepares the reader to appreciate the hero
of chapter 51, who is immune from any and all evils, not as a superhuman being, but as that which is
essentially human, the intellect. The intellect emerges as the true self which survives all, and chapter 51
can be understood consistently as an allegory of the individual intellect's attempt at transcendence and
conjunction with God. This final section of the theory describes not just providence through the intellect
for the intellect" (69). My reading differs
from Raffel's in that I believe that Maimonides does not in fact shift the meaning of selfhood, and that
III.51 is about the whole human being who, through the perfection of the intellect, minimizes the
extent to which he is subject to physical harms and moral luck.

saying "no," Maimonides does not really mean what he says in III.51. Even the virtuous person cannot eliminate or even greatly reduce chance or luck in the external circumstances of his or her life. Some of those arrows flying through the field of battle are bound to fall on him.[14] These commentators then argue for another reading, one which renders III.51 consistent with Maimonides' other statements on providence. On this reading (which Samuel ibn Tibbon finds naturally suggested in *Guide* III.23),[15] the person who attends to God will not literally escape the evils that come his way – especially physical evils (the harms that nature brings) and moral evils (what people do to each other), which tend to be due to circumstances well beyond one's control – but he will nonetheless be less troubled by them. The virtuous person's mind is fixated on the true and lasting good – knowledge of God – and he becomes immune to the lure of mutable goods and inured to the travails of his body. He has achieved a lasting state of spiritual well-being and happiness, one that is not subject to the vagaries of chance or moral luck.

Maimonides says that this is the condition of Job at the end of the biblical story. In his first speech, as Maimonides reads it, Job adopts the Aristotelian view: God is not watching over individuals and is causing suffering for no good reason at all, "because of his contempt for the human species and abandonment of it."[16] After God has spoken, however, Job achieves a state of understanding:

> He knew God with a certain knowledge, he admitted that true happiness, which is the knowledge of the deity, is guaranteed to all who know Him and that a human being cannot be troubled in it by any of all the misfortunes in question.[17]

It is not that the good person experiences no loss or harm in his life; after all, Job lost virtually everything. Rather, consumed with his bond with God and possessing true happiness, he cares less about those losses. He may see evils in his lifetime, but they will not constitute an "affliction" for him. Or, to put it another way, if by 'evil' is meant "true evils" – those that harm the

---

[14] Touati (1990, 198), for example, insists that "it is evident that we should not take literally" what Maimonides says here about the safety of a person caught in the midst of battle.

[15] See the text and analysis in Diesendruck 1936 and the discussion in Raffel 1987 and Ravitzky 1981. Samuel ibn Tibbon, however, does not see this as a possible reading of III.51 itself, and in fact is worried that III.23 is in tension with III.51.

[16] Maimonides identifies each of the speakers in the Book of Job with one of the philosophical views on providence (excepting the Epicurean view): Job = Aristotelian theory, Eliphaz = Torah theory, Bildad = Mutazilite theory, Zophar = Asharite theory, and Elihu = Maimonidean theory; see *Guide* III.23. For a discussion of Maimonides' reading of Job, see Eisen 2004, Chapter 3.

[17] *Guide* III.23, Maimonides 1963, 492–493.

soul – then in this sense no (true) evil will touch the virtuous person. He may lose every material and worldly good that he owns, but his possession of the true good is untouched. The lesson Maimonides sees here is a rather Socratic and Stoic one.[18]

This reading, based on Maimonides' interpretation of Job, is certainly one we can attribute to Maimonides, and makes good sense of much of what the *Guide* has to say in several places about providence and evil (particularly III.23). However, I want to suggest that we should not be so quick to dismiss the first reading of III.51 and write off the surprising passages merely as metaphorical biblical exegesis or simply a matter of the "incoherencies" that Maimonides puts in the *Guide* for his esoteric purposes. But nor do I think that, in order to make sense of III.51, there is any need to introduce divine miracles or human beings becoming like disembodied celestial beings. That is, I think that Maimonides does indeed believe that the virtuous person really can diminish the degree to which chance affects his overall (and not just spiritual) well-being and reduce the role of moral luck in the external circumstances of this life – not only because the virtuous person does not recognize the things brought by chance as real goods or evils, but also because such a person, unlike the non-virtuous person, can exercise greater control over the events in which they engage and over the things that happen to them.

Although I shall not argue this point here, it is Maimonides' view in the *Guide* that the divine emanation or overflow in which the virtuous person with a perfected intellect (whether he be a philosopher – that is, one engaged in speculation – or a prophet) participates involves theoretical knowledge, both "natural science" and "divine science."[19] It thus includes knowledge about the cosmos, and especially about the order of things in this sublunar realm. It is, in fact, a reflection of the creator's own knowledge of his creation, and especially the most general aspects of it, emanating down through the separate intellects that govern each of the celestial spheres. The overflow thus carries information about nature and its laws – among other things, just the kind of understanding that allows an individual to successfully navigate his way around the obstacles to his flourishing that the world regularly presents. Thus, a person who has perfected his intellect in the proper way will not just care less about what might be lost on a ship at sea, but he will also know not to get on the doomed ship in the first place (e.g. because he knows a storm is coming or sees that the ship is poorly constructed or badly captained).

---

[18] This is Touati's preferred reading.   [19] *Guide* III.18, Maimonides 1963, 475.

Perhaps we should not take the relevant passage *too* literally – after all, everyone is bound to get a scratch or bruise now and then, even the virtuous person and even while (perhaps especially while) he is attending to the divine overflow. But I do think that Maimonides basically means what he says here: the person enjoying divine providence through the overflow will have greater control over what happens to him and not just over his responses to it. A person with a deep knowledge of nature will have extraordinary predictive power, and thus will know what the course of nature typically brings in certain circumstances. He will rarely be taken by surprise, and thus in the worldly conditions of his life moral luck will be reduced to an absolute minimum.[20]

I admit that what I am suggesting makes Maimonides' view of providence out to be a very naturalistic and reductive one: the more you know about nature, the better off you are in navigating your way through life. But that is precisely Maimonides' intention here.

Still, even if this is granted to be a plausible and preferable reading of III.51, one that makes sense of that passage's prima facie extreme and implausible claim about providential protection without resorting to miracles or disembodied intellects, there still remains the problem of a tension between the two aspects of Maimonides' theory of providence. What really bothered Samuel ibn Tibbon and his son Moshe ibn Tibbon[21] is how to reconcile the more Stoic element suggested by Maimonides's discussion of Job (and especially III.23) with the account presented in III.51.[22]

My suggested reconciliation is as follows. The intellectual condition of the virtuous person actually does two things. First, it guides him successfully through the world with minimal harm. Second, it makes him indifferent to whatever harms or evils he does happen to encounter despite the protection provided by providence. To put it another way, there are two means of

---

[20] Interestingly, Samuel ibn Tibbon does also consider this as a possible reading of Maimonides' account, only to reject it in the end. He suggests that the virtuous individual will foresee and anticipate any evil that "the human intellect perceives during the mind's contemplation so that it enables him to guard himself from all possible evils, natural, accidental and moral and thus be saved from [them]" (Diesendruck 1936, 359; translation from Raffel 1987, 33). According to Raffel, Samuel proposes "a kind of rational divination" at work here. Samuel decides, however, that this ultimately cannot be what Maimonides means, since such rational insight would not (as Maimonides says) protect an individual from "all evils," especially those brought by nature and those perpetrated by other humans, but only self-inflicted ones. On my reading, the rational insight will bring protection from those other species of evil as well.

[21] And Touati, and many others; for example, Guttman 1973, p. 502.

[22] See Touati 1990. There are other ambiguities and tensions in Maimonides' account; see, for example, Curley 2002.

reducing the role of luck in one's life and especially in the pursuit of happiness: controlling things in the world around you, and controlling your responses to them. The ancient Stoics advocated only the latter; Maimonides believes that both strategies are available to the sage.[23]

Notice that on neither aspect does providence consist in the active and willful intervention of God in human affairs; it is not that God chooses in particular to reward the person who has united himself to the overflow. Rather, quite naturalistically, the knowledge acquired by the virtuous person through the overflow affords him an advantage in the world. "The overflow of the divine intellect ... guides the actions of righteous men, and perfects the knowledge of excellent men with regard to what they know."[24]

Why, then, do virtuous people sometimes suffer? Maimonides' response is that, in essence, they do not. If a person suffers misfortune, it is because he deserves it.[25] If a virtuous person suffers, it is, regardless of appearances, because he has done something that has taken him outside the protection of providence, if only for a short time. The bond to God and the overflow can be broken, by a lapse in attention or redirection of the mind to lesser things:

> If a man's thought is free from distraction, if he apprehends Him, may He be exalted, in the right way and rejoices in what he apprehends, that individual can never be afflicted with evil of any kind. For he is with God and God is with him. When, however, he abandons Him, may he be exalted, and is thus separated from God and God separated from him, he becomes in consequence of this a target for every evil that may happen to befall him. For the thing that necessarily brings about providence and deliverance from the sea of chance consists in that intellectual overflow.

When the bond with the overflow is broken, the virtuous person is no better off than the wicked person. They are both on their own, abandoned to the world, come what may, subject to moral luck:

> Yet an impediment may prevent from some time [the overflow] reaching the excellent and good man in question, or again it was not obtained at all by such and such imperfect and wicked man, and therefore the chance occurrences that befell them happened.

---

[23] Raffel (1987) appears to offer a similar solution when he distinguishes in Maimonides between "providence as consequent upon the practical intellect" and "providence as consequent upon the theoretical intellect" (60).

[24] *Guide* III.18, Maimonides 1963, 475.

[25] Maimonides thus rejects the suggestion that a truly virtuous person might experience undeserved suffering as part of a "trial"; see *Guide* III.24.

Full responsibility for the disconnection from the divine overflow lies with the individual, not God: "It is clear that we are the cause of this 'hiding of the face', and we are the agents who produce this separation."[26]

Similarly, the prosperity of the wicked person is not a true flourishing, since this person is not enjoying the highest good, intellectual perfection. Moreover, the prosperity that has happened to come his way is totally undeserved and does not represent a reward from God for anything he has done. Rather, being unprotected and at the mercy of nature, it so happens that chance has brought him some apparently fine things. But his possession and enjoyment of them is equally subject to fortune, and certain to be short-lived.

II

An even clearer exposition of the close relationship between rational perfection, *eudaimonia*, and a kind of immunity from (or at least reduction of) moral luck is provided by Gersonides in his philosophical magnum opus, *The Wars of the Lord* (*Sefer Milḥamot ha-Shem*).

Gersonides, like Maimonides, is concerned with two species of providence. First, there is what he calls "special" or "individual" providence (*hashgaḥah peratit*). This is the protection that comes only to a certain class of human beings, namely those who, through the use of their intellects, achieve a union with the active or agent intellect – which is, again, the separate intellect of the sublunar realm that embodies a full knowledge of the world it rules, a kind of quasi-divine governing spirit – and a consequent insight into the ways of nature. Second, there is a general providence (*hashgaḥah kelalit*) that extends across all of nature and, thereby, to all human beings. Let us look at these more closely in turn.

The source of evil, Gersonides says, is never God. Nor does it come from the (immaterial) forms of things. Rather, evil has its origins either in matter or in chance or accident. By 'matter,' he means the mixture of elements in material nature (including human bodies) and the human choices that may be influenced by this. By 'chance [*keri*],'[27] Gersonides understands the unfortunate effects upon human beings of occurrences of nature ("land upheavals, earthquakes, fires from the heavens, and so forth"). These

---

[26] *Guide* III.51, Maimonides 1963, 625–626.

[27] *Wars of the Lord* (henceforth, *Wars*) Book IV, Chapter 3, Levi ben Gershom 1987, 168. When I mention the Hebrew text, I am referring to the standard 1866 Leipzig edition, *Sefer Milḥamot ha-Shem* (henceforth, MH); for this use of *keri*, see MH 160.

occurrences are as causally ordered as anything else in the sublunar realm: they are "the evils that befall man from the patterns determined by the arrangements of the heavenly bodies." What is "accidental" and a matter of "chance" is the *evilness* of their results relative to human beings and their ends; it is an evil that is unforeseen and unintended by the natural causes of such things. As Gersonides notes, it is the "*evil* resulting from these events [for human beings] that is due to chance."[28]

Now nature has provided in a general way for all creatures through the endowments of the species. Each type of animal has been given the appropriate means necessary for its survival. And the more noble the creature, the greater its capacities for self-preservation:

> Induction shows that the Agent Intellect provides for existing things in giving them either bodily organs or instinctual powers, by virtue of which the possessors of these faculties can preserve their individual existence and ward off or avoid harm. For example, it endows some animals with horns, cloven hooves, or beaks to keep them from harm or to enable predatory animals to obtain prey. In some animals the Agent Intellect bestows only instinctual desires or skills. An example of an instinctual desire is the natural instinct of a lamb to run away from a wolf upon seeing it, even though it does not know that the wolf will harm it, and [indeed] it has not even seen a wolf previously. Similarly, many birds flee from predatory birds, although they have never seen them previously ... This kind of providence is exhibited in man in a much more perfect form. For man is endowed with a practical intellect from which many kinds of useful arts are derived for his preservation. He is also given an intellect from which are derived the tendencies to flee from harmful things and to obtain advantageous things.[29]

This general providence, similar to that of Maimonides, derives, like all the determined aspects of nature, from the ordinary causal course of nature as this is driven by celestial bodies and through the agent intellect. All individual human beings are thus endowed by nature with the faculties and instincts that they need for survival in a world governed by laws which themselves derive from the same celestial influences. The heavenly spheres provide us with desires, thoughts, and intentions for action that are to our benefit. The general celestial providence thus takes care of all individuals *qua* members of the human species, but not *qua* particulars. It extends to all humans as humans in their interactions both with material nature and with each other, without taking any account of their particularities, especially their moral differences, their virtues and vices. Of course, although this

---

[28] *Wars* IV.3, Levi ben Gershom 1987, 168–169.   [29] *Ibid.*, 166–167

general ordering of nature aims for the best, and generally results in good, sometimes it brings about evil. "Sometimes there necessarily results from these patterns some accidental misfortunes." Although we have, by general providence, the wherewithal to deal for the most part with what fortune brings our way, we are not, by nature alone, prepared to deal with all the threats to our well-being. Nature is still a risky environment, full of potential harm and obstacles to our flourishing.

This is where special providence comes in. Although God has not ordered the patterns (*ha-siddurim*) of the heavens such that no evil is to occur, nonetheless "he has given man an instrument whereby these evils can be avoided – reason [*ha-sekhel*]."[30] Thus, in addition to the astral-based (general) providence, there is also an intellect-based providence available to human beings, through the achievement of which they can escape (or at least limit) the occasional unfortunate effects of general providence.

Because the agent intellect is an intelligent cause, it possesses full knowledge – the "maker's knowledge" – of the order it imposes on the world:

> Since the agent responsible for the [existence] of all beings in the sublunar world must possess the knowledge of the order [obtaining in this world] – just as the craftsman must have an idea of the order obtaining among the things he is to create – and since ... this agent is the Agent Intellect ... it follows that the Agent Intellect possesses the knowledge of the order obtaining in the sublunary world.[31]

By generating the natural sublunar forms, the agent intellect is the cause of substances; and because this separate intellect emanates from even higher intellects and ultimately from God, it knows fully the plan it is thereby carrying out:

> The separate agent responsible for all these things [substances] should know the law, order and rightness inherent in these sublunar phenomena, since these things acquire their very existence from the intelligible order of them in the soul of this separate agent.[32]

The agent intellect contains the concepts of all beings, organized comprehensively and systematically, such that the totality of what the agent intellect knows constitutes an exhaustive body of science. Its knowledge is thus a kind of complete and archetypal blueprint for the world it governs. "The Agent Intellect ... possesses [the knowledge] of the plan and order [of the terrestrial domain]." Gersonides, in fact, calls it "the rational order of the

[30] *Wars* IV.6, Levi ben Gershom 1987, 184.   [31] *Wars* I.6, Levi ben Gershom 1984, 151.
[32] *Wars* V.III.4, Levi ben Gershom 1999, 135.

terrestrial world" and "the law" of the sublunar world,[33] although its science also includes knowledge of all celestial phenomena. It is an eternal and incorruptible order, in contrast to the changing, corruptible, and temporal procession of things and events in the world that instantiates and dynamically exemplifies it. This knowledge in the Agent Intellect exists in "a perfect and unified manner."[34]

Through the proper use of his intellect, an individual human being perfects himself and becomes "closer" to the agent intellect, discerns that Intellect's "maker's knowledge" of the essences of things and of the patterns and laws of nature, and thereby attains a higher degree of "protection" from nature's uncaring ways. The person enjoying special providence is a person who, through the actualization of his intellect and the acquisition of higher knowledge, is better equipped to obtain what is good and avoid any evils impending from the ordinary course of nature. As the human mind comes to an understanding of the true order of the world, its knowledge grows, in fact, to mirror (as much as possible for human beings) the knowledge that is in the agent intellect itself. A person thereby becomes "enlightened." Unlike the general run of people, "who are not within the scope of divine providence except in a general way as members of the human species," this person knows how nature operates; he can predict what, according to nature's laws, the future will bring and generally be able to put nature's ways to his own use.

If true virtue is the pursuit of intellectual perfection – as Gersonides believes[35] – then this special providence is the natural product and reward of virtue. The truly righteous person will, for the most part and just *because* of his intellectual achievements, obtain the goods that this world has to offer and avoid its evils. Sinners, on the other hand, will in general be punished – not directly, through some particular directive from God, but by being left out in the cold. Those who do not pursue virtue, who do not perfect their intellects, will be subject to the vicissitudes of nature, to a high degree of moral luck:

---

[33] *Wars* V.III.13, Levi ben Gershom 1999, 186. Gersonides uses a Hebrew transliteration of the Greek term *nomos* (MH 286).

[34] *Wars* I.6, Levi ben Gershom 1984, 146–147.

[35] Like Maimonides, Gersonides insists that moral virtue is only a necessary precondition for the higher, intellectual virtue of rational perfection; see Gersonides' commentary on Proverbs 1:19: "[This verse] comes to make known that perfection of the virtues is a pre-requisite [literally: preface] for perfection of the intelligibilia, for it is not possible that a person perfect his soul with the intelligibilia if the illness of degenerate virtues is in him." My thanks to Menachem Kellner for bringing this passage to my attention.

When the Torah warns men of evil because of their great sins, it states clearly that this evil will be that God will not look upon them and that He will abandon them to the contingencies of time ... The punishment of sinners consists in God's hiding and indifference. God leaves them to the contingencies of time, and whatever happens to them is determined by the patterns of the heavenly bodies. Nor does God save them from the evil that is to befall them.[36]

[Sinners] are left and abandoned to those accidents that are ordered by the heavenly bodies and ... are not protected by God from the evils that are to befall them, for they are not at the level of perfection such that this kind of divine providence could extend to them.[37]

Without the knowledge possessed by the virtuous, sinners cannot properly and reliably navigate their way through nature, securing the goods they need and protecting themselves accordingly. Things may go well for them, they may flourish and prosper (at least by the lesser, materialistic standards of this life); but then again, they may not. It is all up to chance. Unlike the virtuous, the vicious have not reduced the element of luck in the quality of their lives.

For both Maimonides and Gersonides, then, providence is to be understood in fairly naturalistic terms. While I do not want to ignore or even minimize the important differences between the two thinkers on the issues surrounding this topic,[38] they seem to be in general agreement that the actively virtuous person, precisely through his higher cognitive achievements, enjoys a kind of protection from fortune in his flourishing. This protection, which represents an advantage that one may have in the world, does not come by any special or miraculous actions of God; rather, it is simply the natural consequence of the pursuit of intellectual knowledge.

III

Spinoza, of course, does not really have a theory of divine providence. This is primarily because his metaphysics of God (*Deus sive Natura*) does not allow for an authentically providential deity.[39] However, with Spinoza we

---

[36] *Wars* IV.4, Levi ben Gershom 1987, 173.   [37] *Wars* IV.6, Levi ben Gershom 1987, 181.

[38] For example, Gersonides' account is quite a bit more explicit than Maimonides's account is on the role of the agent intellect, on the nature and content of the knowledge conveyed by the overflow – especially that it includes a knowledge of the order of nature itself – and on the kind of protection it affords. Moreover, Gersonides has a more positive attitude toward astology and seems committed to a kind of astral determinism in nature that is not obviously present in Maimonides' account. For a brief discussion of these differences, see Feldman 2010, 107–108.

[39] See, however, Nadler 2005a for an argument that there is, in a sense, a theory of divine providence in Spinoza.

can still frame things in terms of the relationship between virtue and happiness, between being good and flourishing. And much of what Spinoza says about the relationship between reason, virtue, well-being, and (by implication) moral luck not only echoes what we find in the theories of divine providence in Maimonides and Gersonides, but also can be seen as constituting their natural (and naturalistic) denouement. It would appear, in fact, that what Spinoza is doing is only bringing out what is latent in the naturalistic views of his medieval Jewish rationalist forebears, with whose works he was undoubtedly familiar.[40]

The centerpiece of Spinoza's moral philosophy in the *Ethics* is his account of virtue, which in turn is rooted in his psychological egoism. All beings are essentially and necessarily moved by the pursuit of self-interest and naturally strive for what they believe will aid their preservation. This is a universal law of nature. "Each thing, as far as it can by its own power, strives to persevere in its being" (IIIp6).[41] When this striving for self-preservation – which Spinoza calls a thing's *conatus* – is successful it constitutes virtue, at least in the realm of moral agents. To act virtuously is to do what will truly and most effectively serve to preserve one's being:

> IVp20: The more each one strives, and is able, to seek his own advantage, i.e. to preserve his own being, the more he is endowed with virtue; conversely, insofar as each one neglects his own advantage, i.e. neglects to preserve his being, he lacks power.
>
> IVp22c: The striving to preserve oneself is the first and only foundation of virtue.

Now when human beings are acting rationally in their pursuit of self-preservation, when they act according to reason and "adequate ideas" (rather than beliefs based on the passions, or "inadequate ideas"), they strive naturally for knowledge. Since we are, among all creatures, particularly endowed with reason and the capacity for intellectual understanding, we recognize that our own proper good, our ultimate perfection and well-being, consists in the pursuit of what benefits this our highest part. But what else could benefit our highest intellectual faculties except knowledge?

---

[40] There can be no doubt about Spinoza's familiarity with Maimonides, and with the *Guide* in particular (of which he owned a Hebrew edition), given his explicit critical discussion of Maimonides in the TTP. Spinoza also knew Gersonides, although evidence for his familiarity with the *Wars of the Lord* is somewhat more circumstantial. No works by Gersonides are listed in the inventory of Spinoza's library. However, Spinoza mentions the opinion of "Rabbi Levi ben Gerson" in Adnotatio XVI to Chapter 9 of the TTP (G III.256) on a matter of biblical exegesis. I find it very difficult to believe that Spinoza was not also acquainted with the most important philosophical work of this thinker, who was arguably the most important medieval Jewish philosopher after Maimonides.

[41] All English passages from the *Ethics* are from Curley's translation, Spinoza 1985 (sometimes modified).

Thus, if virtue is the pursuit of what is truly in one's own self-interest; and if the acquisition of knowledge is what is truly in our own self-interest, then human virtue consists in the successful pursuit of knowledge.[42]

But Spinoza is concerned here with the pursuit not just of any ordinary kind of knowledge. Rather, what is most beneficial to a rational being is a particular sort of deep understanding that he calls "intuitive knowledge [*scientia intuitiva*]," or (in his epistemic hierarchy) "the third kind of knowledge." This is an intuitive understanding of things in their relations to higher causes. More precisely, it consists in "adequate ideas" of things – minds and bodies – that clearly and distinctly relate them to the infinite and eternal aspects of God or nature. It is, Spinoza says, the highest form of knowledge available to us.

In contrast to "inadequate ideas," which are formed haphazardly and provide only a relative and superficial acquaintance with things – since such ideas result only from "random experience" and our fortuitous and haphazard experience of bodies as they happen to affect us – adequate ideas are formed in a rational and orderly manner. While inadequate ideas are "the only source of falsity" (IIp41), adequate ideas are necessarily true. These ideas, which reveal the essential natures of things, come in two forms.

What Spinoza calls "the second kind of knowledge," or "Reason [*ratio*]," is the apprehension, through a discursive procedure, of higher principles of nature – including the so-called "common notions," or universal features of all things falling under an attribute – and of how things instantiate and are governed by them.[43] If sense experience presents things only as they happen to appear to a particular person from a given perspective at a given moment in time, Reason and its adequate ideas show how a thing follows necessarily from one or another of God's attributes (Thought or Extension). Through reason one grasps what a thing essentially is and *why* it necessarily is thus. It therefore ultimately presents its object from an "eternal" point of view, *sub specie aeternitatis*, and thus leads to a conception of that item without any relation to time or finite and partial perspective.

> It is of the nature of Reason to regard things as necessary and not as contingent. And Reason perceives this necessity of things truly, i.e., as it is in itself. But this necessity of things is the very necessity of God's eternal

---

[42] See IVp20–p26.
[43] There is a good deal of debate in the scholarly literature as to whether the second kind of knowledge is an understanding of only general truths and principles of nature – "common notions" – or also truths about individual things and their essences. Compare Wilson 1996 (116–119) and Allison 1987 (113–116) with Yovel 1989 (156, 165–166).

nature. Therefore, it is of the nature of Reason to regard things under this species of eternity. (IIp44c2)

While knowledge of the second kind provides this understanding of things through ratiocination – moving step by step through conceptual stages, ultimately placing finite effects in their necessary relationship to infinite causes[44] – the third kind of knowledge, intuition, takes what is known via Reason and grasps it in a single and comprehensive act of the mind, "in one glance" (IIp40s2). In the third kind of knowledge there is an immediate perception of the essence of a thing and of the way it follows necessarily from its ultimate, first causes in nature:

> This kind of knowing proceeds from an adequate idea of the formal essence of certain attributes of God to the adequate knowledge of the formal essences of things. (IIp40s2)

Intuition synthesizes into a metaphysical truth – an essence – what reason knows only discursively. It thereby generates a deep and epistemically superior causal understanding of a thing by situating it immediately and timelessly in relation to the eternal principles of nature that generated and govern it.

The person living according to reason, then, strives to acquire the third kind of knowledge: an intuitive understanding of the natures of things not merely in their finite, particular, and fluctuating causal relations to other finite things, not in their mutable durational existence, but through their unchanging essences. And to truly understand things essentially in this way is to relate them to their infinite causes: substance (God or nature) and its attributes. What we are after is a knowledge of bodies not through other bodies but through Extension and its laws, and a knowledge of minds and ideas through the nature of Thought and its laws. It is the pursuit of this kind of knowledge that constitutes human virtue and the project that represents our greatest self-interest as rational beings:

> Vp25: The greatest striving of the mind, and its greatest virtue, is understanding things by the third kind of knowledge.
>
> Demonstration: The third kind of knowledge proceeds from an adequate idea of certain attributes of God to an adequate knowledge of the essence of things, and the more we understand things in this way, the more we understand God. Therefore, the greatest virtue of the mind, i.e., the mind's power

---

[44] This should make clear that I am sympathetic to the reading of the second kind of knowledge according to which Reason does encompass individuals, and situates them in relationship to other finite but especially also infinite causes.

or nature or its greatest striving, is to understand things by the third kind of knowledge.

Vp29s: We conceive things as actual in two ways: either insofar as we conceive them to exist in relation to a certain time and place, or insofar as we conceive them to be contained in God and to follow from the necessity of the divine nature. But the things we conceive in this second way as true, or real, we conceive under a species of eternity, and to that extent they involve the eternal and infinite essence of God.

Sub specie aeternitatis: when we understand things in this way, we see them from the infinite and eternal perspective of God. When we perceive things in time, they appear in a continuous state of change and becoming; when we perceive them "from the perspective of eternity," what we apprehend abides permanently. We see the necessity of all things in nature, especially all the facts about ourselves and our determinate place in the world.

IV

The virtuous person, then, has pursued and acquired true and adequate ideas, a deep, even "divine" understanding of nature and its ways. Spinoza insists that this knowledge is of the greatest benefit to a human being.

To begin with, there is the fact that an understanding of nature's essences and laws provides the virtuous person with the tools he needs to navigate life's obstacle course. Nature's ways are transparent to him, not opaque. His capacity to manipulate things and avoid dangers is greater than that of the person who is governed by the senses and imagination. A rational knowledge of things is useful in this relatively superficial manner.

More importantly, however, a knowledge of the second and third kinds is, for the virtuous person, the source of an abiding happiness and peace of mind that is resistant to the vagaries of chance. When a person sees the necessity of all things, *sub specie aeternitatis*, and especially the fact that the objects that he values are, in their comings and goings, not really under his control, that person is less likely to be overwhelmed with strong emotions at their arrival or passing away. The resulting life will be tranquil and not given to sudden disturbances of the passions. Herein lie the true natural benefits of virtue. As in the case of Maimonides and Gersonides, it leads to a diminishing of the role of luck in one's living well.

In Part Four of the *Ethics*, Spinoza shows how a life governed by the emotions, or "passive affects," is a life of "bondage [*servitus*]." The passions are those changes in our power that happen in us the causes of which lie outside our own nature. We feel passions when we are being acted upon by the world around us. The spectrum of human emotions are all functions of the ways in which external things affect our capacities. Love, for example, is simply our affective awareness of a thing that brings about some improvement in our constitution; we love the thing that benefits us and causes joy. All of the human emotions, insofar as they are passions, are directed outward, toward things and their tendencies to affect us one way or another. Aroused by our passions and desires, we seek or flee those things that we believe cause joy or sadness. "We strive to further the occurrence of whatever we imagine will lead to joy, and to avert or destroy what we imagine is contrary to it, or will lead to sadness" (IIIp28). Our hopes and fears fluctuate depending on whether we regard the objects of our desires or aversions as remote, near, necessary, possible, or unlikely.

What we often fail to keep in mind, however, is the fact that the things that stir our emotions, being external to us, do not answer to our wills. We have no real power over whether what we hate is near or distant, whether the person we love lives or dies. The objects of our passions are beyond our control (especially in the absolutely deterministic universe that Spinoza describes). Thus, the more we allow ourselves to be controlled by these objects – by their comings and goings – the more we are subject to fluctuating passions and the less active and free (that is, self-controlled) we are. The upshot is a fairly pathetic picture of a life mired in the passions and pursuing and fleeing the changeable and fleeting objects that occasion them: "We are driven about in many ways by external causes, and . . . like waves on the sea, driven by contrary winds, we toss about not knowing our outcome and fate" (IIIp59s). It is, Spinoza says, a kind of disease to suffer too much love for a thing that is mutable and never fully under our power, even when we do, for a time, have it in our possession:

> Sickness of the mind and misfortunes take their origin especially from too much love toward a thing which is liable to many variations and which we can never fully possess. For no one is disturbed or anxious concerning anything unless he loves it, nor do wrongs, suspicions, and enmities arise except from love for a thing which no one can really fully possess. (Vp20s)

The solution to this predicament is an ancient one. Since we cannot control the objects that we tend to value and that we allow to influence our well-being, we ought instead to try to control our evaluations and responses themselves and thereby minimize the sway that external objects and the passions have over us. We can never entirely eliminate or even totally subdue the passions. We are essentially a part of nature and cannot fully remove ourselves from the causal series that link us to the world of external things. We are, Spinoza says, "necessarily always subject to passions" (IVp4). We can, however, counteract the passions, understand and control them, and thereby achieve a certain degree of relief from their turmoil.

The path to restraining and moderating the passions is through virtue. As we have seen, virtue for Spinoza consists in the pursuit of knowledge and understanding: the acquisition of adequate ideas and the intellectual intuition of the essences of things. We have also seen that when we perceive things *sub specie aeternitatis*, through the second and third kinds of knowledge and in relation to God or nature, what we apprehend is the deterministic necessity of all that happens. We see that all bodies and their states and relationships – including the condition of our own body – follow necessarily from the essence of matter and the universal laws of physics; and we see that all ideas, including all the properties of minds, follow necessarily from the essence of thought and its universal principles. Such insight can only weaken the power that the passions have over us. When we come to this level of understanding and realize that we cannot control what nature brings our way or takes from us, we are no longer anxious over what may come to pass and no longer obsessed with or despondent over the loss of some possessions. We regard all things with equanimity, and we are not inordinately and irrationally affected in different ways by past, present, or future events. The result is self-control and a calmness of mind:

> The more this knowledge that things are necessary is concerned with singular things, which we imagine more distinctly and vividly, the greater is this power of the Mind over the affects, as experience itself also testifies. For we see that Sadness over some good which has perished is lessened as soon as the man who has lost it realizes that this good could not, in any way, have been kept. (Vp6s)

Spinoza's ethical theory is, to a certain degree, Stoic, and recalls the doctrines of thinkers such as Cicero, Seneca, and Epictetus:[45]

> We do not have an absolute power to adapt things outside us to our use. Nevertheless, we shall bear calmly those things that happen to us contrary to what the principle of our advantage demands, if we are conscious that we have done our duty, that the power we have could not have extended itself to the point where we could have avoided those things, and that we are a part of the whole of nature, whose order we follow. If we understand this clearly and distinctly, that part of us which is defined by understanding, i.e., the better

---

[45] Still, Spinoza is critical of the ancient Stoics in important respects; see *Ethics* V, preface. For a study of Spinoza and the Stoics, see DeBrabander 2007, James 1993, and Miller (forthcoming).

part of us, will be entirely satisfied with this, and will strive to persevere in that satisfaction. For insofar as we understand, we can want nothing except what is necessary, nor absolutely be satisfied with anything except what is true. (IV, App, Spinoza 1925, II.276; 1985, I.594)

The third kind of knowledge, by revealing how all things depend on God or Nature and its attributes, puts a person in an intellectual union with the highest possible object of human knowledge. As this state of knowing represents our *summum bonum*, the virtuous person strives to maintain it. And because its object is eternal and unchanging, he can do so. What, in the end, replaces the unstable passionate love for ephemeral "goods" – in a life where one's happiness is subject to the insecure possession of such things – is an abiding intellectual love for an eternal, immutable good that we can fully and securely possess, namely, God. The happiness (*beatitudo*) and well-being that this cognitive condition represents is, if not immune to, then at least greatly free from what may come by way of the wheel of fortune. Spinoza's "free person" is active, not passive; that is, he is in a condition whereby what happens to him (especially in his states of mind) follows from his own nature and not as a result of the ways external things affect him. Living as he does "according to the dictates of reason alone," he bears the gifts and losses of fortune with equanimity, does only those things that he (rightly) believes to be "the most important in life," and is not anxious about death.

V

For Spinoza, then, virtue has its rewards. There are certain supreme benefits that it confers, by nature, upon the virtuous person. The striving for and acquisition of understanding and the second and third kinds of knowledge bring a well-being and peace of mind that is essentially under one's control. In the life of such a person the role of moral luck is greatly diminished. Virtue – construed, as it is for Maimonides and Gersonides, as an intellectual achievement – is a source of abiding happiness and freedom from the vicissitudes of chance. Spinoza puts this point in terms of "fortune [*fortuna*]" in the preface to Part Four, where he prepares the reader for the contrast he will draw between the person governed by the passions and the person who lives according to reason:

I assign the term "bondage" to man's lack of power to control and check the emotions. For a man at the mercy of his emotions is not his own master but is subject to fortune, in whose power he so lies that he is often compelled, although he seeks the better course, to pursue the worse.[46]

In the scholium to Vp41, people who "shape their lives according to their lusts," as opposed to what reason dictates, are described as being "ruled by fortune rather than by themselves." The virtuous person, through his rational knowledge, naturally enjoys stable happiness through a kind of protection from nature's callous and indifferent operations and the psychological turmoil they bring. The vicious person, on the other hand, is at the mercy of the elements, living the life of bondage and "tossed about" by the passions.

If one wanted to take the connection with medieval Jewish rationalism one step further, one might even go so far as to say that in Spinoza's system there is room for a kind of divine providence, albeit one that does not employ a providential God. For Spinoza, God or Nature rewards the virtuous. However, God (or Nature) does so not because there is a plan that it conceives and then willfully carries out, but simply because that is how Nature necessarily works. It is a theory of divine providence without teleology. Providence, as Spinoza explains in Chapter 3 of the TTP, is the inviolable causal order of nature, as this is necessarily determined (not chosen) by God/Substance. And a part of that order consists in a system of rewards and punishments – not by intention or design, but by natural causes. The pursuit of virtue brings benefits *by nature*; correspondingly, the life of vice is naturally and necessarily attended by the lack of such benefits.

Nevertheless, even if the language of divine providence is not appropriate here, and however much Spinoza's account may resemble what we find among some ancient Stoics, Spinoza's naturalistic and intellectualist solution to the problem of moral luck bears a stronger connection to the views of his medieval Jewish rationalist forebears than to the Stoic doctrines. As it is for Maimonides and Gersonides, virtue for Spinoza is an achievement of the intellect: human perfection consists in the actualization of our highest cognitive faculty, reason, through the attainment of intellectual understanding. Notice that what is important here is not just *what* one knows (for example, to take the Stoic case, that there are some things that are under my control, and there are other things that are not).[47] In fact, *what* one knows appears to differ, at least in part, between Maimonides and Gersonides, on the one hand, and Spinoza, on the other hand. Of greater

---

[46] Spinoza 1925, II.205; 1985 I.543.
[47] Epictetus, for example, insists (in the first line of his *Enchiridion*) that the most important thing to know is that "some things are up to us [*eph' hemin*], and other things are not up to us."

importance, and what seems really to unite these three thinkers, is the moral value of rational knowledge itself as a secure and non-transitory good and as an essential achievement for flourishing in this life by minimizing the influence of luck. This is the rationalist way to wisdom, joy, and blessedness. "Blessedness consists in Love of God, a Love which arises from the third kind of knowledge. So this Love must be related to the Mind insofar as it acts. Therefore, it is virtue itself" (Vp42). Spinoza's Love of God is not a passion but an intellectual love in which the mind takes cognizance of the eternal object of its understanding.

Spinoza's bold move, however – a move that constitutes his transformation of Jewish rationalism – is twofold. First, he identifies God with nature, and thereby explicitly makes nature itself the supreme object of our cognitive quest. Reason is no longer what binds us to a transcendent deity but rather is what provides our intellectual connection to the cosmos of which we are a part. Second, he argues much more explicitly than either Maimonides or Gersonides does that, while the pursuit of rational knowledge constitutes our supreme perfection and the true path to happiness, its "rewards" and benefits (to return to the question of "divine providence") are merely the natural effects that such understanding brings to a person and are limited solely to this life. Maimonides and Gersonides laid the philosophical groundwork for both of these conclusions, but it took a thinker as audacious as Spinoza to bring it all to a stunning logical conclusion.

CHAPTER 9

"Something of it remains": Spinoza and Gersonides on intellectual eternity

Julie R. Klein

Introduction

The eternity of the mind is among the most difficult and intriguing ideas in Spinoza's philosophy.[1] "The human Mind cannot be absolutely destroyed with the Body," he writes enigmatically in *Ethics* Vp23, "but something of it remains which is eternal." What remains after death, Spinoza argues in succeeding propositions, is intellectual, concluding that the mind's degree of eternity is proportionate to its knowledge. Whatever else we are to make of the fifth part of the *Ethics*, Spinoza identifies the eternity of the mind principally with the third kind of knowing, *scientia intuitiva*, and he holds that clear and distinct knowing engenders "a Love toward a thing immutable and eternal," i.e. God or Nature. This knowledge-based love "can always be greater and greater (by Vp15), and occupy the greatest part of the Mind (by Vp16), and affect it extensively" (Vp20s). In Vp23s, Spinoza promises that "we feel and know by experience that we are eternal," and his famous term, "intellectual love of God [*amor Dei intellectualis*]," captures the simultaneity of affective and cognitive experience (Vp32c). The experience of intellectual knowing and the experience of intellectual love, which Spinoza also calls "the greatest Joy" and "the greatest satisfaction of the Mind" (Vp27, 32) are one and the same experience.

The *locus classicus* for intellectual eternity is found at the conclusion of *De Anima* III.5, where Aristotle explains, in famously puzzling lines, that the active or agent intellect, the *nous poetikos*, "when separated," "is alone just what it is, and this alone is immortal and eternal." As such, the active or

I thank the readers and hearers of early versions of the ideas presented in this essay, especially Jeffrey Bernstein, Idit Dobbs-Weinstein, Mogens Laerke, Helen S. Lang, Steven Nadler, Eric Schliesser, and Noa Shein, whose generous suggestions have resulted in many improvements. All deficiencies are of course due to me alone.

[1] Jonathan Bennett famously declared: "those of us who love Spinoza's philosophy should in sad silence avert our eyes from the second half of Part Five" (Bennett 1984, 375). Nadler 2005c shows the absurdity of Bennett's proposed textual amputation.

acting intellect stands in contrast to the intellect that is acted upon, the *nous pathetikos*, and which is destructible.[2] Historically, interpretations of Aristotle's account of the immortality or eternity of the soul turn on the expression "when separated," which invites questions of how, when, and where the separation occurs. Does the separation exist in thought and discourse, i.e. as a conceptual distinction, or does it exist in the order of real things, i.e. outside the mind? Does it occur after the death of the body, or can it occur while body lives? The *loci classici* for intellectual pleasure are also found in Aristotle. The opening line of the *Metaphysics* announces that "All human beings by nature desire to know" and adduces the delight [*agapesis*] we take in sensation as evidence.[3] *Metaphysics* XII.7 argues that the unmoved mover's actuality, which Aristotle characterizes as eternal intellectual self-contemplation in *Metaphysics* XII.9, involves the highest pleasure.[4] *Nicomachean Ethics* X.7–9 identifies intellectual contemplation as the paramount form of human flourishing, calling it the most divine, most excellent, and the happiest, and Aristotle concludes regretfully that the human knower experiences such happiness only intermittently. In addition to intellect and the other parts of the soul, human knowers are embodied, which results in physical, social, and political needs that that must be met in order for joyful knowing to occur at all, let alone be sustained for some interval.[5]

In this essay, I argue that Part Five of the *Ethics* reflects Spinoza's knowledge of medieval Jewish and Islamic discussions of these classic Aristotelian texts.[6] I have in mind Maimonides (d. 1204), Averroës

[2] *De Anima* III.5 430a20–25. All translations are from Aristotle 1991. The usual translation of *nous pathetikos* is "passive intellect," but a more literal rendering as "intellect that is acted on" better captures the natural motion from potency to act; the two forms of *nous* are intrinsically related as contraries. The elliptical, enigmatic character of *De Anima* III, and the consequent need for interpretive labor, cannot be over-emphasized.

[3] *Metaphysics* I.1 980a20–25. Aristotelian themes are widely dispersed in medieval philosophy, and this theme finds a place in, for example, the seemingly unlikely setting of Bonaventure's Christian Augustinianism; see Lang 1986. Seventeenth-century authors had general access to Aristotelian philosophy as a common intellectual heritage and received idiom, which makes the task of identifying specific connections especially important. In the present chapter, I consider Spinoza's encounter with Aristotle as mediated by the medieval Islamic and Jewish Aristotelians. Readers interested in Spinoza's encounter with the Latin Aristotle should consult Manzini 2009, an important work that identifies an exact Latin edition of Aristotle that Spinoza used (*Opera Omnia*, Basilea, ex officina Joan. Oporini, 1548). Manzini 2011 is also a very useful resource.

[4] *Metaphysics* XII.7 1072b15–30 and XII.9 1074a25–35.

[5] Spinoza makes a similar argument in TIE §§11–14.

[6] For an overview of the recent Spinoza-Maimonides literature, see Nadler 2009. For the purposes of the present chapter, perhaps the most important Maimonidean text is found in *Guide* III.51: "Love of God is proportionate to apprehension [of God]." Spinoza could also have encountered the idea of *amor dei intellectualis* in Leon Ebreo's *Dialoghi d'Amore*, which he owned; see Ivry 1983 for why Leon, who is usually considered a Neoplatonist, should be recognized as an Averroist.

(1137–1198), and Gersonides (1288–1344). The Arabic and Hebrew commentators give, in the main but with important exceptions (e.g. Avicenna), materialist answers to the questions raised by Aristotle's texts. By "materialism," I mean a conceptual horizon in which psychology and cognition are treated as intrinsically connected with, on the one hand, physics, and, on the other hand, ethics and politics. Like Spinoza, these thinkers view the human soul as a "part of nature" (Ep 32) rather than as a "dominion within a dominion" (III Preface, TP I.2), so we can also think of this materialism as a form of naturalism.[7] For Spinoza, whose most famous phrase is perhaps "God, or Nature [*Deus, sive Natura*], "naturalism is an apt term. The opposite of "material" or "natural" here is "transcendent" or "dualist." In this regard, the Jewish and Islamic Aristotelians offer an alternative to mainstream Christian Aristotelianism and its Cartesian successors, all of whom hypothesize the existence of a really separate, purely incorporeal part of the soul or mind, a part whose cognitive powers are essentially independent of sensation.

Steven Nadler's *Spinoza's Heresy: Immortality and the Jewish Mind* (2001) provides the first comprehensive account of Spinoza's relation to his Jewish predecessors on the issue of immortality or the eternity of the mind. Nadler interprets Spinoza's eternity of the mind as "the culmination of a certain trend in Jewish rationalism"; Spinoza, he argues, takes the intellectualist view of the immortality of the soul found in Maimonides and further refined by Gersonides "to its ultimate logical conclusion."[8] As Nadler emphasizes, Spinoza's identification of the eternity of the mind with its experience of the third kind of knowledge repeats Gersonides' position.[9] In the present chapter, I consider Spinoza's use of Gersonides, adding a series of new texts and approaching the topic from a somewhat different angle. I emphasize Gersonides' anticipation of Spinozan immanence, and I argue that Spinoza's model of causation as involvement (Iax4), not only his model

---

[7] See Dobbs-Weinstein 2014.

[8] Nadler 2001, 130–31. Spinoza scarcely uses the word *immortalitas* in his entire oeuvre, and his clear decision to replace the traditional phrase 'immortality of the soul' with 'eternity of the mind' can hardly be accidental. Like Nadler, I reject the claim in Wolfson 1934 that Spinoza defends an essentially rabbinic view regarding the immortality of the soul.

[9] "Spinoza's third kind of knowledge, the body of adequate ideas that persist after one's death, is, for all intents and purposes, the acquired intellect of Gersonides' theory" (Nadler 2001, 123). The Spinoza–Gersonides literature is small but growing. Recent contributions include Dobbs-Weinstein 1998, which focuses on Spinoza's appropriation of Gersonides' account of active and material intellect and characterizes him as a proto-monist, and 2004, which focuses on intellectual desire and pleasure; Garrett 2007, which argues that Spinoza largely concurs with Gersonides' criticisms of Maimonides; and W. Harvey 2012, which is devoted to Spinoza and Gersonides on *conatus*. My own contributions are found in Klein 2003 and 2006.

of intellectual knowledge, precludes any account of individual immortality. Finally, I emphasize the affective dimensions of intellectual knowledge to show the common Aristotelian ground between Spinoza and Gersonides.

In the *Ethics*, Spinoza remarks that "some of the Hebrews" seem to have grasped that "thinking substance and the extended substance are one and the same substance, which is now comprehended under this attribute, now under that." They grasped, too, that "A mode of extension and the idea of that mode are one and the same things, but expressed in two ways," but they saw this thesis "as if through a cloud, when they maintained that God, God's intellect, and the things understood by him are one and the same" (IIp7s). These Hebrews are Jewish Aristotelians, who affirmed Aristotle's claim that the knower and the known are one in knowing but failed to pursue its radically immanentizing implications.[10] Spinoza, I think, must have regarded Maimonides, who espoused an emanationist cosmology, as having philosophized through the cloud of divine transcendence.[11] But Gersonides, who absorbed Averroës' profound critique of emanation, comes much closer to transparency. Crucially, by identifying the active intellect with both the divine intellect and the intelligibility of nature, Gersonides abandons the usual religious distinction between the creator and the creatures and the usual Aristotelian distinction between the supra- and sublunar realms in favor of the idea of a single order of intelligibility.[12] Thus he powerfully anticipates Spinoza's *Deus sive Natura*.[13] Gersonides further advances an immanentizing agenda in holding that essential causes remain in their effects.

In the TTP, Spinoza dismisses Gersonides' exegesis of the Book of Judges but calls him "an otherwise most erudite man [*virum alias erudi-tissimum*]" (TTP 9, Annotation 16). My argument here is that Spinoza made good use of some of his erudite predecessor's metaphysical and

---

[10] Aristotle states the thesis of noetic union at *De Anima* III.4 430a5 and *Metaphysics* XII.7 1027b20. In Maimonides, see *Guide* I.68; the *Book of Knowledge*, "Foundations of the Law" 10:2; and *Eight Chapters*, Chapter 8. W. Harvey 1981 reviews statements of this thesis in Abraham ibn Ezra's *Commentary on Exodus* and Hasdai Crescas's *Or Adonai Light of the Lord* as well. Ravitzsky 1993 calls noetic union "dynamite concealed in the teachings of the Jewish Aristotelians."

[11] Fraenkel 2006 argues for a fascinatingly Spinozan Maimonides, but in my judgment achieves this portrait at the cost of downplaying the crucial conceptual links between creation and prophecy in the *Guide*.

[12] See Davidson 1992b; Dobbs-Weinstein 2006; W. Harvey 2012; Klein 2006; Pines 1991. Not all readers see Gersonides as an immanentizing philosopher; for example, Feldman 1978, 1992, 2010. More generally, as Gatti 2007 observes, immanentizing and Averroistic interpretations meet with resistance from readers more concerned with Gersonides' religious views; see especially Manekin 2003 and Touati 1973.

[13] Gersonides' strategy of retaining language but rejecting or overturning traditional meanings is familiar to readers of Spinoza.

psychological views to explain how the mind can be said to exist both *sub specie aeternitatis* and *sub specie durationis seu temporis*. Spinoza's distinction between irreducibly different attributes of the singular Substance, God, or Nature, as well as his refusal to countenance talk of cross-attribute predication and causation, rely on the same model.

Three shared motifs

Before examining Gersonides' texts, let us briefly consider three Spinozan motifs that he anticipates.

Both thinkers focus on the process of coming to know ourselves as the parts of a larger order that we are. Spinoza views the human intellect as part of the intelligibility of what he synonymously calls God or substance or nature. In IIp11c he calls the human Mind "part of the infinite intellect of God," and he reiterates this conclusion in IIp45 and its scholium, Vp29s, and Vp36 and its scholium. Taken together in their causal connections, all of the minds, i.e. modes of Thought, "constitute God's eternal and infinite intellect" (Vp39s). But it is difficult to discern the causal order of nature, for human beings are immersed in sensation and imagination. Spinoza describes knowing as a process of rethinking imaginative ideas in terms of the intelligible order. Imagination, the first kind of knowledge, produces inadequate ideas, but reason and intellection, the second and third kinds of knowing, operate in terms of adequate ideas (IIp40s2). Because nature is always intelligible (Ip15–16, EIIp45s), all things are knowable through their proximate causes and, ultimately, through the first cause. Spinoza presents the third kind of knowing as a distinctive way of knowing singular things in their relation to the first cause (IIp40s2, Vp36s). In the very last line of the *Ethics*, Spinoza calls *scientia intuitiva* "most clear (*praeclara*)," which, I show in the last section of this chapter, we can understand as transparent or unmediated, though still finite, participation in the intelligibility of nature. In the *Treatise on the Emendation of the Intellect*, Spinoza uses "the knowledge of the union that the mind has with Nature" (¶13) to express the same point.[14]

Where Spinoza speaks of the infinite intellect of God and the intelligibility of substance or nature, Gersonides speaks of the order (*seder*) and law

---

[14] Curley translates *praeclara* as "excellent," which evokes Spinoza's surrounding statements about intellectual knowing as the highest perfection and greatest satisfaction of the mind. His translation also preserves the sense of eminence carried by *prae*, but "most clear" or "pre-eminently clear" would be more literal and would preserve the surrounding references to understanding clearly and distinctly (e.g Vp28dem, p38s). In connection with TIE ¶13, it is worth recalling that ¶11 speaks of this union as occurring only in "intervals."

(*nimus*, derived from the Greek *nomos*) in the soul of the active intellect. Just as Spinoza thinks that there is a single infinite intellect, Gersonides thinks that there is a single active intellect that moves all potential intellects to actuality. Gersonides argues that the intelligible order or pattern in the active or agent intellect exhibits the order in the divine intellect, so that God is the cause of all existents and "the *nomos* of the existent beings, their order and their equilibrium."[15] Like Spinoza, Gersonides thinks that we are always part of the order of existing things, even if we do not understand the causal structure of our participation. To sense is to undergo natural things; to understand them is to apprehend their intelligible content. Following Aristotle and Averroës, Gersonides is particularly interested in the transition from the former to the latter, which he analyzes as a process of abstraction that culminates in union or conjunction with the active intellect, i.e. union with the intelligible order or law of all beings. Gersonidean existent beings are Spinozan modes; the Gersonidean active intellect, which Spinoza calls the attribute of thought, is their total and infinite condition and order.

Second, both Spinoza and Gersonides rely on an account of perspectival or conceptual, as opposed to real, difference. Spinoza's account of "what remains" (Vp20s) of the human mind relies on an account of *how* the idea of the essence of the human body can be thought to exist, and not on an account of the existence of some part of the mind as a thing really distinct from the body. To be more precise, his discussion depends on the simultaneous sameness and difference of the mind and the body. Spinoza holds that the mind is nothing other than the idea of its body, but it is not the body itself (IIp11, p13). IIp7s is especially clear on this point: "the thinking substance and the extended substance are one and the same substance, which is now comprehended under this attribute, now under that." Throughout the *Ethics*, Spinoza uses the qualifier *quatenus* (insofar as) to mark such shifts in perspective, and it is almost impossible to over-emphasize the significance of the term in Spinoza's philosophy for resisting both dualism and the proliferation of real entities.[16] In a very important passage, Spinoza marks the distinction between conceiving a thing *sub specie durationis seu temporis* and *sub specie aeternitatis* with *quatenus*:

---

[15] Gersonides, *Commentary on Song of Songs* 4. All citations from this text, henceforth cited as *Commentary on Song of Songs*, come from Kellner's English translation (Levi ben Gershom 1998), which is based on Kellner's critical edition (Levi ben Gershom 2001). For a parallel text in the *Wars*, which uses more technical language, see I.11: "It is evident that the acquired intellect is itself the order [*siddur*] obtaining in the world [*l'elu ha-devarim*] that is inherent in the Agent Intellect." Feldman translates *l'elu ha-devarim* as "in the *sublunar* world" (emphasis added) (Levi ben Gershom 1984, 213).

[16] Using an electronic text, Laerke 2012 finds 444 instances of *quatenus* in the *Ethics*. He concludes that *quatenus* "exprime plûtot un certain type de liaison des concepts" (262).

We conceive things as actual in two ways [*duobus modis*]: Either insofar as [*quatenus ad*] we conceive them to exist in relation to a certain time and place, or insofar as [*quatenus ad*] we conceive them to be contained in God and to follow from the necessity of the divine nature. But the things we conceive in this second way as true, or real, we conceive under the aspect of eternity [*sub specie aeternitatis*], and to that extent they involve the eternal and infinite essence of God (as we have shown in IIp45 and p45s) (Vp23s).[17]

Gersonides uses the same expression to express the same idea, which he presumably found in Aristotle.[18] In Hebrew, he writes *mi-ẓad* (insofar as). As I shall show below, Gersonides thinks that forms exist simultaneously (1) in actual composites of form and matter and so in determinate times, manners, and places, and (2) infinitely and eternally in the active or agent intellect. Rather than conceiving two "things," *quatenus* and *mi-ẓad* signal two ways of conceiving the same thing.[19] In keeping with Spinoza's terminology in Ip29s, I shall reserve the term "aspectical difference" for conceiving nature under the aspect of eternity (*sub specie aeternitatis*) and under the aspect of time and duration (*sub specie temporis seu durationis*). I use the more general term "perspectival difference" to encompass the difference between Spinozan attributes (e.g. Thought and Extension) as well.

Third and finally, Spinoza formulates discussions of knowing and eternity in terms of degrees and extent. Spinoza frequently employs the idiom "the more . . . the more [*quo magis . . . quo magis*]" to emphasize the proportionate relationship of concrete experiences to intellectual knowing and the proportionate relationship of intellectual knowing and the mind's satisfaction or beatitude. He uses the idiom and "as much as possible [*quamprimus*]" to emphasize the difficulties of attaining intellectual knowledge. Gersonides, too, emphasizes proportionate relationships and argues that finite intellects exhibit degrees of conjunction with the agent intellect: "he who knows the law [*nomos*] of some of the existent beings apprehends God's essence *to some extent* [*b'ofen mah*]."[20] Both thinkers, we shall see, link the language of degrees to the language of desire and striving.

---

[17] Spinoza provides a helpful example of what he means in Ip15s: "Water, insofar as it is water, is generated and corrupted, but insofar as it is substance, it is neither generated nor corrupted."

[18] Perhaps the most prominent occurrence of this kind of qualification is *Metaphysics* XIII.2 1077b12–34, where Aristotle's agenda is to develop the respective objects of metaphysics and mathematics without recourse to Platonism. Gersonides' commentary on Averroës on Aristotle's *Metaphysics* is unfortunately lost. Aristotle's anti-Platonic agenda runs throughout the texts by Gersonides that I discuss in this chapter. Whenever Gersonides takes up intelligibility, of which mathematics is the paradigmatic expression, he takes pains to separate his own position from Plato's.

[19] To my knowledge, Dobbs-Weinstein 1998 is the first to comment on this point.

[20] *Commentary on Song of Songs*, Levi ben Gershom 1998, 4, emphasis added.

Some backgound: varieties of Aristotelianism

Readers of early modern philosophy are often familiar with Latin Christian accounts of the immortality of the soul. Reviewing the basic Latin-tradition account helps us set the alternative traditions in sharper relief. The roots of Descartes's incorporeal, self-subsistent, and ontologically discrete *res cogitans*, for example, are to be found in Augustine's account of the inner man and the displacement of *anima* by *mens*. The immortality of the individual human soul reflects its non-physical nature, and the death of the body releases each soul for its eternal fate. Even as devoted an Aristotelian as Thomas Aquinas posits an individuated, self-subsistent, and absolutely immaterial agent intellect as the intrinsic principle of existence and knowledge in each human soul. In so doing, Thomas resolves ambiguities in Aristotle's *De Anima* and profound debates in the commentary tradition in accord with Christian doctrinal requirements. For Thomas, the individuation of the soul is linked both to cognition, for it guarantees the crucial anti-Averroist principle "This man understands [*Hic homo intelligit*]"; and to justice, inasmuch as individuation anchors his account of moral responsibility and just desserts.[21] By Descartes's time, the Latin Aristotelian tradition discusses the human soul in special, rather than general, metaphysics; like God, the human soul is essentially incorporeal and not bound by nature. Even as later and medieval and Renaissance developments in anatomy and physiology suggested increasingly physical explanations of functions previously attributed to the soul, Christian thinkers affirmed the essentially immaterial character of the human soul, particularly will and intellect, in order to satisfy the requirements of higher cognition, morality, and immortality.

When we turn to the Islamic and Jewish tradition of commentaries on Aristotle's *De Anima*, a rather different picture emerges. The commentaries of Averroës, whose views were targeted in medieval Latin condemnations (e.g. in 1277) and consequently mostly excluded from university curricula, constitute the core of a materialist Aristotelian tradition.[22] Maimonides,

---

[21] See e.g. *Summa theologiae* I, q. 76, a.1. Thomas's comprehensive refutation is found in the treatise *De Unitate intellectus contra Averroistas*. For detailed analysis of Thomas's differences with Averroës on cognition, see Black 2004. It is important to note that Thomas objected vehemently to Averroës' doctrine of a single *material* intellect and to bear in mind that all of Thomas's criticisms reflect his general resistance to what he (correctly) perceived as Averroës' materialism.

[22] Hasse 2007 surveys the survival of Averroistic philosophy in the universities of the Latin West after 1277 and later condemnations. One way to avoid condemnation was to append to any serious discussion a statement that Averroës' views were contrary to the higher teachings of faith. Jewish philosophers, who worked outside the universities, did not face the same constraints.

too, for all of his difficulties with matter and his emanationist metaphysics, affirms that there is no cognition without sensation.[23] Unlike the Christian commentators, the Islamic and Jewish Aristotelians do not find or supply a substantial rational power equivalent to Thomas's individual agent intellect. In this regard, they are more reserved readers, and they continuously wrestle with the seemingly conflicting requirements of Aristotle's various statements about matter, body, soul, intellect, and knowledge. Most important for us, they leave open the possibility of real identity and perspectival or conceptual difference. Following them, then, we need not automatically assume a real distinction between the aspect of the soul that is eternal and the body through which cognition arises and occurs. In *De Anima*, one especially strong hint that neither Platonism nor its successor substance dualism is necessary comes in Book II:

> The objects that excite the sensory powers to activity, the seen, the heard, &c., are outside . . . . What actual sensation apprehends is individuals, while what knowledge apprehends is universals, *and these are in a sense within the soul itself.* That is why someone can think when he wants but his sensation does not depend on himself – a sensible object must be there.[24]

Aristotelian forms are constitutive principles in things, which, when met in actual extra-mental individuals, become universalized in the intellect, while forms exist in the extra-mental world, universals exist in the soul itself. The objects of mathematics provide the clearest example of how Aristotle sorts out the relation between extra-mental existents and intra-mental concepts: "The mind when it is thinking the objects of mathematics thinks of them as separate though they are not separate."[25]

Nor need we think of the intellect as a self-subsistent or ontologically discrete thing. Several considerations apply on this point. First, for Aristotle and the materialist Aristotelians, the intellect is nothing other than, or nothing but, its ideas. The mind is neither a pre-existing nor substantial container for ideas. Nor is the mind equipped with any ideas at birth; Aristotelians regard all knowing as beginning in sensation. Intelligible forms or universals are thus not *in* an intellect; they *are* an intellect.[26] Second, inasmuch as the Aristotelians identify knowledge with conjunction with the

---

[23] *Guide* I.68, Maimonides 1963, I.72.   [24] *De Anima* II.4 417b20–25, emphasis added.

[25] *De Anima* III.7 431b15. See also *Physics* II.2 193b30–194a12 and *Posterior Analytics* I.11 77a5–9. These texts agree with *Metaphysics* XIII.2 1077b12–34, cited above in note 18.

[26] Spinoza regards the so-called faculties of intellect and will as "Either complete fictions or nothing but metaphysical beings, or universals, which we are used to forming from particulars. So intellect and will are to this or that idea, or to this or that volition as 'stone-ness' is to this or that stone, or man to Peter or Paul" (IIp49s). Ep 2 and *Cogitata Metaphysica* I.6 make the same case.

active intellect, it is difficult to see how knowers can be individuated.[27] Third, Aristotle analyzes two "kinds" of intellect or intellectual principles: one active and productive, the *nous poetikos* that "can make all things," the other acted upon, the *nous pathetikos* "capable of becoming all things." *Nous poetikos* is "separable, impassive, and unmixed, since it is in its essential nature activity."[28] "When separated," this active intellect "is alone just what it is, and this alone is immortal and eternal (we do not remember because, while this is impassible, passive thought is perishable); and without this nothing thinks."[29] Nowhere in *De Anima* does Aristotle specify whether intellect in the active sense or intellect in the acted upon sense is single or multiple. Given Aristotle's silence, the medieval Jewish and Islamic Aristotelians are free to argue for the existence of a single active intellect. Averroës' most controversial argument, the so-called unicity thesis criticized sharply in the Latin tradition, defends the existence of a single acted upon intellect.[30]

For the Jewish and Islamic Aristotelians, understanding the material basis and conceptual separability of sensation and intellection turns on the task of explaining the relationship of imagination, whereby the soul stores impressions and which lies in the sensitive faculty of the soul, to the acted upon intellect, which must be moved to actuality by the active intellect in order for knowing to occur. Although Aristotle does not specify the exact processes of abstraction, *De Anima* II–III and *Posterior Analytics* II.19 indicate that cognition strips away material determinations of time, place, and manner from received sensibles, producing an image and also a potential intelligible, i.e. an intellect that is acted upon. When active intellect acts on the potential intelligible, an actual intelligible is produced. In this process, the intellect that is acted upon lies, so to speak, "between" imagination and intellectual actuality. Yet defining the nature, let alone the manner of being, of the acted upon intellect, which somehow receives the dematerialized, and hence departicularized or de-individuated, image from sensation, and which is actualized by the active intellect, is no small

---

[27] Gersonides criticizes Maimonides on this account, but it is difficult to see how his position is actually different. Gersonides explains intellectual differentiation, i.e. immortality obtained by different individual knowers, in *Wars of the Lord* I.13 (Levi ben Gershom 1984, 223–225). Nadler 2001 delves into this issue in detail.

[28] *De Anima* III.5 430a18–20. In Hebrew, the *nous poetikos* is the *sekhel ha-po'el*. Some translators render *po'el* as "active," others as "agent." *Nous pathetikos* is the *sekhel asher ba-koach*. The term 'material intellect' (*sekhel ha-hyiulani*) refers clearly to the material origins of potential intellect and to the way that Aristotelians conceive matter as potentiality.

[29] *De Anima* III.5 430a23–25.

[30] For a comprehensive account of the Arabic tradition on intellection, see Davidson 1992a. Davidson 1992b examines Gersonides' views on intellect.

challenge.[31] And so Aristotle, who so keenly defines the problem, provides little if any insight into its solution.

Averroes addressed the problem three times in three commentaries on *De Anima*, each of which provides a somewhat different solution to the problem.[32] Given the processes of transmission and translation, different linguistic audiences had different ideas about Averroës' views. Averroës' *Long Commentary on De Anima* was available to medieval readers in Arabic and in Latin translation; his *Middle Commentary* was preserved in Arabic and in Hebrew translation; his *Epitome* survived in Arabic and in Hebrew translation.[33] As reader of Latin and Hebrew, Spinoza could have known all three views, either directly or indirectly. The *Long Commentary* was well known among Latin thinkers, and, if Spinoza did not personally read Averroës' works in Hebrew, Gersonides' extensive citations provided a thorough account. Gersonides examines Averroës' view of the material intellect and the question of the immortality of the soul in three works from the middle of his own career: the *Supercommentary on Averroes's Epitome of Aristotle's de Anima*,[34] completed in 1323; the first book of the *Wars of the Lord*, "On the Immortality of the Soul," thought to be completed in 1325;[35] and a third book on the soul, the *Commentary on the Song of Songs*, written in

---

[31] The idea of a pure intellectual potentiality is difficult to understand. In what sense is a pure potentiality, i.e. something unstructured or unformed, receptive for knowing and only knowing? The reason for the potentiality or indeterminacy, i.e. the blankness of the Aristotelian "blank slate," is fairly straightforward. If the *nous pathetikos* had a form of its own, it could not receive the forms of other objects. The forms to be received would be impeded or distorted by any pre-existing forms; their actuality would prevent the acquisition of new forms. Consequently, "that in the soul which is called thought (by thought I mean that whereby the soul thinks and judges) is, before it thinks, *not actually any real thing*" (emphasis added) and "it was a good idea to call the soul 'the place of forms', though this description holds only of the thinking soul, even this is the forms only potentially, not actually" (*De Anima* III.4 428a20–28). That said, the intellect that is acted upon nonetheless is an intellect of some kind and so has some structure or identity. Aristotle regards prime matter as the only absolutely pure potentiality. It never occurs without form and so functions as a theoretical construct.

[32] For an overview of the different genres of commentary and Averroës' various solutions to the Aristotelian problem, see Ivry's introduction to Averroës 2002.

[33] Maimonides held Averroës in high regard as a commentator on Aristotle, and this in turn led to the translation of Averroës' commentaries from Arabic into Hebrew (S. Harvey 1992). As a result, Averroës became *the* philosopher for post-Maimonidean Jews (Glasner 1995; 2002; S. Harvey 2003). Gersonides was the first major Jewish philosopher to encounter Aristotle with a comprehensive knowledge of Averroës' commentaries.

[34] A partial modern edition of the Hebrew text and translation into English of the *Supercommentary* appears in Levi ben Gershom 1981. All references are to this edition, which I henceforth cite as *Supercommentary*.

[35] Gersonides' magnum opus, *Milhmot Adonai* (*Wars of the Lord*), was started in 1317 and finished in 1340, but first published only in 1560 (Riva di Trento). Levi ben Gershom 1866 provides a somewhat improved text, and Seymour Feldman's translation provides extensive editorial notes (Levi ben Gershom 1984, 1987, 1999). There is as yet no complete critical edition.

June or July 1325.[36] Scholars have generally doubted that Gersonides read Arabic, but Glasner has presented convincing evidence to the contrary.[37] Gersonides' connections to astronomers and perhaps others at the Papal Court at Avignon explain his knowledge of Latin, which he calls "the language of the Christians." Thus far, however, no scholar has identified textual evidence pointing to direct knowledge on his part of Averroes' *Long Commentary on De Anima*, but it is most likely that Gersonides was aware of the late thirteenth-century condemnations of Averroës and of Thomas Aquinas's rejection of Averroës' theory of the soul in particular.[38]

As the title suggests, Gersonides' *Supercommentary* is commentary on Averroës' short, topically organized *Epitome of Aristotle's De Anima*. A lengthy note in the *Supercommentary* shows Gersonides' familiarity with Averroes' *Middle Commentary* on *De Anima* and so with Averroes' willingness to rethink his own positions. Taken together, the *Supercommentary* and the *Wars* present a critical assessment of Averroës' and other commentators' treatments of the core issues of imagination, acted upon intellect (which Gersonides also calls, synonymously, the material intellect and the potential intellect), active intellect, and the human acquired intellect (*sekhel ha-nikneh*). Gersonides' aim is to establish the truth about intellectual potentiality and actuality – and not, as for us, to interpret historical texts. Aristotle and his commentators are authoritative only inasmuch as they are right about the question; thus Gersonides at once reads and adds original proposals for resolving outstanding difficulties. By systematically considering the strengths and weaknesses of the commentators' positions, Gersonides articulates what he finds aporetic and so sets the stage for his own answers.[39] The *Commentary on the Song of Songs* treats the biblical poetry as an allegory of the soul's desire for knowledge, i.e. perfection and immortality. According to Gersonides, the verse, "Let him kiss me with the kisses of his mouth," for example, pertains to unification or conjunction with the active intellect.[40] All three texts concern the relation of body and soul, which they discuss in terms of the relation between imagination, the acted upon intellect, agent intellect, and acquired intellect; the most

---

[36] Publication of Gersonides' Bible commentaries began in Ferrara in 1477. Saperstein 2005 sheds light on the important role of Gersonides' philosophical works and biblical commentaries in the circle of Amsterdam Rabbi Saul Levi Mortera, Spinoza's teacher at the Keter Torah yeshiva prior to the *ḥerem*.

[37] Glasner 2002.

[38] Cf. Dobbs-Weinstein 1998, 193–194. The classic study on the impact of Latin Scholasticism is Pines 1967; a more recent analysis is found in Rudavsky 2003.

[39] On Gersonides' use of aporetic questions as a philosophical method, see Klein-Braslavy 2011.

[40] *Commentary on Song of Songs* 17–30 (on verses I:1-I.8).

difficult issue is the status of imaginative forms and material intellect in relation to the active and acquired intellect. While at first glance it may seem that Gersonides multiplies the intellects – the active or agent intellect, the acted upon/potential/material intellect, and the acquired intellect make three – his language of sameness, aspects, and degrees allows us to view intellect from different perspectives or vantage points. Spinoza will use the same language to avoid the same pitfall.

Texts from Gersonides

Gersonides directly tackles the problem Aristotle leaves to his successors. The *Supercommentary* is oriented by Averroës' claim in the *Epitome* that "that which is imagined is identical to that which is intellect." Gersonides interprets Averroës' statement to mean that intellect or the intelligible aspect of the thing "is abstracted from matter, while the imagined thing is in matter."[41] In other words, the imaginative forms are in some sense the same as potential intellect, for, abstracted from matter, the imaginative forms "become intellect."[42] In a related text in *Wars* I.10, Gersonides is at pains to emphasize that the acquisition of intelligibles involves no real or essential change in the imaginative forms; in abstractive knowing, the production of an intelligible does not produce an additional thing.[43] Given these considerations, Gersonides concludes that potential intellect arises from imaginative forms, which are the most dematerialized forms still considered in regard to their origin in sensation. *Qua* intellect, however, potential intellect is, according to Aristotle's requirements, unmixed with the faculty of sensation, and so it is not reducible to the imaginative forms. In Gersonides' technical idiom, potential intellect is a disposition (*hakhanah*) inhering in the imagination.[44] Similarly, potential intellect qua intellect is constituted by intelligibles, but only by potential

---

[41] *Supercommentary*, Levi ben Gershom 1981, 125. [42] *Ibid.*, 139.

[43] Levi ben Gershom 1984, 205. Cf. the *Supercommentary*: "For it is not the case that the intelligibles which are thought are one thing, and the external existence something else; and that the intelligibles are thought in a manner different from the way in which they exist outside the soul, for that which is thought is the existent itself" (Levi ben Gershom 1981, 91). And also *Commentary on Song of Songs*: "You ought to know that the intelligible form is also potentially in those forms which are in these faculties [sc. senses, memory, imagination], even if the potentiality is more distant. For example, after the intellect abstracts the material attributes – by virtue of which this apprehended thing was distinctively particular – from the imaginative form, *that form becomes universal*; that is, it is the universal common to the infinite individuals of that species. In this manner one may solve the problem which prompted the ancients to posit form and numbers or to deny the possibility of knowledge, as was made clear in the *Metaphysics*" (Levi ben Gershom 1998, 6, emphasis added).

[44] For a full technical exposition, see Dobbs-Weinstein 1998.

intelligibles, and for this reason it is not simply reducible to active intellect, which actualizes the potentiality, or to the acquired intellect, which is the result of actualization. As Gersonides explains the relationships, the imaginative forms, potential intellect, active intellect, and acquired intellect are all simultaneously the same and different.

In the *Supercommentary*, Gersonides summarizes the acquisition of intelligibles and the way the human soul achieves immortality in a short, dense text. He writes:

> We say that when the potential intellect has been aroused by the imaginative forms, and the forms have been abstracted from their matters for [i.e. from] a limited number of sensed individuals, and when the potential intellect has been aroused by the Agent Intellect and has formed an infinite judgment concerning those forms, then there occurs to the material intellect *the same order* that is in the soul of the Agent Intellect regarding this intelligible; and the material intellect unites with the Agent Intellect in this way *to some degree* [*'al zeh ha'ofen*], and *it becomes eternal in this respect* [*me-hazad asher hitached bo*]. For the intelligible that it acquired is itself an intellect, *insofar as* it is in the soul of the Agent Intellect. In this respect, the material intellect can form an infinite judgment even though it abstracted only from a finite plurality. For the order in the soul of the Agent intellect encompasses an infinite number of individuals.[45]

After recalling that the acquisition of intelligibles begins in sense experiences of singular things, Gersonides explains how soul's cognitive faculties progressively abstract or dematerialize the form, the potential intellect. When actualized by the active intellect, the potential intelligible has the form of an "an infinite judgment."[46] In this way, the soul apprehends, for example, the abstract idea "tree" on the basis of actual encounters with, and stored images of, individual oaks, pines, firs, maples, palms, etc. The idea of the triangle is acquired in exactly the same way, as are first principles and axioms. More instances of sensation lead to more imaginative forms and a more extensive potential intellect; fewer instances lead to fewer imaginative forms and a less extensive potential intellect. Unlike the active intellect, which encompasses an "infinite number of individuals," i.e. all individuals, any human knower acquires a finite number of intelligibles. Sense experience is determinate, and no human knower can experience the

---

[45] *Supercommentary*, Levi ben Gershom 1981, 159–160, emphasis added. Mashbaum has rendered Gersonides' original "material intellect" (*sekhel ha-hyiulani*) as "potential intellect."

[46] Gersonides replaces Aristotle's universal intelligible with an infinite judgment for reasons having to do with his view of the logic of universals. Nonetheless, Gersonides carries on Aristotle's core notion of an abstract idea that applies to any individual whatsoever. On Gersonides' logic, see Manekin 1991 and Manekin's introductory essay and commentary in Levi ben Gershom 1992.

whole of nature.[47] When dematerialization and unification occur, the knower actively apprehends some portion of the total intelligibility of nature, and that portion constitutes her acquired intellect.

To see the power of Gersonides' analysis, it is essential to realize that the infinite judgment originates in the extra-mental form but exists only in thought. The eternity of the infinite judgment, like its infinite scope, refers to its abstract character, not to its existence in an extra-natural incorporeal realm; as abstract, the universal intelligible, which Gersonides also refers to as an intellect, is conceived without a determinative, individuating material index, and not as a special incorporeal or transcendent kind of real being (e.g. as the Platonic forms are traditionally interpreted).[48] Gersonides understands the immortality of the soul to be just this infinite and eternal intellectual knowledge.[49] Although only individuals exist in the extra-mental world, only sensation and imagination grasp their individual-izing determinations. By emphasizing the sameness of imaginative and intelligible forms and the sameness of the order in the potential or material intellect and the active or agent intellect, Gersonides eliminates any refer-ence to another class of extra-mental entities. Thus Gersonides can affirm the existence of one actual individual thing that can be thought in two ways. In emphasizing differences of respect, Gersonides holds that an actual thing can be experienced in irreducibly different ways without violating its ontological integrity; respectival difference holds together what real differ-ence would divide. The difference between experiencing nature sensibly and intelligibly, i.e. temporally or determinately and eternally or indeter-minately, occurs in the soul. And so Gersonides has his cake and eats it too: sensible experience is crucial to knowing, insofar as all knowing begins in sensation, and knowledge is independent of sensible experience, insofar as forms are separable in thought. It follows from this that experiencing nature in its eternal aspect does not depend on the death of the body.

Gersonidean knowers experience intellectual pleasure in proportion to their degree of intellectual union. Following the models established in Aristotle's *Metaphysics* and *Nicomachean Ethics* quoted at the beginning of

---

[47] On the quantitative distinction between the active or agent intellect and the acquired intellect, see Dobbs-Weinstein 2006.

[48] See e.g. *Supercommentary*, Levi ben Gershom 1981, 165, where Gersonides rejects the idea of "universal forms existing outside the soul."

[49] Thus it is hard to see how his position differs from Maimonides'. The great rabbi and philosopher Hasdai Crescas (*c.* 1340–1410) categorically rejected what he saw as the common view of Averroës, Maimonides, and Gersonides on the immortality of soul. Whatever else Spinoza learned from Crescas (see W. Harvey 1998), he did not concur with Crescas on this issue.

this chapter, Gersonides identifies the extent of the acquired intellect with degrees of joy:

> Therefore, *the greater* the number of intelligibles acquired, *the greater* the union and joy achieved; and when all the intelligibles that are in the soul of the agent intellect occur to an individual, he attains ultimate felicity, joy, and happiness [*takhlit hahazlakhah, v'takhlit ha-areivut, v'hasmeicha*]. In this respect some men are superior to others; for *in proportion* to their greater apprehension of the order in the soul of the Agent Intellect, they unite with it *to a greater degree*, and their bliss, joy, and happiness are greater. Thus our happiness is intense when we think these intelligibles, for this is our appointed felicity.[50]

Gersonides' point is that actuality, understood here as the intellectual apprehension or conjunction that constitutes the acquired intellect, is intrinsically joyful. As we shall see in the next section, Spinoza, too, associates actuality with knowing and joy; the "greatest satisfaction of Mind there can be arises from the third kind of knowledge" (Vp27), which Spinoza also calls "the greatest human perfection" (Vp27dem). In fact each part of the *Ethics* links perfection with greater existence and reality.[51] Reading these texts from a Gersonidean perspective, the Latin *perfectio* (perfection), derived from the verb *facere* (to make or bring about) might equally be understood as "actualization." Likewise the adjective *perfectum* might be understood as "actualized" or "done" in the sense of completed.

Texts from Spinoza

I turn now to the portrait of Spinoza as a late Gersonidean. If Gersonides pushes the limits of the medieval Jewish philosophical tradition in metaphysics and epistemology, Spinoza clearly exceeds them. In what follows, I begin from the sometimes controversial claim that Spinozan knowing, like its predecessor accounts in the materialist Aristotelian tradition, begins with sensation.[52] Spinoza reflects at length on the roles of corporeal impressions, memory, and imagination in analyzing the acquisition of common notions and reason. Reason, in turn, is the necessary but not sufficient condition for *scientia intuitiva*, the third kind of knowledge (Vp28).[53] Here, I argue that

---

[50] *Supercommentary*, Levi ben Gershom 1981, 160–161, emphasis added.
[51] E.g. Ip11s, IIdef6, III Gen. Def. Aff, IVp45s.
[52] Readers who discern a more Cartesian Spinoza or an idealist Spinoza of course reject the idea that knowledge in the strict sense begins in sensation.
[53] Though I cannot discuss the issue in detail here, it is important to emphasize that Spinoza does not think that the second kind of knowledge automatically leads to the third kind; Vp28 states only that the third kind "can arise" from the second. Spinoza thinks that the idea of God can be apprehended only intuitively, i.e. immediately, and not derived by rational or syllogistic means.

Spinoza uses the Aristotelian-Gersonidean tool of respectival difference to distinguish between conceiving the mind *sub specie durationis seu temporis* and conceiving it *sub specie aeternitatis* without introducing any sort of real distinction. Respectival difference also explains the related distinction between conceiving the mind in relation to the body and conceiving without relation to the body. As Spinoza emphasizes in Part Two, the mind is the idea of the body, not the body itself (IIp11, p13). That which is eternal in the mind is the dematerialized idea of the essence of the mind conceived in relation to God under the attribute of thought.

Spinoza also adopts the Gersonidean model of proportionality in explaining the extent to which any knower can achieve eternity, and he is squarely in the Aristotelian tradition, exemplified so vividly by Gersonides, that identifies intuitive understanding – what Gersonides called unification or conjunction – with "the greatest satisfaction of the Mind there can be" (Vp27) and affection with "the greatest Joy." To the extent that we become capable of the third kind of knowledge, we strive more and more for such knowledge, and our satisfaction and joy, which Spinoza calls *amor Dei intellectualis*, increase proportionately. More broadly speaking, when we read Spinoza against the medieval Jewish and Islamic Aristotelian backdrop, his decision to elaborate the nature of *scientia intuitiva* in Part Five, that is, only after lengthy examinations of affective and socio-political life, comes into focus. Parts Three, Four, and the first part of Part Five patiently and painstakingly explicate the bodily, affective, and socio-political dimensions of actively apprehending our constitutive involvement in God or nature as knowledge and joy.[54] As Aristotle's discussion in *Nicomachean Ethics* X.7–9 indicates, human knowers achieve intervals of contemplation in the midst of corporeal life.

A brief outline of Spinoza's account of how we acquire true and adequate ideas via the body goes as follows. In *Ethics* Part Two, Spinoza argues that there are no human minds without human bodies. He takes as axiomatic not only that human beings think (IIax1) but also that "we feel that a certain body is affected in many ways" (IIax4), and he quickly establishes, by recalling core arguments from Part One, that God is an extended, not just a thinking, thing (IIp1, p2).[55] From these beginnings, Spinoza's insistence that human mind is the idea of its actually existing body (IIp11, p13) easily

---

[54] Dobbs-Weinstein 2006 aptly notes that Spinoza's attention to social and political philosophy is far more Maimonidean than Gersonidean. In this, Maimonides is closest to Al-Farabi. Fraenkel 2010 and 2012 connect Spinoza with the Farabian-Maimonidean tradition via the Jewish Averroist Elijah Delmedigo.

[55] As early as Ip15s, Spinoza criticizes proponents of a disembodied God.

follows. In this context, IIp7 and its scholium, which reject both the Cartesian real difference between *res extensa* and *res cogitans* and the traditional theological idea of a real distinction between God and the world, come as no surprise. Given the simultaneous sameness in substance and difference in attributes (thought and extension) and aspects (eternal creator and temporally and durationally determined creatures), problems of interaction disappear. Spinoza's decision to preface an analysis of the mind's cognitive operations with a mini-treatise on physics, i.e. a discourse on extended things and their interactions and exchanges, reflects his own revised conception of extension. Thus the mini-treatise on physics that precedes Spinoza's account of the kinds of cognitions is not, as readers have sometimes regarded it, a physical "digression," but an essential part of the overall argument.

Ethics Part Two focuses on two features of human knowledge: its infinite ontological condition in God (or nature) and its temporal origin in bodily affections. The human mind, Spinoza writes, is "part of the infinite intellect of God" (IIp11c).[56] At the end of Part Two, Spinoza demonstrates that the human mind "has an adequate knowledge of God's infinite and eternal essence" and so can form the idea of God (IIp47). As Spinoza notes in IIp47s, "that men do not have so clear a knowledge of God as they do of the common notions comes from the fact that they . . . are continually affected by bodies." The corporeal origins of knowing, in other words, can obscure the ontological foundation; natural events are happening, but we, despite being parts of nature, may be quite confused about their order and connection.[57] The first kind of knowledge is confused. Strictly speaking, to know a thing is to know it through its causes (Iax4),[58] and ultimately through its first cause, as clear and distinct – or, in Spinoza's technical term, adequate – ideas can be understood through their causal connections in the idea of God. Coming to see the causal order clearly is the work of reason, the second kind of knowledge, and intuition, the third kind of knowledge (IIp45 and IIp45s).

Thus much of *Ethics* Part Two concerns the possible transition from sensing, remembering, and imagining, in which the mind follows the

---

[56] On infinite intellect, see also Ip15–16 and Ip30.

[57] Here we can see an important difference between Spinoza and his Aristotelian predecessors. In Aristotle, natural teleology generally assures the process of abstractive knowing. Spinoza categorically rejected natural teleology, and his account of how human beings often cannot reconfigure imaginative ideas is extremely subtle. I hope in a subsequent paper to consider how Gersonides' invocations of teleology square with his view that the world is eternal after creation.

[58] See also TIE ¶85. In Aristotle see e.g. *Posterior Analytics* I.6.

common order of nature, to reasoning, which follows the mind's internal order. When the mind imagines, it regards images, i.e. affections in the body, as present (IIp17s); when the mind reasons, it attends to "agreements, differences, and oppositions" among things (IIp29s), establishing causal orders and producing clear and distinct ideas. Because the first cause is singular, and because it remains immanently in all things, "the connection of ideas which happens according to the order of the intellect, by which the Mind perceives things their first causes" is the same [*idem est*] in all men" (IIp18s).[59] Part Two actually says relatively little about this order of the intellect, which Spinoza identifies with a third kind of knowledge, which "proceeds from an adequate knowledge of the formal essence of certain attributes of God to the adequate knowledge of [NS: formal] essence of things." It is thus in a way distinct from reason, which knows properties adequately (IIp40s2). In Part Five, Spinoza recalls and reiterates the IIp40s definition of the third kind of knowledge immediately after establishing the nature of the mind's eternity: "the third kind of knowledge proceeds from an adequate idea of certain attributes of God to an adequate knowledge of the essence of things (see its Def. in IIp40s2)" (Vp25dem). Simply put, the third kind of knowing is the cognitive expression of God or nature's immanent causality.[60]

Given Spinoza's constant critique of teleology (see, for example, the appendix to Part One) and his critique of the idea of faculties in IIp47s, we need to bear in mind that, for Spinoza, the acquisition of the kinds of knowledge cannot refer to a process that begins in sensation and is naturally directed to intellection. What most medieval Aristotelians called faculties arranged in a sequential order, Spinoza calls simply kinds of cognition (*genera cognitionis*).[61] Because *genera*, like faculties, are merely *entia rationis*, it makes more sense to rethink the progressive "stages" of abstraction as respectively distinct ways of knowing.[62] In any case, as Spinoza makes abundantly clear, there is no guarantee of achieving even the second kind of knowledge.

Ethics Part Five, too, devotes considerable attention to the mind's relation to the body's affections before turning to the third kind of knowledge. The first twenty propositions examine the Mind's ability to order and connect

---

[59] See also IV App 4.
[60] Spinoza uses the terms *ratio* and *causa* synonymously in Ip11alt dem. On immanence, see especially Ip25c, but also Ip15–16, p25c, p28–29s.
[61] IIp40s2. See also TIE¶¶18–19.
[62] I argue for this view in detail in Klein 2002. In Klein 2006, I argue that Gersonides' claims about the sameness of images and intellectual ideas undermine the idea of faculties.

images according to the intellect and thereby to feel love toward God (*amor erga Deum*). In Part Five, Spinoza connects the Part Two account of clearly and distinctly understanding causal connections with the argument, made in Parts Three and Four, that each kind of cognition has its characteristic affective state. Briefly stated, imaginative ideas coincide with affective instability and bring the prospect of a negative affect with every positive affect; rational ideas coincide with affective stability, and the characteristic affects are purely positive. Intuitive knowledge brings about the mind's highest love and joy. In this first portion of Part Five, Spinoza demonstrates that "the Mind can bring it about that all the Body's affections, or images of things, are related to the idea of God" (Vp14). To do this is to remove the negative affects that either directly attend or wait in the wings of imaginative ideas. Spinoza then demonstrates that successfully connecting ideas of body's affections to the idea of their first cause brings about joy: "He who understands himself and his affects clearly and distinctly rejoices (by IIIp53), and this joy is accompanied by the idea of God (by p14)" (Vp15).[63] Unlike imaginative joy, which is easily "tainted by an affect of Envy or Jealousy," this rational joy increases when we imagine more people experiencing the same love of God that we experience (Vp20). No one's joy is threatened by competition or by fears of loss, for this "highest good we can want from the dictate of reason (by IVp28)" is "common to all men (by IVp36)" (Vp20 dem).[64]

Spinoza introduces the eternity of the mind in Vp20s. He instructs us that Love toward God "is the most constant of all of the affects, and insofar as it is related to the Body, cannot be destroyed, unless it is destroyed with the Body itself." Then he adds the crucial, provocative promissory note: "What the nature of this Love is insofar as [*quatenus*] it is related only to the Mind, we shall see later," and he invites us to "pass to those things which pertain to the Mind's duration without relation to the Body" (Vp20s). Given IIp7s, considering the mind without the body can involve only a Gersonidean perspectival change.[65] Spinoza's use of the qualifier *quatenus*

---

[63] Consequently "insofar as we understand God to the cause of [imaginative] sadness, we rejoice" (Vp18c).

[64] IIp18s also formulates this point very clearly by contrasting different knowers' imaginative interpretations of the same natural thing and by further contrasting the diversity of imaginative ideas with the singularity of intellectual order. What differentiates and so individuates the knowers is "the order and connection of the affections of the human Body." Spinoza distinguishes this imaginative order from "the connection of ideas which happens according to the order of the intellect, by which the Mind perceives things their first causes, and which is the same [*idem est*] in all men" (IIp18s).

[65] That the distinction cannot be a real distinction is made clear in the preface to Part Five as well. There, Spinoza argues that no dualistic account of the mind's mastery of the bodily passions is acceptable, for the real distinction is "a Hypothesis more occult than any occult quality." Nor, as we saw in IIp7s, is reducing mind to body an option.

and the language of relation enable him to think of the same thing or singular mode of nature in more than one way. In Vp40s, Spinoza considers himself to have fulfilled the invitation. His remarks echo IIp11c:

> These are things I have decided to show concerning the Mind, insofar as [*quatenus*] it is considered without relation to the Body's existence. From them, and at the same time from Ip21 and other things – it is clear that our Mind, insofar as it understanding, is an eternal mode of thinking, which is determined by another eternal mode of thinking, and this again by another, and so on, to infinity; so that together, they all constitute God's eternal and infinite intellect (Vp40s).

Part Five, then, shows us a new way to understand ideas introduced earlier in the text. It reflects not only on Part Two, but on major propositions in Part One as well. As knowledge, the third kind of knowledge relates things to their first cause.

Vp21 and Vp22 encapsulate the difference between thinking about the mind in relation to the body and thinking of the mind without relation to the body. Vp21 reflects the standard Aristotelian position that judgments of actual existence concerning bodies involve both intellect and sense. Spinoza makes the case by arguing that the mind expresses its body's actual existence only while its body actually exists, and that it knows other actually existing bodies only through its own body. In other words, in being aware of my body, I am simultaneously aware of other bodies and vice versa; the simultaneous co-presence of bodies explains why such awareness is confused. Imagination, in Spinoza, is the cognitive state of such aggregations and confusions, and judgments based solely on imagination are erroneous (IIp29s). Vp22 reframes the same situation in terms of essences: "Nevertheless, in God there is necessarily an idea that expresses the essence of this or that human Body, *sub specie aeternitatis*." Matheron helpfully glosses the essence of body as its singular, characteristic ratio of motion and rest or its "corporeal equation."[66] The essence of the very same body that we can imagine is clear and distinct rather than confused. Causally connected to other essences and ultimately to God understood under the attribute of thought, it is adequate. The ever-helpful IIp7s points us to mathematics to explain the relation of a ratio or formula and an existing thing: "a circle existing in nature and the idea of the existing circle, which is also in God, are one and the same thing, which is explained through different attributes" (IIp7s). Absent the reference to concrete existence, the idea of the

---

[66] Matheron 1969, 48. Lachterman 1977 advances this insight.

circle is stripped of all reference to time or duration, which are "determined by the whole of corporeal nature" (Ip11, alternative demonstration; see also IIp8c). Just as in Aristotle's account of mathematicals as universals and in Gersonides' account of infinite judgments as abstractions that apply to any individual of a species, the Spinozan abstract essence is eternal.[67] Spinoza's term for this abstract essence is "formal essence." To return to the example in IIp7s, just as there is an eternal idea of the circle, so too is there an eternal idea of the essence of the mind, which is itself an idea of the body. Thus the formal essence does not exist as a special eternal thing (*res*) but only in the act of understanding. It follows from this position that there is no need to wait for the death of the body to experience eternity.

When finally we reach the famous Vp23 and its scholium, the central texts for understanding what Spinoza means by the eternity of the mind, Spinoza has already distinguished ways of thinking about the mind, and he has identified the human intellect with the divine intellect, i.e. the necessary order or intelligibility of nature. Vp23 reads:

> The human Mind cannot be absolutely destroyed with the Body, but something of it remains which is eternal [*Mens humana non potest cum Corpore absolutè destrui; sed ejus aliquid remanet, quod aeternum est*].

In the demonstration, Spinoza recalls that the mind is the idea of its actually existing body (IIp13), and he recalls that duration pertains only to the Mind considered in relation to its actually existing body (IIp8c).[68] Thus only the actually existing body "is explained by duration, and can be defined by time," leaving open the exact nature of the "something that remains that is eternal" (Vp23dem). The demonstration tells us that what remains is conceived "with a certain eternal necessity" and is "nevertheless something [*nihilominus aliquid*]" despite the fact that it has neither duration nor temporality. While an *aliquid* is not nothing, it is also not quite a thing (*res*), a term Spinoza uses throughout the text. The scholium immediately confirms that the *aliquid* in question is an idea of the essence of the body *sub specie aeternatitatis*: "There is, as we have said, *this idea*, which expresses the essence of the body under a species of eternity, a certain mode of thinking, which pertains to the essence of the Mind, and which is necessarily eternal" (emphasis added). Another way to express the point of Vp23 and its

---

[67] Cf. Nadler, who emphasizes that Spinozan eternity has nothing at all to do with temporal categories and so identifies eternity with atemporality (2001, 111–112, 121–123).

[68] "When singular things are said to exist, not insofar as [*non tantum quatenus*] they are comprehended in God's attributes, but insofar [*sed quatenus*] as they are said to have duration, their ideas also involve the existence through which they are said to have duration" (IIp8c).

scholium is to say that there are no things without essences and no essences without things.[69]

Having established the cognitive sense of the mind's eternity, Spinoza returns to the affective character:

> And though it is impossible that we should recollect that we existed before the Body – since there cannot be any traces of this in the body, and eternity can neither be defined by time nor have any relation to time – still, we feel and know by experiences that we are eternal. For the Mind feels those things that it conceives in understanding no less than those it has in the memory. For the eyes of the mind, by which it sees and observes things, are the demonstrations themselves.

In pointing to demonstrations as the "eyes of the mind," Spinoza invites us to contrast rational seeing and corporeal seeing. Specifically, his turn of phrase recalls IVp59s: "Every Desire that arises from an affect which is a passion would be of no use if men could be guided by reason. Let us now see why we call a Desire blind which arises from an affect which is a passion." Considered in the framework of perspectival difference, the striving to know (*conatus intelligendi*, IVp18) and the highest striving of the Mind (*summus Mentis conatus*, Vp25) are both the same as and different from the body's *conatus*. It is not that a really separate mind senses incorporeally, but rather that there are affects characteristic of intellection; without experiencing intellection, we do not feel them. In this regard, Spinoza's Aristotelian view of the intellect is strikingly different from the really disembodied mind familiar from Descartes, whose proposals for mental mastery over the body are dismissed in no uncertain terms in the preface to Part Five, as well as from numerous other canonical Western texts. Kant's moral philosophy provides an especially salient example.

Spinoza's term *amor Dei intellectualis*, "intellectual love of God," joins the cognitive and affective dimensions of the eternity of the mind:

> For from this kind of knowledge there arises (by p32) Joy, accompanied by the idea of God as its cause, i.e. (by Def. Aff. VI), Love of God, not insofar as we imagine him as present (by p29), but insofar as we understand God to be eternal. And this is what I call intellectual love of God (Vp32c).

Just as the "eyes of the Mind" are demonstrations rather than corporeal organs, intellectual love is an affect, but it is not a passion, and so it is neither

---

[69] Unlike many thinkers in the post fourteenth-century Latin tradition, Spinoza does not conceive actual things as a subset of really possible essences that have been actualized. On the contrary, he presumes the Aristotelian view that everything that can exist, will exist.

determined by corporeal predicates nor destructible. In Vp36s, Spinoza identifies this "constant and eternal Love of God" with "salvation, or blessedness, or freedom [*salus, seu beatitudo, seu Libertas*]" and with the biblical term "Glory [*Gloria*]." In keeping with IIp7s, and to emphasize the mind's simultaneous sameness and difference with the body, I would consider translating *salus* here as "health" or, to evoke a term from the *Nicomachean Ethics*, living well or flourishing (*eudaimonia*).[70]

The same question of individuation that caused Gersonides to criticize Maimonides can be asked of Spinoza. In what sense is the third kind of knowledge constitutive of or possessed by an individual knower? To put this question another way, in what sense can a third-order knower be said to have a self? In Part Five, Spinoza puts the Gersonidean model of degrees or extensiveness to use. To the degree that we understand causes, imaginative affects decrease and rational love increases. While the idea of God is always adequate because nature is always intelligible (IIp46), individual knowers continuously undergo more bodily experiences (Vp39s) and so must continuously work to connect ideas of secondary causes to the idea of the first cause. Provided that we do not get stuck in imaginative knowledge (e.g. as described in IIp28dem), more bodily experience can be the source of more intellectual understanding and a higher degree or greater extent of eternity (Vp39). Any individual mind is composed of imaginative as well as intellectual ideas: "the intellect, however extensive it is, is more perfect than the imagination" (Vp39c). As we saw above, IIp18s links individuation principally to imagination, contrasting the patterns of individuals' imaginative, associative links to "the connection of ideas which happens according to the order of the intellect, by which the Mind perceives things their first causes, and which is the same [*idem est*] in all men" (IIp18s). Thus it seems the prospects for individuation are dim, for insofar as we know through the first causes, our intellects are the same.

Yet in Vp27dem, Spinoza explains that, for any intuitive knower, the "highest satisfaction of the Mind [*summa Mentis acquiescentia*]," its "greatest Joy [*summa Laetitia*]" is "accompanied (by IIp43) by the idea of himself and his virtue [*concomitante ideâ sui, suaeque virtutis*]."[71] The third kind of knowledge is "an action by which the Mind contemplates itself, with the accompanying idea of God as its cause [*actio est, qua Mens se ipsam*

---

70   These retranslations or glosses would also accord with Spinoza's idea of freedom, for a freedom that can be experienced without a body only in the sense of being experienced after death is no freedom at all. But this is not the occasion to analyze Spinoza's critique of conventional religion or his wider political philosophy.

71   Vp36dem uses the same term, "accompanied by," to describe *amor Dei intellectualis*.

contemplamur, concomitante idea dei tanquam causa]."[72] In what sense is there a difference between the mind's self-contemplation and the idea of God? And, if there is a difference, does that difference account for individuation? The best answer perhaps lies in Spinoza's enigmatic references to consciousness (*conscientia*), literally, "knowing-with."[73] The final scholium of the *Ethics* informs us that "the wise man, insofar as he is considered as such," is "by a certain necessity conscious of himself, and of God, and of things" (Vp42s). This passage suggests that the third kind of knowledge apprehends how things belong together in ratios and causes.[74] Knowledge of oneself is no different from, and hence no more privileged than, knowledge of God and things, and these forms of knowledge occur together, for they are mutually involved. Thus the term *conscientia*, thought as involvement, militates against individuation.

There is another sense of individuation for which we must account. Gersonides solves (to his own satisfaction, at least) the problem of individual immortality by appealing to the extent of any given material intellect, which accounts for the extent of any given acquired intellect. Gersonides thus invokes both the determinate origins of knowledge in sensible experience and the achievement of abstract knowing. His solution has the great advantages of explaining why human knowers have different ranges of knowledge and why no human knower knows everything. Given different histories of sensation, different knowers achieve different degrees of material intellect and hence different degrees of unification or conjunction with the active intellect.[75] While for all intellectual knowers any given intelligible is

---

[72] See also IVp52.

[73] The issue of consciousness in Spinoza merits a separate study. Coming from Descartes, to be conscious seems obviously to be self-conscious (e.g. Third Meditation, AT VII: 49), but Spinoza is quite critical of this view of consciousness in *Ethics* Iapp and propositions such as IIp35.

[74] See *Ethics* Part One for the first use of this expression.

[75] Cf. Nadler 2001, 125–131, for an analysis that preserves a stronger sense of individuation in Spinoza. I concur with Nadler that different individuals achieve different degrees of intellectual perfection, though I do not share his concerns that arise from considerations of the principle of the identity of indiscernables. To my mind, Nadler and I differ on the issue of immanence, which he generally stresses (e.g. 25–34) but about which he appears to hesitate in the analysis of the eternity of the mind. Nadler proposes that a mind with "perfect knowledge" "would *mirror* God's total and eternal understanding of things" (125 [emphasis added]; see also 87, which uses the same idiom in connection with Gersonides). Similarly, "My suggestion – and it is, I admit, only a suggestion – is that for Spinoza, after a person's death, what remains of the mind eternally – the adequate ideas, along with the idea of the essence of the body – all disperses and *reverts back* to the infinite intellect of God (the attribute of Thought), since they are just God's knowledge of things" (129; emphasis added). Mirroring and reversion back suggest some significant separation between the knower and God or Nature. Thus when Nadler concludes by noting that "If my proposed account is right, then there is just one set of eternal, adequate ideas, a body of knowledge that each of us, in this lifetime, is able to tap into" (130), he pictures us at some remove from the eternal ideas. In Klein 2003, I argue that we are

the same – in the sense that there is only one world and in the sense that all members of the human species are equipped with the same cognitive processes – individual knowers vary in terms of which intelligibles, and in terms of how many intelligibles, constitute their intellects. Spinoza, I suggest, adopts the same kind of solution. Recall that what perishes is the imaginative part of the mind (Vp21), through which we acquired the first kind of knowledge; what remains is "the intellect, however extensive it is" (Vp40c). Yet insofar as the intellect is "an eternal mode of Thinking, which is determined by another eternal mode of thinking, this again by another, and so on to infinity; so that together, they all constitute God's eternal and infinite intellect," it is difficult to discern any individuating features. To put this problem in an image familiar from Plato, where would we cut the joints?[76] Because Spinozan causes and effects "involve" each other, it is difficult to see how an individual can be conceived as a discrete individual in the usual sense. Indeed, IIdef7 treats singular things as singular on the condition they "so concur in one action that they are all the cause of one effect."[77]

Thus the Spinozan eternity of the mind, like its Gersonidean predecessor,[78] amounts to something like an immanent and finite participation in the infinite order of intelligibility.[79] For Gersonides, unification carries the sense of immanence. In Spinoza, the idiom of the power of intuition as unmediated knowledge specifies the immanence established deductively in *Ethics* Part One. Vp36 emphasizes the constitutive role of God and the distinctive power of intuitive knowing. I take the liberty of quoting Spinoza at length:

> Because the essence of our Mind consists only in knowledge, of which God is the beginning and foundation (by Ip15 and IIp47s), it is clear to us how our Mind, with respect to both essence and existence, follows from the divine nature, and continually depends on God.
>
> I thought this worth the trouble of noting here, in order to show by this example how much more the knowledge of singular things I have called

---

constituted as part of this eternal intelligible order, even if we do not know it, and hence that the possibility of knowing adequately and eternally is grounded in this ontological constitution. More generally, I see the immediacy of *scientia intuitiva* as a radically immanent re-articulation of Aristotelian noetic union. Intellectual knowing immediately expresses our participation in the causal order of nature.

[76] *Phaedrus* 265e.

[77] For other provocative passages on causation in Spinoza, see Ip17s and Ep 12, which use idioms of flowing and following.

[78] Gersonides' critique of Maimonides notwithstanding, the latter's account of intellectual immortality is essentially the same.

[79] Thus the idea that the third kind of knowledge amounts to complete mystical union is ruled out.

intuitive, *or* knowledge of the third kind (see IIp40s2), can accomplish, and how much more powerful it is than the universal knowledge I have called knowledge of the second kind. For although I have shown generally in Part I that all things (and consequently the human Mind also) depend on God for both their essence and their existence, nevertheless that demonstration, though legitimate and put beyond all doubt, still does not affect our Mind as much as when this is inferred from the very essence of any singular thing which we say depends on God.

Conclusion

Examining Spinoza's idea of the eternity of the mind in connection with Gersonides's approach to the immortality of the soul makes Spinoza's view comprehensible and, I hope, sets the stage for further study about the range of philosophical views in the medieval tradition and the seventeenth century. Spinoza so often begins in language familiar from canonical Latin thinkers, but he brings to bear concepts and language from the often ignored Arabic and Hebrew traditions. Appreciating Spinoza's complex relationship to Cartesian philosophy, to Hobbes, and to sources in the Latin legal and political canon has proved a great boon to studying his texts. Attention to Spinoza's complex relationship to the Jewish and Islamic medieval thinkers is fruitful in the same way.

Hasdai Crescas and Spinoza on actual infinity and the infinity of God's attributes

Yitzhak Y. Melamed

Introduction

The seventeenth century was an important period in the conceptual development of the notion of the infinite. In 1643, Evangelista Torricelli (1608–1647) – Galileo's successor in the chair of mathematics in Florence – communicated his proof of a solid of infinite length but finite volume.[1] Many of the leading metaphysicians of the time, notably Spinoza and Leibniz, came out in defense of actual infinity, rejecting the Aristotelian ban on it, which had been almost universally accepted for two millennia. Though it would be another two centuries before the notion of the actually infinite was rehabilitated in mathematics by Dedekind and Cantor (Cauchy and Weierstrass still considered it mere paradox),[2] Spinoza's and Leibniz's impenitent advocacy of the concept had significant reverberations in both philosophy and mathematics.

In this chapter, I will attempt to clarify one thread in the development of the notion of the infinite. In the first part, I study Spinoza's discussion and endorsement, in the "Letter on the Infinite" (Ep 12), of Hasdai Crescas's (c. 1340–1410/11) crucial amendment to a traditional proof of the existence of God ("the cosmological proof"),[3] in which he insightfully points out that the proof does not require the Aristotelian ban on actual infinity. In the second and last part, I examine the claim, advanced by Crescas and Spinoza, that God has infinitely many attributes, and explore the reasoning that motivated both philosophers to make such a claim. Similarities between Spinoza and Crescas, which suggest the latter's influence on the former, can be discerned in several other important issues, such as necessitarianism,[4]

I am indebted to John Brandau and John Morrison for the comments on earlier drafts of this chapter. Special thanks to Meir Neuberger and Rabbi Dovid Katz, my Thursday night Crescas *havrusa*.

[1] See Mancosu 1996, 130–139.   [2] See Boyer and Merzbach 1991, 563–568.
[3] By "cosmological proof" I refer to an argument for the existence of a first cause as a requirement for the intelligibility of the existence of the world.
[4] *Or ha-Shem*, II.5.2, Crescas 1990, 209–210.

the view that we are compelled to assert or reject a belief by its representational content,[5] the enigmatic notion of *amor Dei intellectualis*,[6] and the view of punishment as a natural consequent of sin.[7] Here, I will restrict myself to the issue of the infinite, clearly a substantial topic in itself.

In defense of the actually infinite

Spinoza's twelfth letter – dated July 26, 1663, and addressed to his friend, Lodewijk Meyer – is one of our most valuable texts for understanding the core of his ontology. From his late correspondence, we learn that he circulated copies of this letter even in this period,[8] and we may thus assume that the views expressed in it reflect, more or less, his late thought as well. Among Spinoza's friends, the letter was referred to as "the Letter on the Infinite,"[9] and indeed this title reflects its main topic. In this letter, Spinoza develops a detailed taxonomy of infinities, and in the course of this taxonomy he also provides a concise exposition of some of his key notions and distinctions, such as the nature of numbers, the distinction between substance and mode, the threefold distinction among eternity (*aeternitas*), duration (*duratio*), and time (*tempus*), and the distinction between conceiving a thing by the intellect and conceiving it through the imagination.[10]

Toward the end of the letter, after announcing his satisfaction with his discussion ("unless I am mistaken, I have so explained all of the [errors and confusions concerning the Infinite] that I do not think any Problem about the Infinite remains which I have not touched on here or which cannot be solved very easily from what I have said"), Spinoza adds:

> But in passing I should like to note here that the more recent Peripatetics have, as I think, misunderstood the demonstration by which the Ancients tried to prove God's existence. For as I find it in a certain Jew, called Rab Chasdai [*apud Judaeum*[11] *quendam, Rab Ghasdaj vocatum*], it runs as follows: if there is an infinite regress of causes, then all things that are will also have

---

[5] *Or ha-Shem*, II.5.5–6, Crescas 1990, 219–225. Cf. W. Harvey 2010b, 109.

[6] See W. Harvey 1998, 103–104.   [7] *Or ha-Shem*, II.5.3, Crescas 1990, 213.

[8] Spinoza, Ep 81 (Spinoza 2002, 956). Leibniz too had a copy of this letter. There are a few minor divergences between Leibniz's copy and the version of the *Opera Posthuma* (both versions are reproduced in Gebhardt's critical edition). The *Opera Posthuma* transliterates Crescas's Hebrew given name, חסדאי, as Ghasdai, whereas in Leibniz's copy it is Jaçdai. See Leibniz 2001, 115. A more crucial discrepancy will be discussed shortly. For a helpful discussion of Leibniz's comments on Ep 12, see Laerke 2011b, 63–68.

[9] Ep 80, Spinoza 2002, 955.

[10] On Spinoza's understanding of numbers in Ep 12, see Melamed 2000.

[11] The adjective *Judaeum* is quite rare in Spinoza, who usually prefers to speak of "the Hebrews" or "Pharisees."

been caused; but it does not pertain to anything which has been caused, to
exist necessarily by the force of its own nature; therefore, there is nothing in
Nature to whose essence it pertains to exist necessarily; but the latter is
absurd; therefore, the former is also. *Hence the force of this argument does not
lie in the impossibility of there being an actual infinite [actu infinitum] or an
infinite regress of causes, but only in the supposition that things which do not exist
necessarily by their own nature are not determined to exist by a thing which does
necessarily exist by its own nature* [NS: and which is a cause, not something
caused].[12]

Spinoza had already criticized those who "deny the actual Infinite" a few
pages earlier in the letter, claiming that this denial resulted from confusion
and ignorance.[13] It is also worth noting that in Leibniz's copy of the letter,
Spinoza's criticism is directed at the "Peripatetics" (*Peripatetici*) rather than
the "*recent* Peripatetics" (*Peripatetici recentiores*) as in the *Opera Posthuma*.[14]
One way or another, it is clear that the target of Spinoza's criticism is the
argument for the existence of a first cause from the impossibility of an
infinite chain of causes and effects. This argument, which can be traced
back to Aristotle,[15] had a wide circulation among medieval philosophers.[16]
Intriguingly, Descartes seems to have deemed it valid.[17] The argument is
stated succinctly by Maimonides. In the introduction to the second part of
the *Guide of the Perplexed*, he lists twenty-five premises required for the
proof of God's existence, unity, and incorporeality, the third of which reads:
"The Third Premise: The existence of causes and effects of which the
number is infinite is impossible, even if they are not endowed with
magnitude."[18]

Crescas discusses Maimonides' third premise at three different places in
his *Light of the Lord*. In Book I, Part I, Chapter 3, he provides an initial
exposition of the argument. Already at this point he notes:

> It is because of [the] relation between cause and effect that an infinite series
> of causes and effects is impossible [*nimna*]. The argument may be stated as
> follows: An effect by its own nature [*bivhinat azmo*] has only possible
> existence [*efshari ha-metziut*], requiring therefore a determinant [*makhria*]
> to bring about the preponderance of existence over non-existence, which

---

[12] Ep. 12, Spinoza 1925, IV.61–2; 1985, 205 (added emphasis).

[13] Ep. 12, Spinoza 1925, IV.59; 1985, 204.   [14] See Leibniz 2001, 114. Cf. n.8 above.

[15] See Aristotle, *Metaphysics*, a 2 (994a). Cf. *Physics*, VIII.5 (255a18). For Aristotle's rejection of actually
infinite magnitude, see *Physics*, III.5–8.

[16] Wolfson 1929, 482–483.

[17] In the First Set of Replies Descartes notes that "there is no possibility of an infinite regress" of causes
and effects if they all occur simultaneously (Descartes 1964–1976, VII.III).

[18] *Guide* II, Introduction, Maimonides 1963, 235.

determinant constitutes its cause. Now it must inevitably follow that in the aggregate [*klalam*] of an infinite series of causes and effects either all of the members of the series would be effects or some of them would not be effects. If they were all effects, they would all have possible existence. They would require some determinant to bring about the preponderance of existence over non-existence, and so they would necessarily presuppose the existence of a causeless cause [outside the series].[19]

The crux of the argument here is that an infinite series of causes and effects, which are each merely contingent (having only "possible existence") in themselves, constitutes an aggregate which is equally contingent. Without a cause whose existence is necessary in itself, the actualization of the entire infinite chain remains unexplained. In other words, an infinite chain of causes and effects which are merely possible can just as well be actualized as non-actualized, and in order to explain the actualization of the chain, we must ground it in an existing thing which is not merely possible.

Crescas's exposition of Maimonides' third premise is far more elaborate than the original, and it also switches the issue from the impossibility of an actually *infinite* chain (which is the main point of Maimonides' argument), to *modal* considerations about what can explain the actualization of entities that are merely possible (in themselves).[20] From Crescas's later discussions of this argument,[21] we learn that his presentation relies heavily on a commentary on Maimonides' twenty-five premises by a Persian Islamic philosopher of the late thirteenth century, Muhammad ibn Muhammad al-Tabrizi.[22]

An even closer examination of Crescas's presentation of Maimonides' third premise seems to show that Crescas is not only diverting the focus of the argument from the impossibility of the actually infinite, but that he in fact *assumes that actual infinity is possible*. Recall his discussion (in the passage above) of the "the aggregate of an infinite series of causes and effects." An opponent of actual infinity would reject outright the possibility of aggregating an infinite series, claiming that such a process of aggregation

---

[19] Wolfson 1929, 221–223.

[20] Crescas here follows Avicenna, according to whom a possible being is one whose essence neither necessitates its existence nor rules it out. Such a being is possible in itself, and must have an (external) cause sufficient for its existence or non-existence. See *The Metaphysics*, I.6, Avicenna 2004, 31.

[21] Crescas, *Or ha-Shem*, I.2.3, Wolfson 1929, 225.

[22] Al-Tabrizi's discussion is fundamentally influenced and shaped by the Avicennian distinction between possible and necessary existence. Al-Tabrizi's commentary has been translated twice into Hebrew. The first translation is from the mid-fourteenth century. The second has recently been transcribed from manuscript by Hayoun (see Hayoun 1996). For a helpful discussion of Al-Tabrizi's influence on Crescas's physics, see Langermann 2012.

could never be completed. By treating the aggregation of an infinite series as not in the least problematic, Crescas reveals that he has parted ways with the Aristotelian ban on actual infinity.

Following his reconstruction of Maimonides' third premise, Crescas notes that Maimonides rejected actual infinity only "with reference to objects which have order either in position, as magnitudes, or nature, as causes and effects."[23] Crescas then contrasts this view of Maimonides with Averroës' comprehensive ban on actual infinity:

> Averroës, however, finds it to be impossible even with reference to objects which have no order whatsoever, for he maintains that actual number [*ha-mispar ba-foal*] must necessarily be finite. He reasons as follows: Every actual number is something actually numbered [*safur ba-foal*], and that which is actually numbered must be either even or odd, and that which is even or odd must necessarily be finite.[24]

Crescas does not seem to be impressed by Averroës' argument. He responds briefly and firmly:

> For our own part, we will say this with regard to Averroës' argument: While indeed the division of number into odd and even is true and unavoidable, still infinite number, not being limited [*mugbal*], is not to be described by either evenness or oddness.[25]

Crescas's point is simple: the distinction between odd and even numbers is not applicable to an infinite number.

Crescas's second discussion of Maimonides' third premise appears in Book I, Part II, Chapter 3 of *Light of the Lord*. This chapter relies on the initial exposition [*beur*] of the topic (discussed above), and its title describes it as an inquiry [*haqira*] into the issue. Crescas begins by stating that "the argument framed here by Altabrizi, which has been discussed by us in the first chapter of the first part ... is not altogether sufficient."[26] Specifically, he argues that it is *possible* for a cause to have an infinite number of effects. To prove this point he supplies the following argument:

> It must be admitted that that the emanation [*atzilut*] of an infinite number of effects from one single cause would not be impossible, if it were only possible for a single cause to be the source of emanation of more than one effect. And so, inasmuch as it is evident that there can be an infinite number of effects, despite their all being dependent upon a common cause, it must follow that the assumption of a common cause for more than one effect would not make

---

[23] Crescas, *Or ha-Shem*, I.1.3, Wolfson 1929, 223.   [24] *Ibid.*   [25] *Ibid.*
[26] Crescas, *Or ha-Shem*, I.2.3, Wolfson 1929, 225.

it impossible for those effects to be infinite in number. This being the case, assuming now a series of causes and effects wherein the first is the cause of the second, and the second of the third and so for ever, would that I knew why, by the mere assumption of a common cause for the series as a whole, the number of causes and effects within that series could not be infinite.[27]

Crescas's argument is straightforward. It is commonly accepted ("it is evident") that one cause (e.g. God) can have infinitely many *immediate* effects, so that each of the effects depends immediately on the cause. But if the cause can bring about infinitely many immediate effects, there is no reason why it cannot bring about the same infinity of effects ordered in a causal chain (the first being the cause of the second, and the second of the third, and so on).

Notice that in the first sentence of the quote above Crescas attempts to bypass the question of whether it is "possible for a single cause to be the source of emanation of more than one effect." But this scenario is problematic: if one simple (i.e. having no parts) cause brings about (without any aid) more than one effect, there could be no possible explanation for the difference between the effects (since it is the *same* cause which presumably brings about *different* effects).[28] Crescas is keenly aware of this problem (which would haunt anyone who rejects the possibility of brute facts), yet he rightly notes that it has nothing to do with the question of the possibility of the actually infinite. Thus, he suggests that we bracket this question and proceed on the *premise* that such a scenario is possible, in which case, he argues, we have no reason to deny ("we must admit") that a single cause may bring about infinitely many effects.

Summarizing his inquiry (*haqira*) into Maimonides' third premise, Crescas concludes:

> What this premise [*haqdama*] really means to bring out, and what conclusion therefore is actually needful for our purpose, is the existence[29] of a first cause, which is uncaused by anything else, *regardless of the view whether its effects*, when they are one the cause of the other, *are finite or infinite*.[30]

Crescas's third discussion of Maimonides' third premise appears in *Light of the Lord* I.III.2, where he presents his own proof of God's existence. As one can see from the excerpt below, this is simply an amended version of

[27] *Ibid.*
[28] Maimonides discusses this problem in *Guide* II.22; Maimonides 1963, 317. For a detailed discussion of the same issue in Spinoza, see Melamed 2013a, 116–119, and 2013b, 212–214.
[29] I have slightly amended Wolfson's translation in order to adhere to the literal Hebrew.
[30] *Or ha-Shem*, I.2.3, Wolfson 1929, 229. Italics added.

Maimonides' third premise, which incorporates his critique of the rejection of actual infinity:

> Whether causes and effects are finite or infinite, there is no escaping [*lo yimalet*] that there must be some cause of the entirety of them. For if all were effects they would be of possible existence [*efshari ha-metziut*] with respect of themselves, and would require something to give preponderance to their existence over their non-existence, and this is the cause of them all that gives preponderance to their existence, and this is God, may he be blessed.[31]

With Crescas's three discussions before our eyes, we can now understand Spinoza's enthusiastic endorsement (in Ep 12) of his argument. Not only does Crescas provide powerful arguments in favor of actual infinity (a position Spinoza strongly supports), but he also motivates these arguments by a strict rationalism, which requires a reason for the existence of any being. Spinoza would rely on a similar stipulation ("for each thing there must be assigned a reason, or cause, as much for its existence as for its non-existence")[32] in his own proof of the existence of God in *Ethics* Ip11dem. It is therefore not at all surprising that, upon reading Spinoza's presentation of Crescas's argument, Leibniz noted:

> This is rightly observed, and agrees with what I am accustomed to saying, that *nothing exists but that for whose existence a sufficient reason can be provided* [*nihil existere, nisi cuius reddi possit ratio existentiae sufficiens*]. It is easily demonstrated that this sufficient reason cannot be in the series of causes.[33]

Don Garrett has insightfully pointed out that Spinoza's argument for God's existence in Ip11 merges elements from both the ontological and cosmological arguments.[34] The same point seems to be true about Crescas's argument as well. Under the influence of Avicenna,[35] Crescas reoriented the cosmological argument with the aim of proving the existence of a being which is in itself necessary, i.e. a being whose essence involves existence.

My discussion of Crescas has focused on his reformulation of a common argument for the existence of God, an argument which, in his view, did not depend on the rejection of actual infinity. Though I have briefly noted his

---

[31] *Or ha-Shem*, I.3.2, Crescas 1990, 98–99. The translation is by Zeev Harvey; see W. Harvey 1998, 97.

[32] It is not clear to me whether Crescas would require a reason for the *non-existence* of a thing. Al-Tabrizi provides an interesting argument in favor of the view that non-existence does *not* require a cause: "since it is the role of the cause to determine the preponderance of existence over non-existence, and the absent does not exist at all, therefore, it does not require a cause" (Hayoun 1996, 220. My translation).

[33] Leibniz 1923–, VI.iii.283; 2001, 117 (emphasis added). Cf. Laerke 2011b, 63.

[34] See Garrett 1979, 198, 223.   [35] See W. Harvey 1998, 90–91.

critique of Averroës' argument against the possibility of a.
I have not discussed most of the aspects of his broader
infinity, whether in terms of space, time, or the quanti
seems that at least part of Crescas's motivation for reje
actual infinity was the realization that the Aristotelian
uncountability[37] of actual infinity might not hold in the c
counter. Thus, Crescas writes:

> If God knows numbers, since number can be added to without end, then His
> knowledge extends to an infinity of numbers. If he does not know all of
> them, there must of necessity be a bound which he does not know. But then
> the question remains – why is it that he knows the numbers to that bound
> but does not know greater ones? Have weariness and fatigue befallen His
> knowledge?[38]

A full elucidation of Crescas's defense of actual infinity (like a systematic
clarification of Spinoza's support of it) would require a more detailed and
lengthy discussion than can be carried out here. In the remainder of this
chapter, I would like to point out and "inquire" into (to use Crescas's term)
another important doctrine, closely related to this one, which Crescas and
Spinoza share: the view that God has infinitely many attributes.

Why does God have infinitely many attributes?

At the beginning of the *Ethics*, Spinoza defines God as a substance of
infinitely many attributes:

> Idef6: By God I understand a being absolutely infinite, that is, a substance
> consisting of an infinity of attributes, of which each one expresses an eternal
> and infinite essence [*Per Deum intelligo ens absolute infinitum, hoc est, sub-
> stantiam constantem infinitis attributis, quorum unumquodque aeternam, et
> infinitam essentiam exprimit*].

In Ip16dem Spinoza paraphrases this definition: "The divine nature has
absolutely infinite attributes (by Def 6), each of which also expresses an
essence infinite in its own kind." Still, at the beginning of Part Two of the
Ethics, he argues that we know only two attributes: extension and thought.[39]

---

[36] See *Or ha-Shem*, I.2.1 and III.1.4, Crescas 1990, 65–66 and 302–303. Cf. W. Harvey 2010b, 59–61.

[37] In the colloquial, rather than Cantorean, sense of the term.

[38] *Or ha-Shem*, II.1.3, Crescas 1990, 136–137. The English translation is by Rabinovitch 1970, 228.
According to Rabinovitch, Crescas's inquiries into the qualities of infinite magnitudes anticipated
"the foundation of transfinite arithmetic" (1970, 224). Cf. Levy 1987, 212.

[39] *Ethics* IIax5: "We neither feel nor perceive any singular things, except bodies and modes of thinking."

y of Spinoza's readers have puzzled over this tension, wondering why man knowledge of the infinite attributes of God is so severely limited. I have recently shown that Spinoza has solid, principled reasons for maintaining this view, which he states explicitly in Ep 64 and Ep 66.[40]

A way of resolving this tension has been championed by Jonathan Bennett, who famously argued that for Spinoza 'infinite' is a synonym for 'all.' When Spinoza says that God has infinite attributes, he means only that God exists in every possible way. This does not entail that God exists other than as extended and as thinking, i.e. that there are more than two attributes.[41] I have argued elsewhere that this claim of Bennett's is deeply misleading. Both in the *Ethics* and in other texts, Spinoza states numerous times that there are attributes that are unknown to us. Furthermore, he has strong theoretical reasons for asserting that there are infinitely many attributes apart from thought and extension.[42] I will not repeat my arguments here, but I would like to point out briefly three ways in which the Crescas–Spinoza nexus is directly relevant to the question of the infinity of the attributes.

First, one of Bennett's arguments against interpreting the infinity of attributes as implying the existence of more than two attributes is that there was no philosophical or theological tradition stating that God has infinitely many attributes, and thus that Spinoza was under no pressure from tradition to assert this view.[43] I am not impressed by this argument, since Spinoza's philosophy is not particularly loyal to the "philosophical tradition" (whatever one might mean by this expression). Still, it is clear that Spinoza *was* well acquainted with a philosophical and theological tradition that ascribes infinitely many attributes to God, though it was not the tradition under Bennett's spotlight. In his discussion of the divine attributes in the *Light of the Lord*, Crescas develops in great detail the claim that God has infinitely many attributes and that each of his attributes is infinite.[44] Given Spinoza's discussion of Crescas's conception of infinity, it is highly unlikely that he was unaware of this claim, especially since Crescas was not the only medieval Jewish thinker to advance such an argument.[45]

Second, we have already seen that in Ep 12 Spinoza explicitly defends the notion of *actual* infinity against the Aristotelian ban on it. It goes without saying, I believe, that actual infinity cannot equal two (or any finite

---

[40] See Melamed 2013a, 156–165. [41] Bennett 1984, 76. [42] Melamed 2012, §2.

[43] Bennett 1984, 77.

[44] *Or ha-Shem*, I.3.3, Crescas 1990, 106–108. Cf. W. Harvey 2010b, 91–94, and Levy 1987, 204–207.

[45] See W. Harvey 2010b, 94. Another philosopher who argued that God has "countless" attributes which are unknown to us and with whom Spinoza seems to be quite familiar is Descartes (1964–76, III.394).

number). Could Spinoza, then, recognize an infinity which is beyond any finite number (in Ep 12), and yet conceive God's infinity (in Idef6) as being of a lower kind? This seems highly unlikely, given Spinoza's ascription of *absolute* infinity to God in Idef6.

Third, the genuine importance of Bennett's argument against the infinity of attributes lies in the fact that it forces us to elucidate *why* Spinoza defines God as having infinitely many attributes. Incidentally, Spinoza provides an explicit explanation for his claim in Ip10s:[46]

> So it is far from absurd to attribute many attributes to one substance. Indeed, nothing in nature is clearer than that each being must be conceived under some attribute, and *the more reality or being [realitas aut esse] it has, the more it has attributes* which express necessity, *or* eternity, and infinity. And consequently there is also nothing clearer than that *a being absolutely infinite must be defined (as we taught in Def. 6) as a being that consists of infinite attributes*, each of which expresses a certain eternal and infinite essence.[47]

According to this passage, there is a correlation between a thing's degree of reality and its attributes (*Ethics* Ip9). Nothingness has no reality and hence no attributes.[48] Finite things have a finite degree of reality, and thus have a finite number of attributes, and the absolutely infinite being is infinitely real, and thus has infinitely many attributes.

Still, one might perhaps argue that the above correlation commits Spinoza to the claim that God has *more* attributes (and thus is more real) than finite things, but that he need not have *infinitely many* attributes in order to be more real than all finite things; for this, it would suffice for him to have *one* attribute more than the most real finite being.[49]

In order to address this argument, we will briefly revisit Crescas's discussion of the infinity of God's attributes. Crescas develops his view as an alternative to and critique of Maimonides' negative theology, with its assertion that one should ascribe no essential attributes to God.[50] Despite his critique of Maimonides' position, there is one element of Maimonides' theory which Crescas preserves: the claim that God is incommensurable with finite things.[51] Crescas's God has infinitely many attributes, but is still incommensurable with finite things, since there is no common measure

---

[46] It is quite rare for Spinoza to try to motivate his definitions.
[47] This passage is a verbatim quote from Ep 9 (IV/44–45). Italics added.
[48] "The more attributes I attribute to a being the more I am compelled to attribute existence to it; that is, the more I conceive it as true. It would be quite the contrary if I had feigned a Chimaera, or something like that" (Ep 9/ IV/45/22–25).
[49] Cf. Bennett 1984, 76–77.   [50] Maimonides, *Guide* I.53–55.
[51] *Or ha-Shem*, I.3.3, Crescas 1990, 100–106. Cf. W. Harvey 2010b, 88–96.

between the finite and the infinite. Thus, Crescas writes: "It is impossible to be similar to God by having a common measure, since there is no relation [*yahas*] and measure [*erech*] between the infinite and the finite."[52]

If we add the claim that (1) there is no common measure between the finite and the infinite to the claim that (2) the more reality a thing has, the more attributes belong to it (*Ethics* Ip9), we can fully explain Spinoza's reasons for defining God as having infinitely many attributes. Were God to have any finite number of attributes n that is greater than the number of attributes m belonging to the most real finite being, there would still be a common measure and ratio between God and finite things. In fact, n/m would be the precise representation of the relation between God and the most real finite thing.

Do we have any textual evidence showing that Spinoza accepts the claim that there is no common measure between God and finite things? We do. Spinoza asserts this claim in various formulations in several places,[53] the most explicit of which is Ep 54. This letter, moreover, belongs to Spinoza's very late period (its conjectured date is September 1674), and thus cannot be dismissed as an early, "immature," claim:

> This do I know, that between the finite and the infinite there is no relation [*nullam esse proportionem*], so that the difference between God and the greatest and most excellent created thing is no other than between God and the least created thing.[54]

Conclusion

In this chapter I have examined one thread in the development of the concept of the infinite. In the first part we studied Crescas's and Spinoza's advocacy of actual infinity, and explained the importance of Crescas's Avicennian proof of the existence of God for Spinoza's philosophical project as a whole. Specifically, we showed that both Crescas and Spinoza allow for the aggregation of infinite series, and that both work within the broadly Avicennian view that requires a reason for both the existence and non-existence of things. In the second part, we studied the similarities between Crescas's and Spinoza's views of God as having infinitely many attributes, and explained Spinoza's motivation for defining God as a substance consisting of infinitely many attributes.

---

[52] *Or ha-Shem*, I.3.3, Crescas 1990, 106.
[53] I take the last paragraph of E1p17s as well as E2p10 to make this point, though establishing this reading demands a close analysis of these texts.
[54] Spinoza 1925, IV.253; 2002, 899.

Of the many subsequent readers of Spinoza's "Letter on the Infinite," we should note in particular Georg Cantor, who described the letter as "highly important."[55] Obviously, this is not the right place to discuss Cantor's engagement with Spinoza. Still, let me note that the flow of thought from mathematics to metaphysics and back seems to be quite substantial, when we consider the issue of infinity. According to Hermann Weyl, one of the towering figures of modern mathematics and its philosophy, "mathematics is the science of the infinite."[56] While Spinoza would never concede to having the infinite relegated to mathematics,[57] I suspect that both he and Cantor understood that neither field alone could explain the development of this extraordinary notion.

[55] Ewald 1996, II 890.   [56] Weyl 2012, 17.
[57] For Spinoza mathematics is the study of finite quantity. See Melamed 2000.

Bibliography

Abrahamov, Binyamin (2003). *Divine Love in Islamic Mysticism*. London: Routledge.

Abravanel, Isaac (1993). *Perush 'al ha-Torah*. Jerusalem: Bene Arabel.

Abulafia, Abraham (2001). *Or ha-Sekhel*. Jerusalem: Amnon Gross.

Adamson, Peter (2005). "On Knowledge of Particulars," *Proceedings of the Aristotelian Society* 105: 273–294.

(2010). "The Arabic Tradition," in *The Routledge Companion to Ethics*, ed. John Skorupski. London: Routledge, 63–75

Adamson, Peter, and Richard C. Taylor (2005). "Introduction," in *Cambridge Companion to Arabic Philosophy*, eds. Peter Adamson and Richard C. Taylor. Cambridge University Press, 1–9.

Adler, Jacob (1996). "Spinoza's Physical Philosophy," *Archiv für Geschichte der Philosophie* 78: 253–276.

(1999). "Epistemological Categories in Delmedigo and Spinoza," *Studia Spinozana* 15: 205–230.

(2008). "J. S. Delmedigo as Teacher of Spinoza: The Case of Noncomplex Propositions," *Studia Spinoza* 16: 177–183.

(2013). "The Strange Case of the Missing Title Page: An Investigation in Spinozistic Bibliography," *Intellectual History Review* 23: 259–262.

(forthcoming). "The Education of Ehrenfried Walther von Tschirnhaus (1651–1708)," *Journal of Medical Biography*.

Alexander of Aphrodisias (1495). *Enarratio de Anima ex Aristotelis Institutione*, trans. Girolamo Donato. Brescia: Bernardinus de Misintis.

(1887). *De anima liber cum mantissa*, ed. Ivo Bruns. Berlin: Reimer.

(1980). *The De Anima of Alexander of Aphrodisias: A Translation and Commentary*, trans. Athanasios P. Fotinis. Washington, D. C: University Press of America.

(2012). *On the Soul. Part 1, Soul as Form of the Body, Parts of the Soul, Nourishment, and Perception*, trans. Victor Caston. London: Bristol Classical Press.

Al-Farabi, Abu Nasr (1964). *Al-Siyāsah al-Madaniyyah*, ed. Fauzi M. Najjar. Beirut: Imprimerie Catholique.

(1985). *On the Perfect State (Al-Madīnah al-Fadilah)*, ed. and trans. Richard Walzer. Oxford University Press.

(2007). *The Political Regime*, ed. and trans. J. McGinnis and D. C. Reisman, in *Classical Arabic Philosophy*. Indianapolis: Hackett.

Alfonso de Valladolid (Abner of Burgos) (1990). *Ofrenda de zelos (Minḥat Ḳĕna'ot) und Libro de la ley*, ed. Walter Mettman. Opladen: Westdeutscher Verlag.

(1994–1996). *Mostrador de justicia*, ed. Walter Mettmann, 2 vols. Opladen: Estdeutscher Verlag.

Al-Ghazali, Abu Hamid (1997). *The Incoherence of the Philosophers*, trans. Michael E. Marmura. Provo, UT: Brigham Young University Press.

(2011). *Love, Longing, Intimacy, and Contentment* (Book XXXVI of the *Revival of the Religious Sciences*), trans. Eric Ormsby. Cambridge: Islamic Texts Society.

Allison, Henry (1987). *Benedict de Spinoza: An Introduction*. New Haven, CT: Yale University Press.

Alquié, Ferdinand (1981). *Le Rationalisme de Spinoza*. Paris: Presses Universitaires de France.

Altmann, Alexander (1969). "Essence and Existence in Maimonides," in *Studies in Religious Philosophy and Mysticism*. Ithaca, NY: Cornell University Press.

(1987). "Maimonides on the Intellect and the Scope of Metaphysics," in *Von der mittelalterlichen zur modernen Aufklarung. Studien zur jüdischen Geistesgeschichte von Alexander Altmann*. Tübingen: J. C. B. Mohr, 60–129.

Anscombe, G. E. M. (1963). *Intention*, 2nd edn. Oxford University Press.

Arama, Isaac (1868). *'Akedat Yitsḥak*, 5 vols. Lemberg: A. J. Madfes.

Aristotle (1991). *The Complete Works of Aristotle*, ed. Jonathan Barnes, 2 vols. Princeton University Press.

Aspasius (2006). *On Aristotle's Nicomachean Ethics 1–4, 7–8*, trans. David Konstan. Ithaca: Cornell University Press.

Averroës (2002). *Middle Commentary on Aristotle's De anima*, ed. and trans. Alfred L. Ivry. Provo, UT: Brigham Young University Press.

(2003). *Ha-Be'ur ha-emza'i shel Ibn Rushd le-Sefer ha-nefesh le-Arisṭo: be-targum Mosheh Ibn Tibon*, ed. Alfred Ivry. Jerusalem: Israel Academic of Sciences.

Avicenna (1507/1964). *Liber Canonis*. Venice: Paganino de Paganini; rpt., Hildesheim: Olms.

(1892). *Le livre des théorèmes et des avertissements*, ed. J. Forget. Leiden: E. J. Brill.

(1930). *A Treatise on the Canon of Medicine of Avicenna Incorporating a Translation of the First Book*, trans. O. Cameron Gruner. London: Luzac.

(1951). *Livre des directives et remarques (Kitāb al-Irt wa l-tanbht)*, trans. A. M. Goichon. Beyrouth: Commission internationale pour la traduction des chefs-d'oeuvre.

(1960). *Al-Shifā', al-Ilāhiyyāt*, ed. M. Y. Moussa, S. Dunya, S. Sayet, and I. Madkour. Cairo: Imprimeries Gouvernementales.

(1966). *The General Principles of Avicenna's Canon of Medicine*, trans. Mazhar H. Shah. Karachi: Naveed Clinic.

(1973). *The Metaphysica of Avicenna (Ibn Sīnā): A Critical Translation-Commentary and Analysis of the Fundamental Arguments in Avicenna's Metaphysica in the Dānish Nāmai 'ala'i (The Book of Scientific Knowledge)*, trans. Parviz Morewedge. New York: Columbia University Press.

Avicenna (2004). *The Metaphysics of The Healing: A Parallel English-Arabic Text/ al-Ilahīyāt min al-Shifā'*, ed. and trans. Michael E. Marmura. Provo, UT: Brigham Young University Press.

Baer, Yizhaq (1940). "Minḥat Qenaot by Abner of Burgos and its Influence on Ḥasdai Crescas," *Tarbiz* 11: 188–302.

Barbone, Steve, and Lee Rice (2000). Introduction in Spinoza (2000), 1–30.

Barzilay, Isaac (1974). *Yoseph Shlomo Delmedigo, Yashar of Candia: His Life, Works and Times.* Leiden: Brill.

Basnage, Jacques (1716). *Histoire des Juifs.* La Haye.

Batniksky, Leora (2003–2004). "Spinoza's Critique of Miracles," *Cardozo Law Review* 25: 507–518.

Belo, Catarina (2007). *Chance and Determinism in Avicenna and Averroes.* Leiden: Brill.

Bennett, Jonathan (1984). *A Study of Spinoza's Ethics.* Indianapolis: Hackett Publishing.

Berzin, Gabriella (2004). "Happiness, Pleasure, and Good in Maimonides and Hasdai Crescas" (in Hebrew), in *Shefa' Tal: Studies on Jewish Thought and Culture Presented to Bracha Sack*, eds. Zeev Gries, Howard Kreisel and Boaz Huss. Beersheba: Ben-Gurion University of the Negev Press.

Biale, David (2011). *Not in the Heavens: The Tradition of Jewish Secular Thought.* Princeton University Press.

Black, Deborah (2004). "Models of the Mind: Metaphysical Presuppositions of the Averroist and Thomistic Accounts of Intellection," *Documenti e studi sulla tradizione filosofica medievale* 15: 319–352.

(2005). "Psychology: Soul and Intellect," in *Cambridge Companion to Arabic Philosophy*, eds. Peter Adamson and Richard C. Taylor. Cambridge University Press, 308–325.

Blumenthal, David R. (1977). "Maimonides' Intellectual Mysticism," *Studies in Mediaeval Culture* 10: 51–68.

(1987). "Maimonides: Prayer, Worship, and Judaism," in *Prière, mystique, et judaïsme*, ed. R. Goetchel. Paris: Presses Universitaires France, 86–106.

Boyer, Carl B., and Uta C. Merzbach (1991). *A History of Mathematics.* New York: Wiley.

Boyle, Robert (1772). *The Works.* London: J. and F. Rivington.

Brann, H. W. (1977). "Spinoza and the Kabbalah," in *Speculum Spinozanum*, ed. Sitgfried Hessing. London: Routledge and Kegan Paul.

Broydé, Isaac (1906). "Levi ben Gershon," in *Encyclopedia Judaica.* New York: Funk & Wagnalls, 7: 26–32.

Bruaire, C. (1974). *Le Droit de Dieu.* Paris: Aubier Montaigne.

Brykman, Geneviève (1972). *La Judéité de Spinoza.* Paris: J. Vrin.

Chalier, Catherine (2006). *Spinoza Lecteur de Maimonide. La question theologico-politique.* Paris: Les Editions du Cerf.

Charlap, Luba (2001). "Another View on Rabbi Abraham Ibn-Ezra's Contribution to Medieval Hebrew Grammar," *Hebrew Studies* 42:67–80.

Coert, Hendrik Jan (1938). *Spinoza's Betrekking tot de Geneeskunde en haar Beoefenaren*. Mededeelingen van wege het Spinozahuis 4. Leiden: Brill.

Cohen, Hermann (1924). "Spinoza über Staat und Religion, Judentum und Christentum," in *Jüdische Schriften*, ed. Bruno Strauss, 3 vols. Berlin: Schwetschke, 290–372.

Cohen, Morris Raphael (1946). *The Faith of a Liberal*. New York: Holt and Co.

Cohoe, Caleb (forthcoming). Review of *Alexander of Aphrodisias on the Soul* (London: Bristol Classical Press, 2012). To appear in *Journal of the History of Philosophy*, http://philpapers.org/archive/COHROQ, accessed November 20, 2013.

Collier, Andrew (1991). "The Materiality of Morals: Mind, Body and Interests in Spinoza's *Ethics*," *Studia Spinozana* 7: 69–93.

Cooper, Julie (forthcoming). *Secular Powers: Humility in Modern Political Thought*. University of Chicago Press.

Crescas, Hasdai (1990). *'Or Hashem*, ed. Shlomo Fisher. Jerusalem: Sifre Ramot.

Curley, Edwin (1969). *Spinoza's Metaphysics: An Essay in Interpretation*. Cambridge, MA: Harvard University Press.

(1988). *Behind the Geometrical Method*. Princeton University Press.

(1990). "Notes on a Neglected Masterpiece: The *Theological-Political Treatise* as a Prolegomenon to the *Ethics*," in *Central Themes in Early Modern Philosophy*, eds. Jan Cover and Mark Kulstad. Indianapolis: Hackett, pp. 109–159.

(1991–1992). "A Good Man Is Hard to Find," *Proceedings and Addresses of the American Philosophical Association* 65: 29–45.

(1992). "'I durst not write so boldly' or, How to read Hobbes's *Theological-Political Treatise*," in *Hobbes e Spinoza*, ed. Daniela Bostrenghi. Naples: Bibliopolis, 1992, 497–593.

(1994). "Notes on A Neglected Masterpiece: Spinoza and the Science of Hermeneutics," in *Spinoza: The Enduring Questions*, ed. Graeme Hunter. Toronto: University of Toronto Press, 67–76.

(2002). "Maimonides, Spinoza and the Book of Job," in *Jewish Themes in Spinoza's Philosophy*, eds. Heidi Ravven and Lenn Goodman. Albany NY: State University of New York Press.

(forthcoming). "Spinoza's Contribution to Biblical Scholarship," *Proceedings of the Tübingen Conference on the Tractatus Theologico-Politicus*.

D'Ancona, Christina (2005). "Greek into Arabic: Neoplatonism in Translation," in *Cambridge Companion to Arabic Philosophy*, eds. Peter Adamson and Richard C. Taylor. Cambridge University Press, 11–31.

D'Ancona, J. 1940. "Delmedigo, Menasseh Ben Israël en Spinoza," *Bijdragen en Mededelingen van het Genootschap voor de Joodsche Wetenschap in Nederland* 6: 105–152.

Davidson, Herbert (1988). "Averroes' Commentary on Alexander of Aphrodisias' Treatise on the Intellect" [Hebrew], *Jerusalem Studies in Jewish Thought* 7: 205–217.

(1992a). *Alfarabi, Avicenna, and Averroes on Intellect*. New York: Oxford University Press.

(1992b) "Gersonides on the Material and Active Intellects," in *Studies on Gersonides: A Fourteenth Century Jewish Philosopher-Scientist*, ed. Gad Freudenthal. Leiden: Brill, 195–265.

(1992–1993). "Maimonides on Metaphysical Knowledge," *Maimonidean Studies* 4: 1–13.

(2005). *Maimonides: The Man and His Works*. Oxford University Press.

DeBrabander, Firmin (2007). *Spinoza and the Stoics: Power, Politics, and the Passions*. London: Continuum.

Della Rocca, Michael (2008). *Spinoza*. London: Routledge.

Delmedigo, Joseph Solomon (1629–1631). *Novelot Ḥokhmah* (vol. 2 of *Ta'alumot Ḥokhmah*). Basel: Samuel Ashkenazi.

(1864). *Sefer 'Elim*. Odessa: M. E. Belinson.

Den Uyl, Douglas (1983). *God, Man, and Well Being*. Assen, the Netherlands: Van Gorcum.

Descartes, René (1964–1976). *Oeuvres de Descartes*, eds. Charles Adam and Paul Tannery, 12 vols. Paris: J. Vrin.

(1985). *The Philosophical Writings of Descartes*, trans. John Cottingham, Robert Stoothoff, and Dugald Murdoch, 2 vols. Cambridge University Press.

Diesendruck, Zvi (1936). "Samuel and Moses Ibn Tibbon on Maimonides' Theory of Providence," *Hebrew Union College Annual* 11: 341–356.

Dobbs-Weinstein, Idit (1994). "Maimonidean Aspects in Spinoza's Thought," *Graduate Faculty Philosophy Journal* 17: 153–174.

(1998). "Gersonides's Radically Modern Understanding of the Agent Intellect," in *Meeting of the Minds: The Relations Between Medieval and Classical Modern European Philosophy*, ed. Stephen F. Brown. Turnhout: Brepols, 191–213.

(2004). "Thinking Desire in Gersonides and Spinoza," in *Women and Gender in Jewish Philosophy*, ed. Hava Samuelson. Bloomington, IN: Indiana University Press, 51–77.

(2006). "Tensions within and between Maimonides' and Gersonides' Account of Prophecy," in *Écriture et réécriture des textes philosophiques médiévaux*, eds. J. Hamesse and O. Weijers, Textes et études du moyen âge 34. Turnhout: Brepols, 63–88.

(2014). "Aristotle on the Natural Dwelling of Intellect," in *The Bloomsbury Companion to Aristotle*, ed. Claudia Baracchi. New York: Bloomsbury Publishing, 297–310.

Einstein, Albert (1949). *Philosopher-Scientist*, vol. 1, ed. Paul Arthur Schilpp. New York: Harper & Row.

(1954). *Ideas and Opinions*, trans. S. Bargmann. New York: Crown.

Eisen, Robert (2004). *The Book of Job in Medieval Jewish Philosophy*. Oxford University Press.

Ewald, William, ed. (1996). *From Kant to Hilbert: A Source Book in the Foundation of Mathematics*, 2 vols. New York: Oxford University Press.

Fackenheim, Emil (1945). "A Treatise on Love by Ibn Sīnā," *Mediaeval Studies* 7: 208–228.

Feldman, Seymour (1973). "Gersonides on the Possibility of Conjunction," *AJS Review* 3: 99–120.

(1978). "Gersonides on the Possibility of Conjunction with the Agent Intellect," *ASS Review* 3: 99–120.

(1984). "A Debate concerning Determinism in Late Medieval Jewish Philosophy," *Proceedings of the American Academy for Jewish Research* 51: 15–54.

(1992). "Platonic Themes in Gersonides's Doctrine of the Active Intellect," in *Neoplatonism and Jewish Thought*, ed. L. E. Goodman. Albany, NY: State University of New York Press, 255–277.

(1997). "1492: A House Divided," in *Crisis and Creativity in the Sephardic World: 1391–1648*, ed. Benjamin R. Gampel. New York: Columbia University Press, 38–58.

(2008). "The Theory of Eternal Creation in Hasdai Crescas and Some of His Predecessors," *Viator* 11: 289–320.

(2010). *Gersonides: Judaism within the Limits of Reason*. Oxford: Littman Library of Jewish Civilization.

(2012). "On Plural Universes: A Debate in Medieval Jewish Philosophy and the Duhem-Pires Thesis," *Aleph: Historical Studies in Science and Judaism* 12(2): 329–366.

Fischer, I. (1921). "De Geneesheeren onder Spinoza's Vrienden," *Nederlandsch Tijdschrift voor Geneeskunde*, Part 1, 1856–1873.

Fraenkel, Carlos (2006). "Maimonides' God and Spinoza's *Deus sive Natura*," *Journal of the History of Philosophy* 44: 169–215.

(2009). "From Maimonides to Samuel ibn Tibbon: Interpreting Judaism as a Philosophical Religion," in *Traditions of Maimonideanism*, ed. Carlos Fraenkel. Leiden: Brill, 177–212.

(2010). "Spinoza on Philosophy and Religion: The Averroistic Sources," in *The Rationalists: Between Tradition and Innovation*, eds. Carlos Fraenkel, Dario Perinetti, and Justin Smith. The New Synthese Historical Library. Boston: Springer Academic Publishers, 27–43.

(2012). "Reconsidering the Case of Elijah Delmedigo's Averroism and its Impact on Spinoza," in *Renaissance Averroism and its Aftermath: Arabic Philosophy in Early Modern Europe*, eds. Anna Akasoy and Guido Guiglioni. Boston: Springer Academic Publishers, 213–236.

Fraenkel, Carlos and Rudolf Smend (2007). "Spinoza, Baruch (Bento, Benedictus)," in *Encyclopaedia Judaica*, eds. Michael Berenbaum and Fred Skolnik. Detroit: Macmillan Ref, 111–119.

Frank, Daniel H. and Oliver Leaman, eds. (2003). *The Cambridge Companion to Medieval Jewish Philosophy*. Cambridge University Press.

Frankel, Steven (1999). "Politics and Rhetoric: The Intended Audience of Spinoza's *Tractatus Theologico-Politicus*," *The Review of Metaphysics* 52: 897–924.

(2002). "Spinoza's Liberal Theology: A Practical Solution to the Quarrel Between Religion and Revelation," *Archiv für Geshichte der Philosophie* 84: 273–296.

(2011). "Determined to be Free: Spinoza on the Meaning of Freedom," *Review of Politics*: 73: 55–76.

Frede, Michael (2011). *A Free Will: Origins of the Notion in Ancient Thought*, ed. Halszka Osmolska. Berkeley, CA: University of California Press.

Freudenthal, Gad (1995). "Science in the Medieval Jewish Culture of Southern France," *History of Science* 33: 23–58.

Freudenthal, Gad, and Mauro Zonta (2012). "Avicenna among Medieval Jews: The Reception of Avicenna's Philosophical, Scientific and Medical Writings in Jewish Cultures, East And West," *Arabic Sciences and Philosophy* 22: 217–287.

Freudenthal, Jacob (1899). *Die Lebensgeschichte Spinoza's*. Leipzig: Veit.

Funkenstein, Amos (1993). *Theology and the Scientific Imagination from the Middle Ages to the Seventeenth Century*. Berkeley, CA: University of California Press.

Gabbey, Alan (1996). "Spinoza's Natural Science and Methodology," in *The Cambridge Companion to Spinoza*, ed. Don Garrett. Cambridge University Press, 142–191.

Garrett, Aaron (2007). *Meaning in Spinoza's Method*. New York: Cambridge University Press.

Garrett, Don (1979). "Spinoza's 'Ontological' Argument," *Philosophical Review* 88: 198–223.

(1996). "Spinoza's Ethical Theory," in *The Cambridge Companion to Spinoza*, ed. Don Garrett. Cambridge University Press, 267–314.

Gatti, Roberto (2004). "Sensory Experience and Metaphysics in Medieval Jewish Philosophy: Once Again on the Limitations of Human Knowledge according to Maimonides and Gersonides," *Quaestio* 4: 91–112.

(2007). "Matter from the Point of View of Psychology and Noetic: Do the Intelligible Forms Have a Matter? And If Yes, Which Kind of Matter?" *Quaestio* 7: 283–315.

Gebhardt, Carl (1922). *Die Schriften des Uriel da Costa*. Amsterdam: M. Hertzberger.

Gilden, Hilail (1973). "Spinoza and the Political Problem," in *Spinoza: A Collection of Critical Essays*, ed. Marjorie Grene. New York: Anchor Press, 377–87.

Girsel, Maria (2012). *A Publication that Changed the Face of Renaissance Philosophy*, https://web.archive.org/web/20121029110928/http://www.lynge.com/item.php?bookid=35821, accessed October 28, 2013.

Glasner, Ruth (1995). "Levi Ben Gershom and the Study of Ibn Rushd in the Fourteenth Century Author," *Jewish Quarterly Review* 86: 51–90.

(2002). "On Gersonides' Knowledge of Languages," *Aleph* 2: 235–257.

Goichon, A. M. (1938). *Lexique de la langue philosophique d'Ibn Sīnā*. Paris: Desclée de Brouwer.

Goldstein, Bernard (1996). "Astronomy and Astrology in the Works of Abraham ibn Ezra," *Arabic Sciences and Philosophy* 6: 9–21.

Gottlieb, Michah (2007). "Spinoza's Method of Biblical Interpretation Reconsidered," *Jewish Studies Quarterly* 14: 286–317.

Gouldman, Francis (1664). *A Copious Dictionary*. London: John Field.

Gueroult, Martial (1968). *Spinoza*, 2 vols. Paris: Aubier.

Guttmann, Julius (1973). *Philosophies of Judaism*. New York: Aronson.

Guttmann, Julius, and Alfred L. Ivry (2007). "Alexander of Aphrodisias," in *Encyclopaedia Judaica*, ed. Fred Skolnik, 2nd edn. Detroit: Macmillan.

Halevi, Judah (1905). *The Kuzari*, trans. Hartwig Hirschfeld. New York: Routledge.

Hardenberg, Friedrich von (1960–2006). *Novalis Schriften*, eds. R. Samuel, H. J. Mähl, and G. Schulz, 6 vols. Stuttgart: Kohlhammer.

Harris, Jay M. (1993). "Ibn Ezra in Modern Jewish Perspective," in *Rabbi Abraham Ibn Ezra: Studies in the Writings of a Twelfth-Century Jewish Polymath*, eds. Isadore Twersky and Jay M. Harris. Cambridge, MA: Harvard University Press, 129–170.

Harvey, Steven (1991). "Maimonides in the Sultan's Palace," *Perspectives on Maimonides*, ed. J. Kraemer. Oxford University Press, 47–75.

(1992). "Did Maimonides' Letter to Samuel Ibn Tibbon Determine Which Philosophers Would Be Studied by Later Jewish Thinkers?" *The Jewish Quarterly Review* 83: 51–70.

(1997). "The Meaning of Terms Designating Love in Judaeo-Arabic Thought," in *Judaeo-Arabic Studies*, ed. N. Golb. Amsterdam: Harwood, 175–196.

(2000). "On the Nature and Extent of Jewish Averroism: Renan's *Averroès et l'Averroïsme* Revisited," *Jewish Studies Quarterly* 7: 100–119.

(2003). "Arabic into Hebrew: The Hebrew Translation Movement and the Influence of Averroes upon Medieval Jewish Thought," in *The Cambridge Companion to Medieval Jewish Philosophy*, eds. D. H. Frank and O. Leaman. New York: Cambridge University Press, 258–280.

(2013). "Avicenna and Maimonides on Prayer and Intellectual Worship," in *Exchange and Transmission across Cultural Boundaries*, eds. H. Ben-Shammai, S. Shaked, and S. Stroumsa. Proceedings of an International Workshop in Memory of Professor Shlomo Pines. Jerusalem: Israel Academy of Sciences and Humanities, 82–105.

Harvey, Warren Zev (1973). "Ḥasdai Crescas's Critique of the Theory of the Acquired Intellect," Ph.D. Diss., Columbia University.

(1981). "A Portrait of Spinoza as a Maimonidean," *Journal of the History of Philosophy* 19: 151–172.

(1988). "Crescas vs. Maimonides on Knowledge and Pleasure," in *A Straight Path: Essays in Honor of Arthur Hyman*, ed. R. Link-Salinger. Washington, DC: Catholic University of America Press, 113–123.

(1998). *Physics and Metaphysics in Hasdai Crescas*. Amsterdam: J. C. Gieben.

(1999). "The Biblical Term 'Glory' in Spinoza's *Ethics*" [Hebrew], *Iyyun* 48: 447–449 (English summary in 49 [2000]: 111).

(2008). "Maimonides' Avicennianism," *Maimonidean Studies* 5: 107–119.

(2010a). "Spinoza on Ibn Ezra's 'Secret of Twelve'," in *Spinoza's Theological-Political Treatise: A Critical Guide*, eds. Yitzhak Y. Melamed and Michael A. Rosenthal. Cambridge University Press, pp. 41–55.

(2010b). *Rabbi Hasdai Crescas* [Hebrew]. Jerusalem: Zalman Shazar Center.

(2012). "Gersonides and Spinoza on Conatus," *Aleph* 12: 273–297.

Hasse, Dag N. (2007). "Averroica secta: Notes on the Formation of Averroist Movements in Fourteenth-Century Bologna and Renaissance Italy," in

Averroes et les Averroismes juif et latin, ed. J.-B. Brenet. Textes et études du moyen âge 40. Turnhout: Brepols, 307–331.

Hawking, Stephen (2010). *The Grand Design*. New York: Bantam Books.

Hayoun, Maurice-Ruben (1996). "Moses Maimonides und Muhammad al-Tabrisi: Ausgabe der hebraeischen [anonymen] Uebersetzung des Kommentars al-Tabrisis zu den XXV Leitsaetzen des Maimonides im II. Teil des *Moreh Nebuchim*," *Trumah. Zeitschrift der Hochschule für Jüdische Studien Heidelberg* 5: 201–245.

Heereboord, Adriaan (1665). *Philosophia Naturalis*, in *Meletemata Philosophica*. Amsterdam: Apud Joannem Ravesteinium.

Heurne, Johan van (1609). *Institutiones Medicinae*, ed. Otto van Heurne, 2nd edn. Leiden: Ex officinal Plantiniana Raphelengii.

Hourani, George F. (1966). "Ibn Sina's 'Essay on the Secret of Destiny'," *Bulletin of the School of Oriental and African Studies* 29: 25–48.

(1972). "Ibn Sina on Necessary and Possible Existence," *Philosophical Forum* 4: 74–86.

Hubbeling, H. G. (1977), "The Logical and Experiential Roots of Spinoza's Mysticism," in *Speculum Spinozanum*, ed. Siegfried Hessing. London: Routledge and Kegan Paul.

Ibn Ezra, Abraham (1874). *Sefer ha-'ibur*. Lyck: Im selbstverlage des vereins M'kize Nirdamin (Poland).

(1977). *Perushe ha-Torah le-rabbenu Avraham ibn Ezra: bereshit*, ed. A. Weiser. Jerusalem: Mossad ha-rav Kook.

(1984). *Yesod Dikduk hu Sfat Yeter*, ed. N. Allony. Jerusalem: Mossad ha-Rav Kook.

(1988a). *Ibn Ezra's Commentary on the Pentateuch: Genesis*, Vol. 1, trans. Norman H. Strickman and Arthur M. Silver. New York: Menorah Publishing Co.

(1988b). *Ibn Ezra's Commentary on the Pentateuch: Exodus*, Vol. 2, trans. Norman H. Strickman and Arthur M. Silver. New York: Menorah Publishing Co.

(1988c). *Ibn Ezra's Commentary on the Pentateuch: Deuteronomy*, Vol. 5, trans. Norman H. Strickman and Arthur M. Silver. New York: Menorah Publishing Co.

Ibn Shem Tov, Joseph ben Shem Tov, *Commentary on the Ethics*, Oxford: Budley Mich. 404 (01. 197) [Neub. 1431] fol. 566.

(1555). *Kevod 'Elohim*. Ferrara: Abraham Usque.

Isaac bar Sheshet (n.d.). *She'elot u-Teshuvot*. New York: Merkaz ha-Sefarim.

(1979). "On the Influence of *Or ha-Sekhel* on Moses Narboni and Abraham Shalom" [in Hebrew], *AJS Review* 4: 1–6.

(1988). *Studies in Ecstatic Kabbalah*. Albany, NY: State University at New York Press.

(2000). "Abraham Abulafia and *Unio Mystica*," in *Studies in Medieval Jewish History and Literature*, eds. I. Twersky and J. M. Harris. Cambridge, MA: Harvard University Press, 3: 147–178.

Ivry, Alfred (1983). "Remnants of Jewish Averroism in the Renaissance," in *Jewish Thought in the Sixteenth Century*, ed. Bernard Dov Cooperman. Cambridge, MA: Harvard University Press, 243–265.

(1984). "Destiny Revisited: Avicenna's Concept of Determinism," in *Islamic Theology and Philosophy: Studies in honor of George F. Hourani*, ed. Michael E. Marmura. Albany, NY: State University of New York Press, 160–171.

(2009). "Maimonides' Psychology," in *Maimonides and His Heritage*, eds. Idit Dobbs-Weinstein *et al*. Albany, NY: State University New York Press, 51–60.

James, Susan (1993). "Spinoza the Stoic," in *The Rise of Modern Philosophy*, ed. Tom Sorrell. Oxford: Clarendon Press, 289–316.

(1997). *Passion and Action: The Emotions in Seventeenth Century Philosophy*. Oxford University Press.

(2012). *Spinoza on Philosophy, Religion, and Politics: The Theologico-Political Treatise*. Oxford University Press.

Janssens, J. (1996). "The Problem of Human Freedom in Ibn Sīnā," in *Actes del Simposi Internacional di Filosofia de l'Edat Mitjana*, ed. Paloma Llorenk. Vic-Girona: patronat d'Estudis Osonencs, 112–118.

Joël, Manuel (1866). *Don Chasdai Creskas' Religionsphilosophische lehren in ihrem geschichtlichen einflusse*. Breslau: Schletter.

Jospe, Raphael (2009). *Jewish Philosophy in the Middle Ages*. Brighton, MA: Academic Studies Press.

Kashap, Paul (1987). *Spinoza and Moral Freedom*. Albany, NY: State University of New York Press.

Kellner, Menachem (1976). "Gersonides and his Cultured Despisers: Arama and Abravanel," *The Journal of Medieval and Renaissance Studies* 6: 269–296.

(1991). "Reading Rambam: Approaches to the Interpretation of Maimonides," *Jewish History* 5: 73–93.

(1994). "Gersonides on the Role of the Active Intellect in Human Cognition," *Hebrew Union College Annual* 65: 233–259.

(2013). "Gersonides' To'aliyyot: Sixteenth Century Italy Versus Nineteenth-Century Poland," in *As a Perennial Spring: A Festschrift Honoring Rabbi Dr. Norman Lamm*, ed. Bentsi Cohen. New York: Downhill Publishing.

King, Lester S. (1970). *The Road to Medical Enlightenment*. London: Macdonald.

(1974). "The Transformation of Galenism," in *Medicine in Seventeenth Century England*, ed. Allen G. Debus. Berkeley, CA: University of California Press.

Kisner, Matthew J. (2011) *Spinoza on Human Freedom: Reason, Autonomy and the Good Life*. Cambridge University Press

Klatzkin, Jakob (1926–1933). *Thesaurus Philosophicus Linguae Hebraicae*. Berlin: Eshkol.

Klein, Julie (2002). "By Eternity I Understand: Eternity According to Spinoza," *Iyyun: The Jerusalem Philosophical Quarterly* 51: 295–324.

(2003). "Spinoza's Debt to Gersonides," *Graduate Faculty Philosophy Journal* 24: 19–43.

(2006). "'Gersonides' Approach to Emanation and Transcendence: Evidence from the Theory of Intellection," in *Intellect and Imagination. Proceedings of the Eleventh International Congress of the Société Internationale Pour L'étude de La Philosophie Médiévale (Porto, 26–31 August 2002)*, eds. M. C. Pacheco and J. F. Meirinhos. Turnhout: Brepols, 653–664.

Klein-Braslavy, Sara (2006). "Maimonides' Exoteric and Esoteric Biblical Interpretations in the *Guide of the Perplexed*," in *Study and Knowledge in Jewish Thought*, ed. Howard Kreisel. Beer-Sheva: Ben-Gurion University of the Negev, 137–164.

(2011). *Without Any Doubt: Studies in Gersonides' Methods of Inquiry* (Supplements to the *Journal of Jewish Thought and Philosophy* 13). Leiden: Brill.

Klever, W. N. A. (1991). *Verba et Sententiae Spinozae, or, Lambertus van Velthuysen (1622–1685) on Benedictus de Spinoza*. Amsterdam: APA–Holland University Press.

Klibansky, Raymond *et al.* (1964). *Saturn and Melancholy*. New York: Basic Books.

Knuuttila, Simo (1993). *Modalities in Medieval Philosophy*. London: Routledge.

Kraemer, Joel L. (2008). *Maimonides: The Life and World of One of Civilization's Greatest Minds*. New York: Doubleday.

Kreisel, Howard (1994). "On the Term *Kol* in Abraham ibn Ezra: A Reappraisal," *Revue des Etudes Juives* 153: 29–66.

Lachterman, David (1977). "The Ethics of Spinoza's Physics," *Southwestern Journal of Philosophy* 8: 71–111.

(1991). "Laying Down the Law: The Theological-Political Matrix of Spinoza's Physics," in *Leo Strauss's Thought: Toward A Critical Engagement*, ed. Alan Udoff. Colorado: Lynne Rienner, 123–153.

Laerke, Mogens (2011a). "Spinoza's Cosmological Argument in the *Ethics*," *Journal of the History of Philosophy* 49: 439–462.

(2011b). "Leibniz's Cosmological Argument for the Existence of God," *Archiv für Geschichte der Philosophie* 93: 58–84.

(2012). "Deus quatenus ... sur l'emploi de particules réduplicatives dans l'*Éthique*," in *Lectures Contemporaines de Spinoza*, eds. C. Cohen-Boulakia, P.-F. Moreau, and M. Delbraccio. Paris: Les Presses de l'Université Paris-Sorbonne, 261–275.

Lancaster, Irene (2003). *Deconstructing the Bible: Abraham Ibn Ezra's Introduction to the Torah*. London: Routledge Curzon.

Lang, Helen S. (1986). "Bonaventure's Delight in Sensation," *The New Scholasticism* 60: 72–90.

Langermann, Y. Tzvi (1993). "Some Astrological Themes in the Thought of Abraham ibn Ezra," in *Rabbi Abraham ibn Ezra: Studies in the Writings of a Twelfth-Century Polymath*, eds. Isadore Twersky and Jay M. Harris. Cambridge, MA: Harvard University Press.

(1999). *The Jews and the Sciences in the Middle Ages*. Aldershot, Hampshire: Ashgate.

(2012). "No Reagent, No Reaction: The Barren Transmission of Avicennan Dynamics to Hasdai Crescas," *Aleph* 12: 161–188.

Leaman, Oliver (1995). *Evil and Suffering in Jewish Philosophy.* Cambridge University Press.

Leibniz, Gottfried Wilhelm (1923–). *Sämtliche Schriften und Briefe*, ed. Deutsche Akademie der Wissenschaften, multiple vols. in seven series. Darmstadt/Leipzig/Berlin: Akademie Verlag.

(1985). *Theodicy: Essays on the Goodness of God, the Freedom of Man and the Origin of Evil*, trans. E. M. Huggard. La Salle, IL: Open Court.

(2001). *The Labyrinth of the Continuum*, trans. Richard T. W. Arthur. New Haven, CT: Yale University Press.

Lenz, Martin. "Whose Freedom? Spinoza's Compatibilism," www.academia.edu/1569124/Whose_Freedom_-_Spinozas_Compatibilism.

León Hebreo (1937). *Dialoghi d'Amore*, trans. F. Friedeberg-Seeley and Jean H. Barnes as *The Philosophy of Love*. London: Soncino.

Levene, Nancy (2004). *Spinoza's Revelation*. Cambridge University Press.

Levi ben Gershom (1560). *Milḥamot Hashem*, ed. Jacob Marcaria. Riva di Trento: Jacob Marcaria.

(1866). *Sefer Milḥamot ha-Shem*. Leipzig: Carl Lorck.

(1888). *Be'urim on Ezra, Nehemiah, and Chronicles*. Krakow: Eisig Gräber.

(1981). *Supercommentary on Averroes' Epitome of Aristotle's de Anima*, in "Chapters 9–12 of Gersonides' Supercommentary on Averroes' *Epitome of the de Anima*: The Internal Senses," J. S. Mashbaum, Ph.D. dissertation. Brandeis University, UMI.

(1984). *The Wars of the Lord*, Vol. 1, trans. Seymour Feldman. Philadelphia: Jewish Publication Society.

(1987). *The Wars of the Lord*, Vol. 2, trans. Seymour Feldman. Philadelphia: Jewish Publication Society.

(1992). *The Logic of Gersonides: A Translation of "Sefer ha-Heqqesh ha-Yashar" (The Book of the Correct Syllogism) of Rabbi Levi ben Gershom, with Introduction, Commentary, and Analytical Glossary*, trans. Charles H. Manekin, New Synthese Historical Library Series. Dordrecht: Kluwer.

(1993–). *Be'ur on Pentateuch*, eds. B. Braner, E. Freiman, and C. Cohen. Ma'aleh Adummim: Ma'aliyyot.

(1998). *Commentary on Song of Songs*, trans. Menachem Kellner. New Haven, CT: Yale University Press.

(1999). *The Wars of the Lord*, Vol. 3, trans. Seymour Feldman. Philadelphia: Jewish Publication Society.

(2001). *Perush l'Shir ha-Shirim*, ed. Menachem Kellner. Ramat Gan: Bar Ilan University Press.

Levinas, Emmanuel (1990). "The Spinoza Case," in *Difficult Freedom: Essays on Judaism*. London: The Athlone Press, 111–118.

Levy, Tony (1987). *Figures de l'infini. Les mathématiques au miroir des cultures*. Paris: Éditions du Seuil.

Levy, Ze'ev (1972). *Spinoza's Interpretation of Judaism: A Concept and Its Influence on Jewish Thought*. Tel Aviv: Sefirot Poelim [Hebrew].

(1989). *Baruch or Benedict: On Some Jewish Aspects of Spinoza's Philosophy*. New York: Peter Lang.

Lewis, Charlton Thomas, and Charles Short (1879). *A Latin Dictionary*. Oxford: Clarendon Press.

Lobel, Diana (2000). *Between Mysticism and Philosophy*. Albany, NY: State University of New York Press.

Locke, John (1877). *An Essay Concerning Human Understanding*. London: William Tegg and Co.

Lucas, Jean-Maximilien (1863). *La Vie de M. Benoît de Spinoza*, in *Oeuvres complètes de B. de Spinoza*, ed. J. G. Prat. Paris: L. Hachette, 1: iii–xxxvi.

Luzzatto, S. D. (1970). *Meḥqerei-hayahadut (Studies in Judaism)*. Jerusalem: Maqor.

Machiavelli, Niccolo (1998). *The Prince*, trans. Harvey Mansfield. University of Chicago Press.

Maimon, Solomon (1793). *Solomon Maimon's Lebengeschichte von ihm selbst beschrieben*. Berlin: N. P.

Maimonides, Moses (1856–1866). *Le Guide des égarés*, French trans. Salamon Munk, 3 vols. Paris: Franck.

(1872). *Moreh Nebukhim*, Hebrew trans. Samuel ibn Tibbon with commentaries of Ephodi, Shem Tov ben Joseph ibn Shem Tov, Asher Crescas, and Isaac Abrabanel. Warsaw: Goldman.

(1912). *The Eight Chapters of Maimonides on Ethics*, trans. Joseph I. Gorfinkle. New York: Columbia University Press.

(1931). *Dalālat al-Ḥā'irīn*, eds. S. Munk and I. Joel. Jerusalem: Junovitch.

(1962). *Book of Knowledge*, ed. and trans. Moses Hyamson. Jerusalem: Boys Town.

(1963). *Guide of the Perplexed*, trans. Shlomo Pines. 2 vols University of Chicago Press.

(1989). *Mishneh Torah*, trans. Eliyahu Touger. New York: Moznaim Publishing Corp.

Malcolm, Noel (2002). *Aspects of Hobbes*. Oxford: Clarendon Press.

Mancosu, Paolo (1996). *Philosophy of Mathematics and Mathematical Practice in the Seventeenth Century*. New York: Oxford University Press.

Manekin, Charles H. (1988). "Problems of 'Plenitude' in Maimonides and Gersonides," in *A Straight Path: Studies in Medieval Philosophy and Culture: Essays in Honor of Arthur Hyman*, eds. R. James Long and Charles H. Manekin. Washington, DC: Catholic University Press, 183–194.

(1991). "Logic and its Applications in the Philosophy of Gersonides," in *Gersonide en son temps*, ed. Gilbert Dahan. Louvain-Paris: E. Peeters, 133–149.

(1997). "Freedom Within Reason? Gersonides on Human Choice," in *Freedom and Moral Responsibility: General and Jewish Perspectives*, eds. Charles H. Manekin and Menachem Kellner. College Park: University Press of Maryland, 165–204.

(2003). "Conservative Tendencies in Gersonides' Religious Philosophy," in *The Cambridge Companion to Medieval Jewish Philosophy*, eds. Daniel H. Frank and Oliver Leaman. New York: Cambridge University Press, 304–344.

(2007). *Medieval Jewish Philosophical Writings*. Cambridge University Press.

Manzini, Frédéric (2009) *Spinoza. Une lecture d'Aristote*. Paris: Presses Universitaires de France.

ed. (2011). *Spinoza et ses scolastiques. Retour aux sources et nouveaux enjeux*. Groupe de Recherches Spinozistes, Travaux et documents 13. Paris: PUPS.

Marx, Alexander (1935). "Texts by and about Maimonides," *Jewish Quarterly Review* 25: 371–428.

Matheron, Alexandre (1969). *Individu et communauté chez Spinoza*. Paris: Editions de Minuit.

Maull, Nancy (1986). "Spinoza in the Century of Science," in *Boston Studies in the Philosophy of Science: Spinoza and the Sciences*, eds. Marjorie Grene and Debra Nails. Dordrecht: D. Reidel, 3–14.

McKeon, Richard (1928). *The Philosophy of Spinoza*. New York: Longmans, Green & Co.

Méchoulan, Henri (1991). *Être juif à Amsterdam au temps de Spinoza*. Paris: Albin Michel.

Meijer, Lodewijk (1660a). *Disputatio Philosophica Inauguralis, de Materia, Ejusque Affectionibus Motu, et Quiete*. Leiden: Ex Officinâ Francisci Hackii; reproduction in *Chronicon Spinozanum* 2 (1922): 185–195.

(1660b). *Disputatio Medica Inauguralis de Calido Nativo, Ejusque Morbis*. Leiden: Ex Officina Francisci Hackii.

Melamed, Yitzhak Y. (2000). "The Exact Science of Non-Beings: Spinoza's View of Mathematics," *Iyyun – The Jerusalem Philosophical Quarterly* 49: 3–22.

(2009). "Spinoza's Metaphysics of Substance: The Substance-Mode Relation as a Relation of Inherence and Predication," *Philosophy and Phenomenological Research* 78 (1).

(2012). "Spinoza's Deification of Existence," *Oxford Studies in Early Modern Philosophy*, 6: 75–104

(2013a). *Spinoza's Metaphysics: Substance and Thought*. Oxford University Press.

(2013b). "Response to Colin Marshall and Martin Lin," *Leibniz Review* 23: 207–222.

(forthcoming). "The Building Blocks of Spinoza's Metaphysics: Substance, Attributes, and Modes," in *The Oxford Handbook of Spinoza*, ed. Michael Della Rocca. Oxford: Oxford University Press.

Menasseh ben Israel (1995). *Nishmat Ḥayyim*. Jerusalem: Yerid ha-Sefarim.

Middleton, W. E. Knowles (1966). *A History of the Thermometer and Its Use in Meteorology*. Baltimore, MD: Johns Hopkins University Press.

Mignini, Filippo (1984). "Theology as the Work and Instrument of Fortune," in *Spinoza's Political and Theological Thought*, ed. Cornelis de Deugd. Amsterdam: Royal Netherlands Academy of Arts and Sciences.

Miller, Jon (forthcoming). *Spinoza and the Stoics*. Cambridge University Press.

Mitchell, Stephen, ed. (1991). *The Enlightened Mind.* New York: Harper Collins.

Moses of Narbonne (1852). *Be'ur le-Sefer Moreh Nevukhim.* Vienna: K. K. Hof- und Staatsdruckerei.

Müller, Ingo (1991). *Iatromechanische Theorie und ärztliche Praxis im Vergleich zur galenstischen Medizin.* Stuttgart: Franz Steiner.

Nadler, Steven (1999). *Spinoza: A Life.* Cambridge University Press.

(2001). *Spinoza's Heresy: Immortality and the Jewish Mind.* Oxford University Press.

(2005a). "Spinoza's Theory of Divine Providence: Rationalist Solutions, Jewish Sources," *Mededelingen vanwege Het Spinozahuis* 87.

(2005b). "Rationalism in Jewish Philosophy," in *A Companion to Rationalism,* ed. Alan Nelson. Boston: Blackwell Publishing, 100–118.

(2005c). "Hope, Fear, and the Politics of Immortality," in *Analytic Philosophy and History of Philosophy,* eds. Tom Sorrell and G. A. J. Rogers. New York: Oxford University Press, 201–217.

(2006). *Spinoza's* Ethics: *An Introduction.* New York: Cambridge University Press.

(2008). "Theodicy and Providence," in *The Cambridge History of Jewish Philosophy: From Antiquity through the Seventeenth Century,* eds. Steven Nadler and Tamar Rudavsky. Cambridge: Cambridge University Press, 619–658.

(2009). "The Jewish Spinoza," *Journal of the History of Ideas* 70: 491–510.

(2011). *A Book Forged in Hell: Spinoza's Scandalous Treatise and the Birth of the Secular Age.* Princeton University Press.

Nagel, Thomas (1979). "Moral Luck," in *Mortal Questions,* ed. Thomas Nagel. Cambridge University Press, 24–38.

Narboni, Moses (1852). *Commentary on Maimonides' Moreh ha-Nebukhim,* ed. J. Goldenthal. Vienna: Imperial and Royal Press.

Nehorai, M. Z. (1988). "Maimonides and Gersonides: Two Approaches to the Nature of Providence," *Da'at* 20: 51–64 [Hebrew].

Niehoff, Maren (2011). *Jewish Exegesis and Homeric Scholarship in Alexandria.* Cambridge University Press.

Norris, Christopher (1991). *Spinoza and the Origins of Modern Critical Theory.* Cambridge, MA: Basil Blackwell.

Nuriel, Avraham (1980). "Providence and Governance in the *Guide of the Perplexed,*" *Tarbiz* 49: 346–55 [Hebrew].

Offenberg, Adri (1977). "Spinoza Autodidacte?," in *Spinoza. Troisième centenaire de la mort du philosophe,* ed. Judith C. E. Belinfante. Paris: Institut Néerlandais, 30–31.

Owens, Joseph (1963). *An Elementary Christian Metaphysics.* Milwaukee: Brunce Publishing.

Parens, Joshua (2012). *Maimonides and Spinoza: Their Conflicting Views of Human Nature.* University of Chicago Press.

Pereboom, Derk (2001). *Living Without Free Will.* Cambridge University Press.

Petrus de Abano (1523). *Conciliator Differentiarum Philosophorum ac Medicorum.* Papie: Mandato et expensis Gerardi de Zeis, et Bartholomei de Morandis.

Pfeffer, Jeremy (2010). "Authorship in a Hebrew Codex ... MS 199: Tracing Two Lost Works by Delmedigo," *Christ Church Library Newsletter* 6.3: 1–6.

Pines, Shlomo (1963). "The Philosophic Sources of *The Guide of the Perplexed*," in Maimonides 1963.

(1967). "Scholasticism after Thomas Aquinas and the Teaching of Hasdai Crescas and his Predecessors," *Proceedings of the Israel Academy of Sciences and Humanities* 1: 1–101.

(1968). "Spinoza's *Tractatus Theologico-Politicus*, Maimonides, and Kant," *Scripta Hierosolymitana* 20: 3–54.

(1979), "The Limitations of Human Knowledge According to Al-Farabi, ibn Bajja, and Maimonides," in *Studies in Medieval Jewish History*, ed. I. Twersky. Cambridge, MA: Harvard University Press, 82–109.

(1979–1997). *Collected Works*, 5 vols. Jerusalem: Magnes Press.

(1983). "Medieval Doctrines in Renaissance Garb? Some Jewish and Arabic Sources of Leone Ebreo's Doctrines," in *Jewish Thought in the Sixteenth Century*, ed. B. Cooperman. Cambridge, MA: Harvard University Press, 365–398.

(1987a). "Spinoza's *Tractatus Theologico-Politicus* and the Jewish Philosophical Tradition," in *Jewish Thought in the Seventeenth Century*, eds. Isadore Twersky and Bernard Septimus. Cambridge, MA: Harvard University Press.

(1987b). "Some Distinctive Metaphysical Conceptions in Themistius' Commentary on Book Lambda," in *Aristoteles Werk und Wirkung, Paul Moraux gewidmet*, ed. J. Wiesner, Vol. 2. Berlin: Walter de Gruyter, repr. Pines 1979–1997, Vol. 3, 267–294.

(1990). "Truth and Falsehood Versus Good and Evil: A Study in Jewish and General Philosophy in Connection with the *Guide of the Perplexed*," in *Studies in Maimonides*, ed. Isadore Twersky. Cambridge University Press.

(1991). "Note sur la métaphysique et sur la physique de Gersonide," in *Gersonide en son temps*, ed. G. Dahan. Louvain: Peeters, repr. Pines 1979–1997, Vol. 5, 590–594.

Polgar, Isaac (1984). *'Ezer ha-dat*, ed. Jacob S. Levinger. Tel Aviv: Chaim Rosenberg School for Jewish Studies, University of Tel Aviv.

Popkin, Richard (1987). *Isaac la Peyrère (1596–1676): His Life, Work and Influence.* Leiden: Brill.

(1992). "Spinoza, Neoplatonist Kabbalist?," in *Neoplatonism in Jewish Thought*, ed. Lenn E. Goodman. Albany, NY: State University of New York Press, 387–409.

(1996). "Spinoza and Bible Scholarship," in *The Cambridge Companion to Spinoza*, ed. Don Garrett. Cambridge University Press, 383–407.

Preus, J. Samuel (2001). *Spinoza and the Irrelevance of Biblical Authority.* Cambridge University Press.

Rabinovith, Nachum L. (1970). "Rabbi Hasdai Crescas on Numerical Infinities," *Isis* 61: 224–230.

Raffel, Charles M. (1987). "Providence as Consequent Upon the Intellect: Maimonides' Theory of Providence," *Association for Jewish Studies Review* 12: 25–71.

Rapoport, Solomon Judah Leib (1885–86). *'Igrot Shir*. Przemyśl: Eisik Gräber.

Ravitzky, Aviezer (1981). "Samuel ibn Tibbon and the Esoteric Character of the *Guide of the Perplexed*," *Association for Jewish Studies Review* 61: 87–123.

(1988). *Drashat ha-pesaḥ le-Rav Ḥasdai Crescas u-meḥkarim be-mishnato ha-filosofit (Crescas "Sermon on the Passover" and Studies in His Philosophy)*. Jerusalem: Israel Academy of Sciences and Humanities.

(1993). "On the Study of Medieval Jewish Philosophy," *Archivio di filosofia* 61: 151–166.

Ravven, Heidi (2001a). "Some Thoughts on What Spinoza Learned from Maimonides About the Prophetic Imagination, Part One: Maimonides on Prophecy and the Imagination," *Journal of the History of Philosophy* 39: 193–214.

(2001b). "Some Thoughts on What Spinoza Learned from Maimonides About the Prophetic Imagination, Part Two: Spinoza's Maimonideanism," *Journal of the History of Philosophy* 39: 385–406.

(2001c). "The Garden of Eden: Spinoza's Maimonidean Account of the Genealogy of Morals and the Origin of Society," *Philosophy and Theology* 13: 3–47.

(2013). *The Self Beyond Itself: An Alternative History of Ethics, the New Brain Sciences, and the Myth of Free Will*. New York: The New Press.

Ravven, Heidi, and Lenn E. Goodman, eds. (2002). *Jewish Themes in Spinoza's Philosophy*. Albany, NY: State University of New York Press.

Reines, Alvin (1972). "Maimonides' Concepts of Providence and Theodicy," *Hebrew Union College Annual* 43: 169–205.

Reisman, David C. (2005). "Al-Farabi and the Philosophical Curriculum," in *The Cambridge Companion to Arabic Philosophy*, eds. Peter Adamson and Richard C. Taylor. Cambridge University Press, 52–71.

Révah, I. S. (1959). *Spinoza et Juan de Prado*. Paris: Mouton.

Rivière, Lazare (1656). *Institutiones Medicae*. Lyons: Sumptibus Antonii Cellier.

Rosen, Stanley (1987). "Spinoza," in *History of Political Philosophy*, eds. Leo Strauss and Joseph Cropsey. University of Chicago Press.

Rudavsky, T. M. (2001). "Galileo and Spinoza: Heroes, Heretics, and Hermeneutics," *Journal of the History of Ideas* 62: 611–631.

(2003). "The Impact of Scholasticism upon Jewish Philosophy in the Fourteenth and Fifteenth Centuries," *The Cambridge Companion to Medieval Philosophy*, eds. Daniel H. Frank and Oliver Leaman. New York: Cambridge University Press, 345–370.

(2010). *Maimonides*. Boston, MA and Chichester: Wiley-Blackwell Press.

Sadik, Shalom (forthcoming). "The 'Will Of God', 'God's Knowledge' and 'the Will of Man' in the Thought of Rabbi Issac Polgar," *Daat* 76: 147–172 [Hebrew].

Sainz de la Maza Vicioso, Carlos (1990). "Alfonso de Valladolid: Edición y estudio del manuscrito lat. 6423 de la Biblioteca Apostólica Vaticana," Ph.D. dissertation, Universidad Complutense. Madrid: Editorial de la Universidad Complutense de Madrid.

Saperstein, Marc (1991). "Saul Levi Morteira's Treatise on the Immortality of the Soul," *Studia Rosenthaliana* 25: 131–148.

(2005). *Exile in Amsterdam: Saul Levi Morteira's Sermons to a Congregation of "New Jews."* Cincinnati: Hebrew Union College Press.

Sarna, Nahum (1993). "Abraham Ibn Ezra as Exegete," in *Rabbi Abraham Ibn Ezra: Studies in the Writings of a Twelfth-Century Polymath*, eds. Isadore Twersky and Jay M. Harris. Cambridge, MA: Harvard University Press, 1–27.

Savan, David (1986). "Spinoza: Scientist and Theorist of Scientific Method," in *Spinoza and the Sciences*, eds. Marjorie Grene and Debra Nails. Dordrecht: D. Reidel, 95–124.

Scholem, Gershom (1941). *Major Trends in Jewish Mysticism.* New York: Schocken Books.

Schwartz, Daniel (2012). *The First Modern Jew: Spinoza and the History of an Image.* Princeton University Press.

Schwartz, Dov (2005). *Central Problems of Medieval Jewish Philosophy.* Leiden: Brill.

Seeskin, Kenneth (2005). *Maimonides on the Creation of the World.* New York: Cambridge University Press.

Sela, Shlomo (1999). *Astrology and Biblical Exegesis in the Thought of Abraham Ibn Ezra* [Hebrew]. Ramat Gan: Bar Ilan University Press.

(2003). *Araham Ibn Ezra and the Rise of Medieval Hebrew Science.* Boston: Brill.

Sela, Shlomo, and Gad Freudenthal (2006). "Abraham Ibn Ezra's Scholarly Writings: A Chronological Listing," *Aleph* 6: 13–55.

Sennert, Daniel (1641). *Institutionum Medicinae Libri Quinque*, in Vol. 1 of his *Opera Omnia.* Venice: Apud Franciscum Baba, 239–846.

Shalom, Abraham (1575). *Neveh Shalom.* Venice: Zu'an di Gara'.

Shatz, David (2003). "The Biblical and Rabbinic Background to Medieval Jewish Philosophy," in *The Cambridge Companion to Medieval Jewish Philosophy*, eds. Daniel H. Frank and Oliver Leaman. Cambridge University Press, 16–37.

Siebrand, Heine (1986). "Spinoza and the Rise of Modern Science in the Netherlands," in *Boston Studies in the Philosophy of Science: Spinoza and the Sciences*, eds. Marjorie Grene and Debra Nails. Dordrecht: D. Reidel, 61–94.

Siegel, Rudolph E. (1968). *Galen's System of Physiology and Medicine: An Analysis of His Doctrines and Observations on Bloodflow, Respiration, Humors, and Internal Diseases.* Basil: Karger.

Simon, Uriel, and Raphael Jospe (2007). "Ibn Ezra," "Abraham Ben Meir," in *Encyclopaedia Judaica*, eds. Michael Berenbaum and Fred Skolnik. Detroit: Macmillan Reference, 665–672.

Sirat, Colette (1985). *A History of Jewish Philosophy in the Middle Ages.* Cambridge University Press.

Skulsky, Harold (2009). *Staring into the Void: Spinoza, the Master of Nihilism.* Newark: University of Delaware Press.

Slote, Michael (1990). "Ethics Without Free Will," *Social Theory and Practice* 16: 369–383.

Smith, Steven (1997). *Spinoza, Liberalism, and the Question of Jewish Identity.* New Haven, CT: Yale University Press.

(2003). *Spinoza's Book of Life: Freedom and Redemption in the Ethics.* New Haven, CT: Yale University Press.

Smithius, Renate (1995). "Abraham Ibn Ezra's Astrological Works in Hebrew and Latin: New Discoveries and Exhaustive Listings," *Aleph* 6: 239–338.

Sorabji, Richard (1980). *Necessity, Cause, and Blame: Perspectives on Aristotle's Theory.* Ithaca, NY: Cornell University Press.

Spinoza, Benedictus (1869). *Korte Verhandeling van God, de Mensch, en Deszelfs Welstand,* ed. Carl Schaarschmidt. Amsterdam: F. Muller.

(1910). *Spinoza's Short Treatise on God, Man and His Wellbeing,* trans. A. Wolf. London: A. and C. Black.

(1925). *Spinoza Opera,* ed. Carl Gebhardt, 4 vols, Heidelberg: Carl Winters Universitätsverlag (repr. 1972).

(1985). *The Collected Works of Spinoza,* Vol. 1, trans. Edwin Curley. Princeton University Press.

(1995). *Spinoza: The Letters,* trans. Samuel Shirley. Indianapolis: Hackett.

(2000). *Political Treatise,* trans. Samuel Shirley. Indianapolis: Hackett.

(2001). *Theological-Political Treatise,* trans. Samuel Shirley, 2nd ed. Indianpolis: Hackett.

(2002). *Complete Works,* trans. Samuel Shirley, ed. Michael Morgan. Indianapolis: Hackett.

(2004). *Theological-Political Treatise,* trans. Martin Yaffe. Newburyport, MA: Focus Publishing.

(2007). *Theological-Political Treatise,* trans. Michael Silverthorne and Jonathan Israel. Cambridge University Press.

Stern, Josef (2005). "Maimonides Epistemology," in *The Cambridge Companion to Maimonides,* ed. Kenneth Seeskin. New York: Cambridge University Press.

Strauss, Leo (1968). *Liberalism: Ancient and Modern.* New York: Basic Books.

(1997). *Spinoza's Critique of Religion,* ed. and trans. E. M. Sinclair. University of Chicago Press.

Strickman, Norman H. (2011). "Abraham ibn Ezra's 'Yesod Mora'," *Hakirah* 12: 139–169.

Stroumsa, Sarah (2009). *Maimonides in His World: A Portrait of a Mediterranean Thinker.* Princeton and Oxford: Princeton University Press.

Suringar, G. C. B. (1864). "Invloed der Cartesiaansche Wijsbegeerte of het Natuur- en Genees-Kundig Onderwijs aan de Leidsche Hoogeschool," *Nederlandsch Tijdschrift voor Geneeskunde* 8: 153–170.

Szpiech, Ryan (2010). "In Search of Ibn Sina's 'Oriental Philosophy' in Medieval Castile," *Arabic Sciences and Philosophy* 20: 185–206.

Talmage, Frank. (1999). "Apples of Gold: The Inner Meaning of Sacred Texts in Medieval Judaism," in *Apples of Gold in Settings of Silver: Studies in Medieval Jewish Exegesis and Polemics*, ed. Barry Dov Wolfish. Toronto: Pontifical Institute Publ., 108–150.

Temkin, Owsei (1973). *Galenism*. Ithaca: Cornell University Press.

Themistius (1999). *Paraphrase de la "Métaphysique" d'Aristote*. French translation from Hebrew and Arabic by Rémi Brague. Paris: J. Vrin.

Thomas Aquinas (1947). *The Summa Theologica of St. Thomas Aquinas*, trans. Fathers of the English Dominican Province. Chicago: Benzinger Brothers, available online at www.ccel.org/a/aquinas/summa/FP.html.

(1968). *On the Unity of the Intellect Against the Averroists*, trans. Beatrice H. Zedler. Milwaukee: Marquette University Press.

(n.d.). *Quaestiones Disputatae de Anima*, http://dhspriory.org/thomas/QDdeAnima.htm, accessed 27 November 2013.

Thorndike, Lynne (1955). "The True Place of Astrology in the History of Science," *Isis* 46: 273–278.

Totaro, Pina (2002). "'Ho Certi Amici in Ollandia': Stensen and Spinoza – Science versus Faith," in *Niccolò Stenone (1638–1686) Anatomista, Geologo, Vescovo*, eds. Karen Ascani *et al.* Roma: Erma di Bretschneider.

Touati, Charles (1973). *La pensée philosophique et théologique de Gersonide*. Paris: Éditions de Minuit.

(1990). "Les deux theories de Maïmonide sur la providence," in *Prophètes, talmudistes, philosophes*. Paris: Editions de Cerf.

Twersky, Isadore (1972). *A Maimonides Reader*. New York: Behrman House.

Vajda, Georges (1955). "The Doctrine of R. Moses b. Joseph Halevi on Providence," *Melilah* 5: 163–168 [Hebrew].

(1957). *L'Amour de Dieu dans la théologie juive du Moyen Âge*. Paris: J. Vrin.

Valabregue-Perry, Sandra (2010). *Concealed and Revealed: "Ein Sof" in Theosophic Kabbalah* [Hebrew]. Los Angeles: Cherub Press.

Van Bunge, Wiep (2001) "Baruch of Benedictus: Spinoza en de 'Marranen'," *Mededelingen vanwege het Spinozahuis* 81.

Vaz Dias, A. M. and W. G. Van der Tak (1932). *Spinoza. Mercator & Autodidactus. Oorkonden en andere authentieke documenten betreffende des wijsgeers jeugd en diens betrekkingen*. The Hague: Martinus Nijhoff. English translation in *Studia Rosenthaliana* 16 (1982): 103–195.

Velthuysen, Lambert van (1657). *Tractatus Du Medico-Physici, Unvs, De Liene, Alter, de Generatione*. Utrecht: Typis Theodori ab Ackersdijck & Gisberti à Zyll.

(1680). *Tractatus de Cultu Naturali, & Origine Moralitatis*, in his *Opera*. Rotterdam: Typis Reineri Leers, 2: 1363–1570.

Verbeek, Theo (2003). *Spinoza's Theological-political treatise: Exploring "the Will of God."* London: Ashgate.

Vermij, Renk H. (2002). "The Calvinist Copernicans: The Reception of the New Astronomy in the Dutch Republic: 1575–1750," *History of Science and Scholarship in the Netherlands* 1: 241–242.

Vlessing, Odette (1996). "The Jewish Community in Transition: From Acceptance to Emancipation," *Studia Rosenthaliana* 30: 195–211.

Waxman, Meyer (1920). *The Philosophy of Don Hasdai Crescas*. New York: Columbia University Press.

Weiss, Raymond L. (1991). *Maimonides' Ethics*. University of Chicago Press.

Werblowsky, R. J. Zwi (1959). "Philo and the Zohar, Part II," *Journal of Jewish Studies* 10: 113–135.

Weyl, Hermann (2012). *Levels of Infinity*, trans. Peter Pesic Mineola, NY: Dover.

Williams, Bernard (1981). *Moral Luck*. Cambridge University Press.

Wolfson, Harry A. (1929). *Crescas' Critique of Aristotle: Problems of Aristotle's Physics in Jewish and Arabic Philosophy*. Cambridge, MA: Harvard University Press.

(1934). *The Philosophy of Spinoza*, 2 vols. Cambridge, MA: Harvard University Press..

(1976). *The Philosophy of the Kalam*. Cambridge, MA: Harvard University Press.

Wilson, Margaret (1996). "Spinoza's Theory of Knowledge," in *The Cambridge Companion to Spinoza*, ed. Don Garrett. Cambridge University Press, 89–141.

Yovel, Yirmiyahu (1989). *Spinoza and Other Heretics*. Vol. 1: *The Marrano of Reason*. Princeton University Press.

Zohar. . . 'im ha-Be'urim ha-Nifla'im ha-Sulam (1974–1975). Jerusalem: n.p.

Le Zohar (1981). Translated into French by Charles Mopsik. Paris: Verdier.

Zweifel, Eliezer ben David ha-Kohen (1856). Letter 15, to Senior Sachs. *Kerem Ḥemed* 9: 80–85.

Index

Made in the USA
Middletown, DE
11 December 2019

80464287R00139